The Inclusion Imperative

The Inclusion Imperative

How real inclusion creates better business and builds better societies

Stephen J Frost

KoganPage

LONDON PHILADELPHIA NEW DELHI

First published in Great Britain and the United States in 2014 by Kogan Page Limited

2nd Floor, 45 Gee Street
London EC1V 3RS
United Kingdom

1518 Walnut Street, Suite 1100
Philadelphia PA 19102
USA

4737/23 Ansari Road
Daryaganj
New Delhi 110002
India

www.koganpage.com

ISBN   978 0 7494 7129 3
E-ISBN   978 0 7494 7130 9

British Library Cataloguing-in-Publication Data

A CIP record for this book is available from the British Library.

Library of Congress Cataloging-in-Publication Data

Frost, Stephen, 1977-
   The inclusion imperative : how real inclusion creates better business and builds better societies / Stephen Frost.
      pages cm
      ISBN 978-0-7494-7129-3 – ISBN 978-0-7494-7130-9 (ebk)   1. Diversity in the workplace. 2. Multiculturalism.   3. Intercultural communication.   4. Olympic Games (30th : 2012 : London, England)–Case studies.   5. Paralympic Games (14th : 2012 : London, England)–Case studies. I. Title.
      HF5549.5.M5F765 2014
      658.3008–dc23
                                                                                            2013044130

Typeset by Amnet
Print production managed by Jellyfish
Printed and bound by CPI Group (UK) Ltd, Croydon CR0 4YY

For Dad

CONTENTS

LIST OF FIGURES

LIST OF TABLES

ABOUT THE AUTHOR

Stephen Frost is a globally recognised inclusion expert, and Principal of Frost Included (www.frostincluded.com), an inclusive leadership and consulting practice. From 2007–12 he served as Head of Diversity and Inclusion for the London 2012 Olympic and Paralympic Games.

At London 2012, he was responsible for designing, implementing and delivering results in Diversity and Inclusion across a 200,000 workforce, £1.1 billion procurement budget, 57 delivery functions and 134 venues. His team achieved unprecedented workforce inclusion and established new standards in supplier diversity. It was the first time any Olympic or Paralympic Games had ever delivered such an inclusion programme.

From 2004–07 Stephen established and led the workplace team at Stonewall, Europe's largest gay-equality organisation: establishing and growing the Diversity Champions programme; launching the UK's first lesbian and gay recruitment guide; establishing the LGBT Leadership programme in conjunction with Harvard University; and developing the Workplace Equality Index, which has become a standard performance measure across many global employers.

Stephen started his career in advertising where he worked on disability and age awareness campaigns and has worked in consultancy and communications in the USA, China, Greece, Tanzania and Israel. He teaches at Harvard University, USA, Sciences Po, France and in organisations worldwide. He advises the International Paralympic Committee, Novartis, BP and the governments of the UK and Singapore on inclusive leadership and diversity best practice.

He was a Hertford College Scholar at Oxford, a Fulbright Scholar at Harvard and is a Fellow of the Royal Society of Arts. He is Vice President of the Chartered Institute of Personnel and Development (www.cipd.co.uk) and was elected recipient of the 2010 Peter Robertson Award for Equality and Diversity Champions. In 2011 he was named one of the top 100 influential LGBT people in the UK, and a Young Global Leader by the World Economic Forum. Harvard University awarded him a Visiting Fellowship in order to complete this book.

He can be contacted via www.frostincluded.com.

ACKNOWLEDGEMENTS

In 1994, the Yorkshire Schools Exploring Society taught me 'I am part of all that I have met'. I have been fortunate in life to meet some extraordinary people; smart people who care, many of whom share my passion for Diversity and Inclusion.

Marty Linsky and Dean Williams, for the leadership lessons that have stood the test of time and inspired a generation. Marie Danziger, for helping me find my voice and always believing in me. Steve Kelman, for focused advice (and lunch). Max Bazerman, for telling me to forget the agent and go direct. Iris Bohnet, for the Davos chat, the Fellowship invitation and the best supervision possible. Victoria Budson, Megan Farwell and the whole team at the Women and Public Policy Program who provided me not just with a Fellowship, but also with the space, time and support to get this done.

Loreen Arbus, Pamela Gallin, Francine Le Frak and the Harvard Women's Leadership Board. Margaret Traub, Phyllis Dicker, Tim McCarthy, and the team at the Carr Centre for Human Rights.

Mrs Hall, Mr Tibbitts, Mr Hartley, Mrs Galloway, Dr Coones, Paul Bennett, Felicity Callard, Ben Page, Tony Gomez-Ibanez; the teachers in my life who have got me from the beginning and been selfless in their help, advice and counsel.

Young Global Leaders Benjamin Skinner, Michelle Wucker, Lorna Sollis, Valerie Keller, Andrew Lee, Gina Badenoch, Stefan Reichenbach, Lucian Tarnowski and Mark Turrell, for the support and friendship. Kennedy School Leadership Teaching Assistants Shannon McAuliffe, Netaly Ophir Flint, Michael Koehler, Brent Hire, Tim O'Brien, Francisco Lanus, Chris Lien and Andrew Johnston. Fellow Harvard colleague Paola Cecchi Dimeglio, for the sage and selfless advice.

Paul Deighton, the best Chief Executive in the world ever, really. Jean Tomlin, from whom I learned so much. Charlie Wijeratna, David Luckes and Dan Perret for hiring me. Sue Hunt, who defined triumph in adversity. Charles Allen, for the mentoring and wine. Tanni Grey-Thompson, for allowing us to believe in the British establishment again. Greg Nugent, Terry Miller, James Bulley, Debbie Jevans, Floella Benjamin, John Amaechi, Paul Elliott, Mike Brace, Ayesha Qureshi, Paul Ntullia and Barbara Soetan, for defining how a Diversity Board can drive change.

The Diversity and Inclusion team, who surpassed themselves and made history, Tom Secker-Walker, Lauren Finnegan, Jackie Parkin, Andrew Moncrieffe, Mark Todd, Margaret Hickish, Lou Oastler. The countless interns, Ben Supple, Garmina Jain, Laura Birkman, Jennifer Choi, Anne Babalola, Abdul Hassan, Kohinur Aktar, volunteers and corporate refugees Bernie Oastler, Joe Troedsen, Pierre-Louis Fayon and Darren Naylor who constantly inspired us through their selfless commitment. This book is also dedicated to one of our team who did not make it to the finishing line, the unique and brilliant talent that is David Morris.

All the friends who helped me with the proposal and who conscientiously scrutinised early drafts and provided honest and essential feedback, Dean Cerrato, Micaela Connery, Andrea Coomber, Joseph Dancey, Brooke Ellison, Steve Girdler, Tanni Grey-Thompson, Laurent Grossi, Steve Humerickhouse, Sue Hunt, Mike Innes, Danny Kalman, Andrew Lee, Michele Lucia, Laurie Neville, Tom Secker-Walker, Nick and Cherayar Selmes, David Young.

Mathew Smith, Nancy Wallace and the team at Kogan Page for believing in this project from its inception, and for counsel during the journey.

To my Mum, the nicest human being in the world, Emma my sister and hero – and in memory of Dad. I love you unconditionally, I owe you everything and this book is for you.

Most of all, thank you to the men and women of London 2012 whose courage, creativity and talent showed the world what can be achieved when a diverse team pulls together and achieves its individual and collective potential.

Stephen Frost, London

FOREWORD

I visited London in February 2010. Stephen Frost, the Head of Diversity and Inclusion at London 2012, had badgered my office for a long time and I was rather impressed with what he was doing, so I agreed to help.

I visited the Olympic Park and saw with my own eyes the transformation that was taking place. I met local school children and then returned to the London 2012 Offices to meet the Board. After a cup of tea with Princess Anne, I addressed the London 2012 staff, followed by a session just with the Heads of Department.

Not content with that, Stephen then had me address the great and the good at the Royal Society of Arts. I told him then that I would 'fix him', in a non-violent way.

But I was so glad I visited London 2012, and talked to the men and women who were planning and staging the greatest show on the planet. I was glad because I wanted to look into their eyes and tell them that they were not just hiring people, they were changing lives. They were not just building venues, they were transforming communities. They were not just staging an event, they were producing a spectacle that could inspire and change the world.

That day, I launched the Leadership Pledge. I put my reputation on the line that these men and women were going to do as I said and hire a diverse slice of humanity. They did. They produced the most diverse workforce any Organising Committee has ever had and these people then delivered the most diverse Games there has ever been.

I am proud of that.

Nelson Mandela said 'The Games in London will inspire athletes as well as young people... it is a diverse and open city [and] I can't think of a better place to unite the World'.

I think it did that. This is the story. Let us now hope that others follow suit.

Archbishop Emeritus Desmond Tutu,
Nobel Laureate
Cape Town, October 2013

Introduction

Diversity and Inclusion are organisational imperatives still viewed by many as 'nice to have', or even a net cost. This book has been a decade in the making, and it demonstrates why the exact opposite is true.

This book now offers talented people, who care about bettering the world through their organisation, a credible strategic framework, tested policies and tools, as well as an authoritative case study.

It offers the inspiring story of London 2012 and analyses those new and successful methods and techniques that are now available, and applicable to your own situation.

One of the key promises made by the 2005 London Olympic and Paralympic bid in Singapore was to create a 'Games for everyone'. This was to use the UK's rich diversity to achieve unprecedented inclusion in the world's biggest and most complex event.

When London became the surprise victor, the London Organising Committee of the Olympic and Paralympic Games (LOCOG) had to shift from a campaigning organisation to a delivery project. No company, government or previous Organising Committee had ever delivered on diversity promises before to the extent required by the bid. Many corporations and governments had discussed Diversity and Inclusion but few had ever achieved systemic breakthrough in their own processes, let alone on a wider societal scale.

Under unprecedented scrutiny, facing competing agendas, lacking in resources and with an immovable deadline, we therefore had to be bold and brave, establishing risky and untested policies if we were to stand any chance of meeting expectations. This is the untold social legacy back-story to the well-known public event.

Diversity is a topic rarely out of the news, from the lack of women on Boards to terrorism to racial profiling. Yet so many existing diversity policies, based on compliance programmes and training, are tired and ineffective. They are at best token, at worst counterproductive. However, just because current policies are ineffective does not mean there is not an urgent need to address questions of Diversity and Inclusion in our society. We need new inclusion policies if we are to work and live together effectively.

The circumstances surrounding the London Olympic and Paralympic Games provided a once in a lifetime opportunity to challenge existing thinking on diversity policies and to try new approaches, with the incentive of a fixed end date. This was the first time such a programme was implemented in the Olympic or Paralympic Games and this book is a unique opportunity to share a cadre of created best practice, to pass on to future projects and contribute to international policy.

A book of this nature is needed by policymakers and practitioners to reach business communities currently disengaged from current 'Diversity 101' policies. Far from being 'worthy' or 'politically correct' (ideas explained within the book), it is, by necessity, quite the opposite, and a bold and humorous rejection of much of what has gone before.

The objective was to write a book based on the work of LOCOG from 2008–12 in the area of Diversity and Inclusion. In particular, the book seeks to focus on those systems that had most effect and have wider applicability; for example, interview bundling leading to more diverse hires, or greater transparency in the procurement system leading to increased competition, reduced costs and, at the same time, increased supplier diversity.

The work from this period was reviewed from December 2012 to May 2013 alongside key publications, documents and sources, which have informed the narrative. There already exists a plethora of humourless or inadequate 'diversity' texts, focusing on multi-culturalism and how to undertake diversity policies in corporations from a compliance perspective. Compliance rarely creates best practice. This book is dramatically different.

This book will appeal to Chief Executive, Director and Managing Director level professionals, HR professionals, academics, policymakers, students and all who aspire to leadership roles, as well as the general public and Olympic and Paralympic followers who will be interested in the inside story of the greatest event the UK has ever staged. After the sport has finished, this book is a contribution to the debate around legacy and ongoing social and diversity initiatives.

The Inclusion Imperative demonstrates why existing diversity policies fall short, not least because they, like many organisations, are ill-equipped to deal with the exponential rate of change characteristic of the times we are now living in. Moreover, the book demonstrates how new *Real Inclusion* strategies can be an integral part of business success. There are five principal reasons why.

First, for gaining new customers and retaining the ones you already have. The world outside the organisation is changing faster than the world within the organisation. Without radically reflecting that world, the organisation will fail to keep up, lose market share, and may even die.

Second, for employee recruitment and retention. Employees are customers too and by treating everyone 'the same' under the illusion of 'fairness' an organisation loses the marginal added value each individual's discretionary effort could bring to the party.

Third, for growth through productivity. Barriers to growth are not just inflexible labour markets and taxes; they are also subconscious bias, implicit associations and sexist and homophobic attitudes that are deeply inefficient, as well as distasteful.

Fourth, for better group decision-making and innovation based on mathematical models. The latest research demonstrates how diversity trumps ability in many group decision-making processes, especially in new areas of growth.

Finally, there are ethical issues to consider – there is not just a moral imperative to reach out and include diverse talent in order to ensure inclusivity in increasingly fast-paced policy developments and economic changes. There is also a business case to be articulated based on emotional appeal.

The book is important for our world right now. This is the first and perhaps only occasion that the Olympic Games and Paralympic Games have been staged with Diversity and Inclusion as central tenets of delivery. As many diversity programmes and efforts have failed to date, the immovable deadline presented by the world's biggest event offered a 'do or die' scenario for inclusion. A window of attention has been opened. The story needs to be reviewed before it closes.

The book is also a fresh, humorous and intelligent rejection of past theory. Just because current policies have failed, and 'diversity training' is so 'cringe-worthy', does not mean the issues are any less important. People who care about inclusion (and/or realise we need it) have been waiting for a book like this to offer evidence to inform intelligent arguments for change. To be an example one can point to without embarrassment, to be able to engage even the most ardent foe of 'diversity' with a witty riposte as to why inclusion is actually in their interest too.

Perhaps most important of all, this book is applicable to other organisations. The bulldozer that is the Olympic Games can create paradigm change, over-riding established competing factions, conflicting agendas and localised interest/lobby groups as well as offering data sets and sample sizes of sufficient size to deduce meaningful and transferable results. But if the London Olympic and Paralympic Games can create change with minimal resources and time, then other organisations should be able to go one better. London 2012 has proven it can be done.

There is much talk of legacy. You are holding a key part of it right now, in your hands. Diversity and Inclusion unquestionably made London 2012 a better Games. In fact, they were a key differentiator. London 2012 showed the world how real inclusion can create better business and contribute to building better societies. We hope you too will now become part of the inclusive legacy of London 2012.

Lord Paul Deighton
Commercial Secretary to the Treasury and LOCOG Chief Executive 2006–12
Baroness Tanni Grey-Thompson
Paralympian and Member of the House of Lords
Jean Tomlin OBE
LOCOG HR, Workforce and Accreditation Director 2006–13

PART ONE
Courage

Introduction to Part One

Why do real inclusion?

This is a book about how to achieve real inclusion – to improve your organisation, and then the world. It makes use of the extraordinary platform offered by the Olympic and Paralympic Games, but it is a book designed to be accessible to anyone who cares about how we live and work together more effectively as a society, regardless of their interest in, or views about, the Games.

If you want to change the world, then you should start with your organisation. While change at an individual level is often worthwhile, it is usually too small-scale to make a real impact in the wider system.[1] And while change at a wider societal scale can indeed be systemic, it is often beyond the reach of mere humans. So the organisation is often the best laboratory to work in. It is a slice of society, where an individual can work with a team to make an effective intervention.

This is a book written by a practitioner, for practitioners. Moreover, this is for leaders who want to make a difference. You will find three interwoven themes within: inclusion as a method of leadership (Inclusive Leadership); how inclusion made a step-difference to the world's biggest and most complex event (London 2012); and finally how inclusion can also add significant value to your organisation.

It is written by an individual, working with a team, who together made an effective intervention and think there is merit in sharing the learning with other colleagues in the system. That's you. For anyone who says it can't be done or doesn't know why we would do it in the first place, read the pages that follow, and then make up your own mind.

There are few opportunities in professional life to bring together a set of people, resources and circumstances and rewrite the rules in real time. But the Games offered that opportunity. The deadline, the intense scrutiny and the high expectations combined to create circumstances that required new solutions. It was high risk because if things had gone wrong, the media would have let everyone know about them. The Games went well in the end, and so many in the media did not. This book, therefore, is now an opportunity to share some of the learning that was forged in the heat of battle.

Success was by no means guaranteed during the journey. The pressure was immense at times, with a requirement for speedy decision-making on the basis of incomplete information when the result was far from clear. I remember the headhunter telling me upon the eve of being offered the job that I should consider it long and hard because it could potentially ruin my CV. Jean Tomlin, LOCOG Director of HR, Workforce and Accreditation, was constantly aware of being only two decisions away at any one moment from career suicide.

Some will say that the results and methods developed in London 2012 were unique and applicable only to the Games. I disagree. Many of the concepts and methods developed are highly applicable to other organisations that I know and have worked with. These organisations have simply enjoyed the luxury to date of not facing the circumstances we faced, and so have not been compelled to enter such uncomfortable territory. Moreover, many of the concepts and methods developed would work even better in organisations that, with this book, have the benefit of hindsight and, most likely, more time and resources as well.

It is not a story of universal success. There were failures. But some of those failures were necessary to demonstrate the need to change strategy and move on from the policies of the past. And all of the failures taught us something. There were difficult conversations, normally avoided in traditional professional practice for the sake of remaining professional. There were workplace tensions, often avoided in more mainstream organisations by people associating with people like themselves. At LOCOG, people did not have that luxury. They did not have time to determine whom they wanted to work with and who not; they were often thrown together in short timeframes and expected to come up with results regardless. In this sense, it was a window into the future, an example of how work is transforming, from fixed 'departments' to flexible teams that can 'swarm' a problem and offer collectively derived solutions, akin to crowd-sourcing in social media.

Originating in Ancient Greek philosophy, courage is counted as one of the four cardinal virtues, along with prudence, justice and temperance. In other words, it is pivotal. Any person seeking to confront, change or improve a difficult situation must be able to sustain this characteristic. Courage is not reckless. As discussed in Aristotle's *Nicomachean Ethics*, it is the antithesis of recklessness, as well as cowardice.[2] In many books about change and leadership, courage is often forgotten or overlooked. It is either intentionally or unintentionally omitted. I think that is unfortunate, and perhaps slightly dishonest and disrespectful to the lot of the practitioner. It is they, after all, who have the responsibility to push through the change programme. Here, I argue it is the first of three essential ingredients, followed by creativity and talent, required in order to achieve real inclusion.

In his 1957 book *Profiles of Courage*, former US President John F Kennedy examines the traits of eight senators in their quest to achieve legislative and social change.[3] While they are all men, and the book is in some ways a creature of its time, it introduced the idea that inclusive leadership does require a qualitative element of courage, in addition to a quantitative element of calculation. Courage, in the context of achieving an inclusive organisation, is keeping the issue on the table when so many people believe it would be more convenient to drop it. It is pointing out, and then dealing with, the proverbial elephants in the room. Assuming the strategy is creative, the practitioner talented and the purpose worthwhile, courage is then separating your self from your role, braving the inevitable storm, and avoiding being shot down in the process.

There is important work to do, and the clock is ticking.

Notes

1 Individual agency is undeniably important though, read Stephen Covey, *The Seven Habits of Highly Effective People* (Simon & Schuster, 1989).

2 http://en.wikipedia.org/wiki/Nicomachean_Ethics.

3 John F Kennedy *Profiles in Courage* (Harper and Brothers, 1956). See also Geoffrey Best *Churchill, a Study in Greatness* (Penguin, 2002). Both these men were able to offer authentic leadership, which, especially for the time, was courageous.

Inside the tent: the seven stages of life in an organising committee

01

Paul Deighton, the highly capable and humorous former Chief Executive Officer of the London Organising Committee (LOCOG), summarised the process of staging the Games in a seven-stage model. He was paraphrasing one of his predecessors, Sandy Holloway, the Chief Executive of Sydney 2000. The stages were, in very specific order: celebration; shock; despair; search for the guilty; persecution of the innocent; celebration (again); and, finally, the inevitable glorification of the uninvolved.

This is actually a useful framework to attempt to explain the background and context of the London 2012 Games, and specifically to articulate and explain the animal that was the London Organising Committee. The nature of the organisation appears in some ways unique: its temporary nature with an immovable deadline, the level of scrutiny and limited resources being key factors. However, for the most part, it was simply an intensified experience of what persists in most organisations. Other more mainstream organisations simply do not have to endure the level of external analysis LOCOG was subject to. Most companies are not public experiments. Since LOCOG was, we can all learn from the experience.

Introducing the organisation

There was a paradox evident in the organisation: the intense level of scrutiny encouraged a risk-averse approach, yet the force of circumstances dictated the opposite. Whereas the scrutiny did indeed encourage a risk mitigating, conservative approach to tackling problems, the immovable deadline, lack of resources and multiple other constraints forced the opposite approach. It was this latter approach that prevailed. Experimentation became a necessity, and the resulting laboratory was a wonderful learning environment in which to learn. As Tony Sainsbury, a colleague and Games veteran, observed 'it's the only place in professional life where you can gain 15 years of experience in 5'.[1]

LOCOG was a private organisation, and therefore not subject to the public sector 'equality duties'; legally mandated action to 'promote' equality.[2] It was a temporary organisation, growing from fifty or so individuals in 2005 to an army of 200,000 staff, volunteers and contractors in order to stage the Games in 2012. It was also the first time the Paralympic Games' preparations had been brought into the same organisation as the Olympic Games, with both Games being prepared by the same staff under the same leadership of Chair Seb Coe and Chief Executive Paul Deighton.

LOCOG's primary purpose was to deliver the Games; to prepare both Olympic and Paralympic Games and to stage an inspirational Games for the athletes, the Olympic and Paralympic family and the viewing public. Even though its mission was 'to use the power of the Games to inspire change', LOCOG's primary purpose was explicitly not social change, it was event staging. One of the best summaries, truly, of life in an Organising Committee was parodied in the BBC Comedy series *Twenty Twelve*, which included incidents such as losing foreign delegations due to bus drivers not knowing routes, legacy and sustainability fighting for airtime, different interpretations of 'Inclusion day' and so on, many of which were, in fact, true.

When Jeremy Hunt, the Secretary of State for Culture, Media and Sport – the sponsoring government department – was asked what he thought of LOCOG, he replied 'competent'.[3] That was a fair summary of how LOCOG was perceived by many stakeholders. 'Private sector' was used frequently by public sector colleagues.

The reality was that LOCOG was headed by an ex-banker, with a cohort of professional corporate people in its ranks. It was also, however, extremely diverse in terms of the backgrounds and world-views of its key players. There were those from a strongly commercial background, bankers, lawyers and management consultants, who wanted to run LOCOG as a for-profit entity. There were those from a strongly public sector background, civil servants, charity personnel and government secondees, who wanted LOCOG to live up to its perceived social responsibilities as a priority. There were also those who were somewhere in-between, including international colleagues, and 'Games junkies' who had staffed multiple Games before, moved from host city to host city, and who felt that the focus should only be on operational delivery.

The consequence of these often wildly different world-views was a constantly contested territory in which to operate. No two meetings would be the same. In some, commercial interests would triumph. In others, social interests would dominate. In some, legacy would be front of mind, and in others it would all be about the operational here and now. As Head of Diversity and Inclusion for the Organising Committee, my responsibility was to ensure we staged a Games where, according to our own PR, 'everyone is invited, everyone is welcome and everyone can take part'. In the job description it said 'this role will be accountable for the development of the "Diversity strategy" and will influence across the organisation to ensure that diversity forms part of everything that we do at LOCOG'.

Re-defining success

The Olympic Games is a truly unifying event. Every four years, more countries than are members of the United Nations assemble in a global city to compete on the sporting field. It is the largest peacetime event in the world, and the most complex to organise.

The complexity of the Games derives not just from their size, but also from the sheer range and diversity of stakeholder constituents and client groups involved. The number of nations, the number of nations who have no/strained diplomatic relations and the number of athletes creates unique challenges. As does the number of media, the pressure on existing transportation and security systems, the potential for new hazards and unforeseen challenges.

The complexity of the project also derives from the need to satisfy different definitions of success. For many inside the organisation it was a technical exercise. It was possibly the largest and most complex technical exercise imaginable, but it was still a technical test. Delivering 26 simultaneous world championships for the Olympic Games over 134 venues, with a workforce of 200,000 and the entire world watching, followed by 20 more simultaneous world championships two weeks later for the Paralympic Games, was the ultimate technical challenge. The Olympic Games is comprised of 26 world championships (39 disciplines) across 34 venues, 8.8 million tickets, 10,490 athletes, 302 medal events, 21,000 media and broadcasters, 19 competition days (including football), 2,961 technical officials, 204 National Olympic Committees, 5,770 team officials and 5,000 anti-doping samples. In order to cope with this challenge, people understandably resort to technical know-how as per Table 1.1.[4]

Past Games had endured real technical challenges, from venue readiness at Athens 2004, terrorism at Munich 1972 and Atlanta 1996 to boycotts at Moscow 1980 and Los Angeles 1984. Given this, it is perhaps understandable that many would have relied on what we already know and have learned over the years. They would have proclaimed success as simply the successful staging of the event, as indeed happened in London in July, August and September 2012.

For others inside and outside the organisation, it was more than that. Technical excellence was a prerequisite to success, but not success in and of itself – £9 billion and the chance of a lifetime constituted too great an input to only produce a technical output, no matter how impressive. We needed to change the system, we needed to engage in adaptive work. On paper, this latter group won. 'Legacy' became the key word, and the mission of the organisation became 'to use the power of the Games to inspire change'.

In some ways, this was a gift for inclusion. To use 'the power of the Games' to inspire social change, to make the world a better place, was in many ways the ultimate organisational mission statement. However, it was carefully worded so as to be open to multiple interpretations. The faction who lost the 'paper war' still remained in the technical driving seat; the most complex event in the world requires technical excellence as a precondition to any other aspiration, no matter how noble. So while the mission of the organisation was indeed 'inspiring change' that was a value that had to be fought for, not taken as given, in the technical race to the finishing line.

'Success' therefore remained open to interpretation. There was relative unanimity concerning the successful technical delivery of the event, but

TABLE 1.1 Technical versus adaptive work

Type of Work	What's the Work?	Who Does the Work?
Technical	Apply current know-how	Authorities
Adaptive	Learn new ways	The people with the problem

Adapted from Ron Heifitz and Marty Linsky, *Leadership on the Line* there was relative ignorance at the start about 'success' in terms of inclusion. We therefore had to create a definition of success that respected the technical prerequisite, but was sufficiently bold to justify the opportunity of a lifetime the Games had provided. Diversity and Inclusion presented an adaptive challenge of changing the system, which many people did not initially want to take on, either consciously or subconsciously, especially if 'the system' worked fine for them already. For one, many good people were turned off by their current perceptions of Diversity and Inclusion based on their experience to date in other organisations. In addition, time, money and lack of resources in general presented very real obstacles. This was, in a very real sense, all about achieving diversity on a deadline.

'Success' for Diversity and Inclusion at LOCOG had to start with a re-definition of the subject matter and an intelligent articulation of a genuine business case for action. This is detailed in Chapters 3 and 4. We began with the mission, to use the power of the Games to inspire change, and this was translated into 'Everyone's 2012', allowing everyone to take part. There were technical goals laid out at the start, with target zones for workforce and procurement diversity, for example. However, the specific definitions of success, and moreover the spirit of success, only came alive mid-way through the project when we asked the departments to define inclusion success for themselves. Their discretionary effort, courage, creativity and talent produced results that we could not have envisaged on paper five years out.

Celebration

The first stage in Paul's model was celebration. London was not expected to win the hosting of the 2012 Games, and this is where the Diversity and Inclusion story begins – as an accident of history.

On 6 July 2005, all the media cameras in the Singapore conference hall were in front of the Paris delegation, waiting for the reaction to the announcement. Back in France, the Champs-Elysées and the square in front of the Paris town hall were packed with jubilant French citizens. President Jacques Chirac had already left Singapore for the G8 summit, confident of victory and a prize he had helped secure for the French Republic.

The British Prime Minister Tony Blair, on the other hand, stayed until the last minute, despite being the host of the G8 summit, which was taking place in Scotland. He held court in a hotel suite and received a steady stream of visitors, including many that the French President had not met. There was comparatively little attention given to the London delegation, David

Beckham aside. People in London and around the UK did stop for the announcement, but only to hear the expected French victory and then commiserate with each other in a typically British fashion.

The UK had bid for the Games three times before, once with Birmingham for the 1992 Games (held in Barcelona) and then twice with Manchester for the 1996 Games (held in Atlanta) and the 2000 Games (held in Sydney). Three bids, three losses. It was felt that London, the nation's capital, was the last chance to maintain national pride – and lose with dignity. Losing to Paris would be palatable, because it had been a good campaign and the bid had improved greatly in the months leading up to the Singapore decision. And this was losing to Paris, in many people's minds the old enemy. It was also home of all things Francophone, which might have appealed greatly to the Francophone International Olympic Committee.

All of this made the reaction to Jacques Rogge's words all the more electric. As the International Olympic Committee President opened the envelope to announce the winner, I was glued to the television in the cramped, small, old office of Stonewall, the lesbian and gay charity, opposite Victoria station in London. I had my French 'pen-friend' of 20 years on the mobile phone, confident of victory. It was indeed an historic moment. I was surrounded by Stonewall colleagues as we temporarily suspended work for the lunch hour in order to watch the BBC, congratulate the French and then get back to our desks.

When Jacques Rogge took the envelope from a young Singaporean girl, opened it, read 'the Games of the thirtieth Olympiad are awarded to the city of… London' there followed a second of disbelief, as though time had stood still, followed by the most almighty roar. A roar not just from my colleagues in the office, but a roar from the streets below, a roar from the television of the folks assembled in Trafalgar Square and a roar from the bid team in Singapore as the cameras scrambled past the bemused French in order to catch live TV feed of London Mayor Ken Livingstone hugging Minister Tessa Jowell who was hugging Seb Coe who was hugging David Beckham.

In Paris, on the other hand, there was silence. It was a palpable silence that rolled across the square in front of the Hotel de Ville, that rolled down the Champs-Elysées and that even extended to Benoit on the other end of my mobile phone. The silence was followed by mutterings of disbelief, by disquiet about an 'Anglophone plot', about the role of Tony Blair and the supposed inherent irregularities in the International Olympic Committee voting system.

But in London, the mood was triumphant. It was not triumphant for simply winning against the odds, not even triumphant in *Trafalgar Square*, of all places, for beating the old adversaries the French. It was triumphant for a coming together, for the assembled individuals on the pavement in London, or in offices that day, to turn to a colleague or even a stranger and to hug them. London had promised to deliver a Games for everyone, 'Everyone's London 2012', and we had taken 30 young people from the East End of London, constituting 30 per cent of the London delegation, to make our point to the powers that be.

Diversity and Inclusion were a central part of the bid. London had made a virtue of this, promising to make London a Games for everyone, and it contrasted markedly with the French presentation, which showcased technical excellence and one white man speaking after the next. The French presentation was awe-inspiring, but it was 1980s male-created *gigantisme*, not modern inclusiveness pertinent to the times. Nelson Mandela had said 'The Games in London will inspire athletes as well as young people... it is a diverse and open city [and] I can't think of a better place to unite the world.' From Singapore to London, and in many parts of the world to some degree, there was genuine celebration.

Shock

The second stage in the 'seven stages' is a dramatic word. But less than 24 hours later, on Thursday 7 July 2005, four terrorists detonated home-made explosives on the London transport system, killing 52 people, injuring 700 and bringing one of the world's capitals to its knees. Three of the four were British nationals of Pakistani descent living in Leeds, Yorkshire. It was the ultimate expression of the negative effects of diversity.

To go from jubilation to tragedy, celebrating diversity to despising it, in less than 24 hours was a cruel turn of events; however, a new reality was dawning. Security would have to change from what had been promised in the bid, to what would become necessary in this new reality.

The Host City Contract was an all-encompassing document that legally binds a host city to deliver all the infrastructure, services, security, transport and logistics necessary to host the world's biggest and most complicated event. It specified commitments, one of the major ones being security. It did not specify budgets. Therefore London was committing to an outcome, not a defined monetary amount. Beijing had cost upwards of $32 billion. London was not in a position to spend a similar amount of money, especially after the 2008 economic crisis. Financially it would have been irresponsible, and politically it would have been extremely difficult.

More than anything, many senior people did not expect London to win, and so they had not given serious thought to the consequences of a winning bid. Before they had time to consider the implications, the contract was signed and London was legally bound to host the Games of the Thirtieth Olympiad.

Despair

The third stage is one way to describe some of the meetings that were held in the early years following the win. There appeared simply not enough resources available to deliver the contract. The most challenging episode in the lifetime of the Organising Committee probably revolved around the budget and the necessary increase from what was budgeted in the bid, to what would become necessary in operational delivery once all the consequences of decisions and interdependencies had been established.

The original budget was a 'wildly underestimated' £2.3 billion.[5] One of the trickiest pieces of PR possible was to then explain the new budget of £9.3 billion. It should be noted that this was the budget for the public sector Olympic Delivery Authority, not LOCOG.[6] It was the Olympic Delivery Authority budget that was paying for the redevelopment of an entire part of an old city, London's East End. However, in the public mind, LOCOG/Olympic Delivery Authority, private/public distinctions were somewhat irrelevant, the budget had increased from 2 to 9 billion. Interestingly, by the final stage, see below, the budget was finalised at £8.9 billion and the government was able to trumpet savings to the public purse of £377 million.

Outsiders could be forgiven for thinking that we had vast resources at our disposal. However, resources were incredibly stretched and there was a constant drumbeat of cost cutting, budget revisions and a focus on 'creative resourcing' in order to stay within budget. Budget discipline was one of the Chief Executive's imperatives, and he was successful in achieving it. In an interview with *The Pink Paper*, I was asked how much money had been allocated to Diversity and Inclusion. I answered £2 billion, the LOCOG total budget. We were so integrating Diversity and Inclusion into the organisation that every penny would be used to an inclusive end. The actual resources available for Diversity and Inclusion were £1.3 million over four years. This is substantially less than many corporations who have a far smaller remit than LOCOG.

Deadlines are common practice in corporate life. But at LOCOG, they *were* corporate life. No matter whether it was Sunday evening prepping for the week ahead, Tuesday morning in the 8 am management committee meeting or Friday afternoon exhausted in the office, everyone knew at any time exactly how many days there were to go. We knew how many Fridays there were to go. We knew how many more management committee meetings there were to go. We knew how many monthly status meetings there were to go. Good meetings would fly by from day to day and week to week. Frustrating meetings would be ticked off, safe in the knowledge that they could not continue indefinitely. The mother of all immovable deadlines was a rallying call to put conversations and frustrations on the table, to communicate, to make a decision and then move on. Everyone knew that at 8 pm on 27 July 2012 everything would cease to matter – and no matter what state we were in, the Games would start.

So we had an immovable deadline. This mother of all deadlines was both a challenge and a resource, the former being perhaps more obvious. In negotiations with suppliers or stakeholders they would know you had to get things done and often held the initial advantage in any negotiating situation. In any normal organisation, what didn't get done would either be moved to the next quarter/year business plan, sent to committee, or deprioritised. In LOCOG, what didn't get done, didn't get done.

However, this deadline became in many ways more of a resource as time went on. Because we set out the relatively simple Diversity and Inclusion framework early on, and communicated it constantly, it was not a new concept as the deadline approached. That allowed the use of the deadline more to force outstanding conversations on to the table and to call out procrastination or obstruction. In that sense, it was our friend; less fear inducing and more issue resolving.

Search for the guilty

When times get bad, the search for the guilty often commences. Who got us in to this mess? Many of the campaign team who ran the bid were now absent from the Organising Committee. Understandably so, as the skill sets required to campaign for a Games are wildly different from those required for operational delivery. Some of the original bid team stayed on, and some of those people had an unpleasant time. The search for the guilty largely revolved around the budget, but there was limited mileage in that since the financial situation was what it was. The search moved on to the infamous 'bid promises' that were (or were not) contained in the bid book.

This was particularly true of the 'legacy commitments' ranging from sustainability to getting children involved in sport. Sustainability sounded good in the bid, but some operational folks regarded it as a distraction when it came to operational delivery. The team on the ground worked very hard to compensate for this. The budget controversy paled into insignificance in comparison with the debate around those who said what number of kids would stop eating junk food and start playing hockey.

Bosses and celebrities with egos were facts of everyday life at LOCOG and a co-dependency of the cult of the individual is the culture of silos. In order to avoid blame and claim success, information was king. Many departments would be fiercely territorial of their own patch, refusing point blank to share information with other teams, lest it gave them either an advantage or a perceived unfair share of the credit. There always had to be someone else available to take the blame, should it be required. This is not the extent of the nightmare it may at first appear. It is logical that in a high-stakes endeavour, with limited time and an immovable deadline, people will be extremely focused on making it to the finishing line.

However, the Diversity and Inclusion team was cross-functional in nature. We worked with all departments and so were one of the few functions that challenged the siloed mentality and nature of the organisation. We therefore had to work hard to build trust in order to gain information. This was especially true when it came to benchmarking departments against other teams, which could directly affect their reputation and appraisal. The fact that we were able to build up the trust required in such a short space of time is testament to the approach adopted, namely to listen and consult, rather than lecture and audit.

I was acutely aware of how 'Diversity and Inclusion' could be used by the organisation as its social safety net and a useful scapegoat should it get into hot water over some perceived social failing. One goal, therefore, was to assertively build alliances throughout the organisation and make sure that this was a low probability.[7]

Persecution of the innocent

This is an unfortunate, often regrettable, but frequently occurring consequence of the search for the guilty. Scapegoating, according to some Olympic veterans, is a favourite pastime in Organising Committees where the scrutiny is intense and the need to stay alive and avoid association with inevitable failures is very real. In order to overcome a problem, someone can be exited or demoted to symbolise the correction of a perceived problem and allow the organisation to move on, irrespective of whether it has actually overcome the obstacle. For example, it is classic poor HR practice that when a staff member is being bullied, harassed or victimised by somebody, it tends to be the victim, as opposed to the perpetrator, that is moved.

Again, this might sound deeply unpleasant. However, looking at it from a rational systems perspective, rather than an emotional personal one, this is actually a common occurrence. The only difference is that LOCOG was more transparent and readable than most organisations. The persecution of the innocent is one way to describe the scapegoating of those who were quietest, complained least and had the least influential friends – or those who were perceived as a threat. LOCOG attracted a huge diversity of talented individuals from all walks of life – banking, law, consultancy and professional services, public sector, third sector, the arts, campaigning and lobbying, communications and so on. Many of these people came with dramatically different world-views and some of them sought to impose their view of reality on everyone else. It was a cauldron of strong personalities. In the absence of organisational baggage, lack of traditions, customs or protocol, it was something of a free-for-all and survival of the fittest. In actual fact, as with all imperfect organisations, it was often the survival of the most political and strategic.

Celebration (again)

On 27 July, when the Games began (or, for the staff, 9 September when they ended) there was due celebration as London hosted what is regarded as the best Games ever. How do we judge success? One useful mechanism would be to analyse the experience of some of LOCOG's nine client groups (see Table 8.1 on p 133).

The athletes were universal in their praise. LOCOG's attention to detail, the training venues spread around the UK and the location of the residential village on the park minimising commuting times to events all combined to provide a best-in-class athlete experience. One of the biggest successes was the performance of the athletes, especially the home team, Team Great Britain. Besides the performances of Usain Bolt and Bradley Wiggins, it was noteworthy how the Games were dubbed the 'Women's Games' by leading commentators. Sarah Attar became the first-ever Saudi woman to represent her country in an Olympic stadium. Even though she came 30 seconds behind the second-last athlete in the 800 m event, she received a standing ovation and positively biased commentary from 150 m before the finishing line. It was the first time every country had included women in their teams.

Pierre de Coubertin, the founder of the modern Olympic movement, had characterised women's sport as 'impractical, uninteresting, unaesthetic and incorrect'.[8] In 2012, Jessica Ennis became a household name in the UK, as did Missy Franklin and Gabby Douglas in the United States. Nur Suryani Mohamed Taibi, a Malaysian shooter, represented her country while eight months' pregnant. It was the first time women's boxing was included since 1904 and the US women, for the first time ever comprising a majority of the US team at 51 per cent, brought home 63 per cent of the US gold medal haul.

The British press and international print and broadcast media were housed on the Park too, in purpose-built facilities with the best food and wine possible as well as dedicated shuttles to their hotels in Mayfair and Bloomsbury. The Olympic and Paralympic family and technical officials enjoyed dedicated service, reserved commuting lanes and reserved seats. The workforce, the men and women who actually staged the Games, were treated as a client group and rightly so. More on them later.

Perhaps more than any of these groups, however, the number-one client group and true test of the Games success was the 60 million general public in the UK, from London to the Shetlands, from Wales to Northern Ireland, from Yorkshire to Cornwall. A largely cynical British public had been trans-formed into an enthusiastic nation of flag-waving Olympic and Paralympic supporters. This was in large part due to the success of Team Great Britain, but also due to the Torch Relay, which had visited every part of the Isles, passing within 10 miles of 95 per cent of the population in the 70 days before the Games began.

The glorification of the uninvolved

For many individuals, the ideal scenario had been to outsource risk for the last five years as much and as frequently as possible, and then reclaim the issue late in the day if, and when, success was assured. LOCOG had in some ways a flat hierarchy, although several colleagues challenged me on my acceptance of this over the years. Paul and the Directors would be sup-ported by the Heads of Department (including the Head of Diversity and Inclusion – myself) who would in turn be supported by a series of managers. Every single person in LOCOG deserves credit for his or her contribution to the Games. While, as in many organisations, the glory was bestowed disproportionately on the higher echelons, the deadline determined that someone, somewhere, at some level had to handle the risk. For that fact alone, the unsung brave heroes, lost in the middle of the organisation, deserve the most glory of all.

It is amazing who appears on the scene when the sun is shining. And in the afterglow of London 2012's universally recognised success, more celebrities, politicians, business folks, career enhancers and networking types appeared on the scene than even I thought possible. The glorification of the uninvolved was indeed upon us.

I will never forget a reception hosted in March 2013 by the Commission for a Sustainable London 2012 in recognition of the achievements of the Games. I knew many of the LOCOG Sustainability team well, from having worked alongside them as colleagues the previous five years, and I knew how smart and dedicated they were. During the entire reception, Commissioner after Commissioner was congratulated for their 'oversight' but there was no recognition of any of the actual team on the ground who did all the work.

Walk the line

The seven stages provide an original framework to understand the organism that was LOCOG, but they are purposefully provocative in order to convey a simple point: LOCOG was a crucible, a laboratory without existing rules. It was a forum where we could try new policies, often out of necessity. It was harder than I ever imagined it would be, but it simultaneously offered an unprecedented opportunity to achieve business and social change in new ways. Undertaking work in the LOCOG reality invited the famous quote 'ask for forgiveness, not for permission'.

The leadership challenge was to walk the line: to not fall into the trap of many traditional diversity practitioners of being so off message that you were ignored, but to not be so on message that you created no differentiation and were subsumed into the machine. That line became a recurrent theme in driving change. On one side of it was the real risk of assassination, of being shot down and taken out of the game for pushing too hard. On the other side was the endless desert of inertia. It was helpful to realise that people were not necessarily opposed to change, they were opposed to loss. That realisation was one of the key anchors that helped define where, in fact, the line was on a daily basis.

Self and role

Another important realisation was the distinction between self and role. In the intensity of the experiment, things could get personal. If people, even avid supporters, perceived Diversity and Inclusion as too much of an opportunity cost to their 'day job' they would react against it. The danger was that they would also react against the proponents of that message and in so doing lower the practitioner's credibility to continue with the work. It was of critical importance that the message (Diversity and Inclusion) was not personalised, especially by those who did not want to hear it. It is, after all, about the message. It is not about you. In order to de-personalise the message it was essential to build alliances and to have other colleagues, inside and outside the organisation deliver the message in addition to, or preferably instead of, you. It's harder to assassinate a whole herd than a lone beast.

In this respect, I occasionally failed to take my own advice. With some members of the communications team, I took their initial rejection of Diversity and Inclusion personally, rather than appreciate that they were rejecting my role. Their rationale was that they were already supportive of the overall idea of Diversity and Inclusion, they were busy, and they didn't need additional items on their to-do list. However, by reacting personally to their initial rejection I allowed them to confuse the message with the messenger. It was only as they began to hear the message from other people, especially external VIPs in the media, that the penny dropped.

LOCOG was in many ways a free market for talent. As a temporary construction, it had little organisational baggage, few barriers to entry (except talent and the volume of competition) and it achieved unprecedented diversity. That diversity created a contested space as different people and world-views collided. It was not the proverbial bed of roses propagated in traditional diversity training sessions – this crucible, this laboratory experiment had been testing, even unpleasant, at times.

But that group conflict was necessary for adaptive, rather than merely technical, work to occur. Colleagues from the public sector, familiar with 'equality impact assessments' (EIAs) and 'freedom of information requests' (FOIs) were in meetings on the same side of the table as colleagues from banks and law firms who had no idea what an 'EIA' or an 'FOI' was.[9] When lobby groups started requesting FOIs they soon learned. Several people from the Sports department, who had worked in sport all their life, at first resented the coexistence of consultants and others from professional services firms who quite simply danced to a different tune. 'Alpha males' were challenged, in some cases, for the first time in their professional lives. They were surrounded by talented people who were very different from themselves. They therefore had to work harder, they had to do more homework, and they had to come up with clever arguments and creative solutions if they were going to persuade the wider group of the merits of their proposed course of action. They could not rely on nods, winks and implicit understandings. That code had been broken.

The resulting creative tension produced an amazing outcome. Diversity had been far from the fluffy face of how so many people may have originally perceived it, but it had undoubtedly been effective in contributing to some creative solutions. Diversity and disequilibrium, by definition the opposite of groupthink and equilibrium, were essential ingredients in creating the best Games ever.

Takeaways – inside the tent: the seven stages of life in an organising committee

1 There will always be technical work to do. Diversity and Inclusion is adaptive work, and needs to be framed effectively if it is to be embedded in the systems and processes of the organisation.

2 Inclusive leadership is of central importance in driving change. In addition to separating role from self and walking the line, the use of deadlines and other non-personal parameters can help do the work for you.

3 Diverse realities are messy. Diversity is not a bed of roses, it is by definition a collection of different, often opposing world-views, which can make inclusion even more difficult to achieve.

Notes

1 Conversation with the author, Beijing, August 2008. We were both working on London's 'handover' responsibilities from the Beijing Organising Committee and taking part in the 'Observer programme' run by the Organising Committee to transfer learning from one Games to the next.

2 http://www.equalityhumanrights.com/advice-and-guidance/public-sector-equality-duty/introduction-to-the-equality-duty/.

3 Address to heads of department, 2011.

4 Adapted from Ron Heifitz and Marty Linsky *Leadership on the Line* (Harvard Business Press, 2002), p 14, 'distinguishing technical from Adaptive Challenges'. See also Dean Williams, *Real Leadership* (Berrett-Koehler, 2005).

5 *Telegraph Newspaper*, Jacquelin Magnay 23 October 2012 http://www .telegraph.co.uk/sport/olympics/9627757/London-2012-Olympic-Games-comes-in-at-377m-under-budget-government-announces.html.

6 See Chapter 2 for further explanation.

7 More detail is provided in Part Two.

8 http://www.visualnews.com/2012/08/09/1896-olympics/. For further reading on this apparent contradiction in the 'celebration of humanity', read Pierre De Coubertin *Olympism; Selected writings* (International Olympic Committee, 2000) especially pp 711–12.

9 Equality Impact Assessments (EIAs) are exercises undertaken largely by public sector organisations or large infrastructure projects to determine if an initiative will cause any undue negative impacts on certain sectors of society. From the results, they can then propose mitigating measures. Freedom of Information requests are public requests for otherwise private information, the logic being that there is a public right to know about an otherwise 'secret' issue.

Outside the tent: the Olympic and Paralympic movements

02

Former US President Lyndon Johnson observed that it was 'better to have them inside the tent pissing out, than outside pissing in'. That could not be more true than in the case of LOCOG and the organisation of the Games. LOCOG did not organise the Games in a vacuum. The organisation was part of a larger system, just as every organisation is part of a larger system. And in a very real sense, the system organised the Games, just as the system often determines the fate of any organisation.

Above the organisational level, therefore, it is necessary to understand the external forces acting upon LOCOG. Stakeholders offered resources and expertise. They also offered wildly different viewpoints and agendas, requiring management. The practitioner is not only operating within and navigating an organisation (which is their job on paper), they are also obliged to navigate, or at least be aware of, the external system if they want to create systemic change. The challenge was to identify which bits of the system could be most helpful in bringing that change about.

The Olympic Games

The Olympic Games and Paralympic Games are simultaneously the most well known and least understood movements in the world. Well known, because they enjoy a global television audience in the billions. Less known, because what the client sees is only the output, often very different from the internal processes, politics and systems necessary in the preparation. Many of their peculiarities act as a proxy for a bygone age where less enlightened approaches to diversity still ruled supreme. To lead change in this world requires courage, as deep vested interests with deep historical roots are at stake.

The Olympic Games are well known. The ancient Games were held in Olympia, Greece from the 8th century BC to the 4th century AD. The modern Games originate from 1896 when a Frenchman, Baron Pierre De Coubertin, revived the ancient Games of Olympia after founding the International Olympic Committee in 1894. The 1896 Games brought together 14 nations and 241 athletes, who competed in 43 events, having been inspired by such events as the Much Wenlock Games in England's rural Shropshire. By 2012 they were the pre-eminent global event, sporting or otherwise, and the rings are one of the most recognised symbols and brands in the world.

The history of the Olympics and inclusion is mixed. When the Games were held, a truce was observed, the now famous 'Olympic truce' symbolising a downing of arms between and among enemies, to create peace, if only for a period of time. The ceremonies were also important religious occasions, yet the modern-day International Olympic Committee is staunchly secular. Women first competed at the Games in Paris in 1900, the second modern Olympics. This was before women had gained the vote in many Western countries. Especially noteworthy, given the Francophone nature of the International Olympic Committee and its headquarters in Switzerland, France did not grant women voting rights until 1944 and Switzerland not until 1971. The 1904 St Louis Games were perhaps the most homogenous ever, with 580 of the 650 athletes being from the United States, and this was seen as a low point for the Olympic movement, the movement having since become more diverse with every subsequent Games.

The Olympics is also full of contradictions. It embodies ancient tradition but it has to keep pace with modern technological advancements. Pierre de Coubertin's original vision of a purely amateur event has given way to the inclusion of professional athletes. His original vision of education and culture alongside sport has struggled, although London has gone a long way to revising the educational and cultural aspects of the Games. The Olympics is in many ways embracing of the diversity of humanity yet as we have discussed above, Pierre de Coubertin was of the view that only men should be allowed to partake.

Other challenges of the modern era include boycotts, bribery, doping and terrorism. The Olympic platform allows unknown athletes – and ideas/causes – the opportunity to achieve national and international exposure, for good and bad. It allows a variety of causes to make their pitch for global recognition and media interest, including the competing agendas of varied stakeholders. In Beijing 2008, there was significant protest against China's human rights record, in various global locations that were host to the torch relay. This caused tension with LOCOG because we could not be seen to be condoning human rights abuses but had a diplomatic obligation to stand alongside a fellow Olympic city. It did, however, play a key factor in persuading LOCOG to stage a domestic torch relay in 2012, as opposed to an international one.

The Paralympic Games

The Paralympic Games are much less well known. Originating in 1948 when pioneering neurologist Sir Ludwig Guttmann devised a series of sporting events at Stoke Mandeville hospital in England's Buckinghamshire, it was an effort to help the rehabilitation of soldiers returned from World War Two. It was designed to take place concurrently with the Olympic Games happening in London at that time. He wanted to build on his experience to date witnessing the rehabilitative power of sport for spinal injuries sustained in combat. In 1952 the Dutch joined in, creating the first international event for disabled athletes. They are now the second biggest sporting event in the world, including athletes with a range of physical and mental/intellectual disabilities ranging from visual impairment to amputees and cerebral palsy.

There are several reasons the Paralympics have struggled for equal prominence with the Olympics. They have a shorter history, with fewer accumulated resources. They have also struggled to effectively market disability sport to a predominantly non-disabled or able-bodied majority. At the Beijing 2008 Olympic Games the American broadcaster NBC had over 1,200 staff. Only a handful remained for the Paralympic Games two weeks later. Even in 2012, the Paralympics received widespread coverage in Europe but hardly any in the United States. There is also the diversity of disability among the athletes, and the associated politics that go with that. The Paralympic Games are now organised in parallel with the Olympic Games, yet the International Olympic Committee recognises other events such as the Special Olympics, for athletes with intellectual disability and the Deaflympics, for athletes with hearing impairments. In London 2012, athletes with intellectual disability were re-admitted for the first time since Sydney in 2000, when Spain was disqualified for including team members who later turned out not to have an intellectual disability.

The International Paralympic Committee is the global governing body for the Paralympic Games, equivalent to the International Olympic Committee for the Olympic Games. The International Paralympic Committee is head-quartered in Bonn, Germany, largely due to the fact that when the German government returned to Berlin, their departure freed up some good-value accommodation. Formed on 22 September 1989, it is very young in compari-son with the International Olympic Committee. It is also still in development. For example, the Federation representing deaf athletes was a founding mem-ber of the International Paralympic Committee but decided to withdraw after a few years and continue their own development of the Deaflympics. In 2003, the International Paralympic Committee launched a new logo for the movement with the three agitos from the Latin *agito*, I move. These are the Paralympic equivalent of the rings, but much less well known.

The social and medical models of disability: towards inclusion?

As with the Olympics, there are contradictions and paradoxes associated with the Paralympics. In the UK, the 'social model' is the dominant disability paradigm. The social model places the burden of responsibility for improved accessibility on wider society. For example, a supermarket would be expected to ensure step-free access to its premises, rather than suppose a disabled person could navigate steps with adapted crutches or other support.[1] The 'medical model' of disability, however, emphasises individual responsibility for improved accessibility. For example, a disabled person would be expected to train/adapt/receive support in order to overcome barriers, such as steps. However, due to the diversity of disability in the Paralympics, there are sev-eral 'categories' in which the athletes compete. This 'classification system' is by its very nature an extremely medical model, and even offensive to propo-nents of the social model of disability.

The 'allowable disabilities' are divided into six broad categories: amputee; cerebral palsy; intellectual disability; wheelchair; visually impaired; and 'the others', which are athletes with disabilities that do not fall into the other five categories. The categories are classified from sport to sport and the situation can arise where an athlete has spent years training in one category only to be moved to another by officials at the Games, potentially changing over-night from world champion in one class to a lower ranking competitor in a different class. Infinite diversity is challenging to manage, and difficult to categorise into classes, in spite of the operational necessity of sometimes doing so.

The history of inclusion in the Paralympic movement in relation to the Olympics is interesting. Many commentators have asked why the two largest sporting events in the world cannot be combined so as to make them inclusive of disabled and non-disabled people alike, as the Commonwealth Games tries to do. In fact, disabled people did compete in the Olympic Games before the advent of the Paralympics in 1948. German American gymnast George Eyser, with one artificial leg, was the first disabled athlete to compete in the Olympic Games, taking part in St Louis in 1904.

More recently, disabled athletes competing in the Olympics include Natalie Du Toit from South Africa, Marla Runyon, the blind US runner who competed in Atlanta and an Italian archer who was a wheelchair user.[2] Coming full circle, Oscar Pistorius, a double amputee, competed in London 2012 and passed through several qualifying stages. Inclusion, in this sense, is dependent upon the time when people accept it – the BBC commentary was enlightening in this respect. Although the media were content, even enthusiastic, to allow Pistorius to compete in the Olympics – 'have a go' Oscar – they were not content to see him beat 'professional, able bodied' athletes. That would have been too controversial and uncomfortable for them. Disabled people are, by definition, supposed to be less able than 'able bodied' people.

Ever since, the Paralympic movement has had to contend with the idea of greater inclusion with the Olympics, at the expense of its own moment in the sun. This dichotomy was brought into sharp focus with London 2012 when LOCOG was the first Organising Committee to integrate both Games in one organisational structure. The benefits for the Paralympics were that all the resources, talents and skills devoted to the Olympics were now available to them too. The downside was that they were integrated and did not receive the distinction they had perhaps become accustomed to in recent years. A parallel may be drawn with the advancement of gay rights in UK legislation with the amendment of the Equality Bill in 2005. No longer could lesbian and gay people be turned away from hotels or denied hospital visiting rights to see a partner, but at the same time, no longer could straight people be refused entry to a gay club. Inclusion is a two-way street.

The Paralympic Games embraced disabled athletes other than wheelchair users from the 1976 summer Games onwards. In 1988, the Paralympics began to be held directly following the Olympic Games, in the same city, using the same facilities. The International Paralympic Committee and the International Olympic Committee formalised this arrangement in 2001 and have since extended this through to 2020.

London 2012, a step change for inclusion

The values of the two movements, and the histories they embody, are conducive to inclusion. The Olympic values are excellence, friendship and respect. The Paralympic values are determination, courage, inspiration and equality. In the Olympic Charter, the International Olympic Committee states its commitment to equality and human rights for all:

> The practice of sport is a human right. Every individual must have the
> possibility of practicing sport, without discrimination of any kind and in the
> Olympic spirit, which requires mutual understanding with a spirit of friendship,
> solidarity and fair play. [...] Any form of discrimination with regard to a
> country or a person on grounds of race, religion, politics, gender or otherwise is
> incompatible with belonging to the Olympic Movement.

The Charter does not explicitly refer to gay, age or disability equality. One could infer, given the language, that the intent is very much inclusion in its broadest sense. The International Olympic Committee voiced concern about a new anti-gay law in Russia in advance of the Sochi 2014 Winter Olympics.[3] However, the absence of specificity continues to be a campaigning point for lobby groups who, with some validation, regard the International Olympic Committee as laggard in this area. The Paralympic Charter, on the other hand, explicitly refers to outlawing discrimination on the basis of political, religious, economic, disability, gender, sexual orientation or racial reasons.

The London Games were an intervention in this history, and not all of it was foreseen at the time the organisation was designed. By bringing both Games into one Organising Committee it challenged the prior method of Games organisation, where two separate organisations, one with significantly less resources, would organise two separate games.

But LOCOG went further. Besides organising both Games with the same staff and resources, it also merged the logos and branding. The Olympic branding is the most heavily protected brand imaginable, as anyone who has worked with the International Olympic Committee will confirm. To use the same logo outline shape for both the Olympic rings and the Paralympic agitos was radical. Again, to discuss the International Paralympic Committee's dilemma, it undoubtedly gave them more profile than ever before. But it also reduced their distinctiveness as apart from the Olympics. The legacy to date, however, with the pronounced 'bounce' in the fortunes of the International Paralympic Committee suggests London's strategy had real sustainable value for the movement.

Chairman Seb Coe is on record as stating:

We want to change public attitudes towards disability, celebrate the excellence of Paralympic sport and to enshrine from the very outset that the two Games are an integrated whole.[4]

The political ramifications of this are significant for both the Olympic movement and Paralympic movement. Seb's leadership on this issue also set the scene for much of the inclusion work that followed.

The host country players

While LOCOG was an effective intervention in the global history of the Olympic and Paralympic movements, literally changing the course of their histories, the national scale was a different situation. To help place the organisation of the Games in context it is necessary to understand some of the key players involved.

There was the Olympic Delivery Authority, a public sector organisation and therefore subject to the public sector equality duties as well as freedom of information requirements.[5] As we shared an office, as well as an email suffix, we became quite integrated; however, the different political environments we operated under led to interesting situations, from strategic differences, such as separate diversity strategies, to minor but still potentially important differences, with certain information being public and some not, for example. The Olympic Delivery Authority's primary purpose was to deliver the Olympic Park and all venues on time, within the agreed budget and to specification, minimising the call on public funds and providing a sustainable legacy.

The Greater London Authority under the direction of the Mayor of London was a key player. Its objective was to maximise the economic, social, health and environmental benefits of the Games, particularly through regeneration and sustainable development in East London.

Under the first left-wing Mayor, Ken Livingstone, the Greater London Authority was a key player in the selection of London as host city, following Mayor Livingstone's insistence that the focus of London's bid should be the redevelopment of its poorest boroughs rather than the utilisation of existing venues in predominantly more affluent West London. Under the second more right-wing Mayor, Boris Johnson, the Greater London Authority's focus shifted to more purely economic benefits, rather than focusing on the social per se. The Greater London Authority had a bizarre matrix management system that the employees didn't understand, let alone those of us outside the organisation who had to interact with it. The bottom line was that what the mayor wanted was generally the organisational position.

Except that, unlike many other global capitals, the central authority of the mayor was relatively weak. The 32 London Boroughs enjoyed relatively strong power in the capital and controlled many functions that would be controlled centrally in other capital cities. So what Robin Wales, Mayor of Newham, or Jules Pipe, Mayor of Hackney, wanted in their patch would often trump what Boris (or London 2012) wanted. The Olympic Park was largely in Newham, and Robin Wales was a prominent voice on the Board of LOCOG. The Park also flowed into Hackney and Tower Hamlets. Greenwich and Waltham Forest were also co-located by the Park and these five Boroughs together constituted the 'Five Host Boroughs'. A sixth was added later, Barking and Dagenham, further to the east.

Central government's involvement was (in theory) channelled through the Department of Media, Culture and Sport and the newly created Government Olympic Executive. The challenge was that a sub department (Government Olympic Executive) of a relatively weak department (Department for Culture, Media and Sport) was always going to struggle to attain the necessary traction with LOCOG and the Olympic Delivery Authority when they were in direct contact with Number 10, the Home Office, Ministry of Defence, police and so forth. Many in LOCOG resented the perceived interference of civil servants in a private company and at times great lengths would be gone to in throwing the bureaucrats off the scent of anything they might be interested in. Even though LOCOG was a private company and privately financed, the government acted as lender of last resort and reminded LOCOG of that fact when information was not forthcoming to their liking.

There was also the British Olympic Association and Paralympics Great Britain who were primarily concerned with their respective athletes. Of these varied organisations with their differing agendas, the principal four, LOCOG, Olympic Delivery Authority, Greater London Authority and Department for Culture, Media and Sport came together at the Olympic Board, supported by the Olympic Board Steering Group (OBSG). The collective mission was to host an inspirational, safe and inclusive Olympic and Paralympic Games and leave a sustainable legacy for London and the UK.

The history of London 2012 will vary according to which of the above organisations is talking, but as the Games progressed well, there was surprising unanimity among the varied stakeholders with a genuine sense of collective mission to stage a brilliant Games. It was mainly in terms of earlier debates where there could be friction. For example, LOCOG, responsible for staging the events, wanted to ensure fully accessible venues for every sport. However, it did not receive the keys to those venues until a year before the Games, and was therefore dependent on the Olympic Delivery Authority building to the required standard. Often they did, or beyond, but often there was no 'client' in LOCOG to direct the Olympic Delivery Authority when they were in their early construction phase 2005–09. This resulted in problems when the client came on stream as LOCOG hired. If LOCOG hired too early, there was a cost implication as well as that person not being fully utilised. If LOCOG hired too late, there was a cost saving, but often at the expense of client requirements being met.

On paper, LOCOG was the least likely to champion Diversity and Inclusion. It was the only major player that was private sector and not subject to the public sector equality regulations. It was primarily concerned with staging the Games, whereas the other major players had wider remits; regeneration, legacy and so forth. Yet, as this book argues, it was precisely because of that commercial freedom and independence from government compliance/interference that real inclusion was possible, debunking standard thinking in standard compliance-driven equalities policy. If the goal was greater inclusion, be it in terms of jobs, contracts, or thought leadership, this book shows how LOCOG, free of public sector regulation to some degree, more entrepreneurial in culture, more dynamic and more commercial, achieved more in the inclusion space.

It was, however, a team effort and alliances had to be built. Many of the Government Olympic Executive staff I dealt with were helpful, and some became good allies. They cared about social legacy and came to see the LOCOG Diversity and Inclusion programme as a cost-effective way of making change.[6] They also regarded LOCOG as something of a private sector anomaly, an experiment, and, as there was little cost risk associated with the Diversity and Inclusion programme, they were very happy to see it proceed. Similar allies for inclusion resided in most of the other organisations.

The sponsors

The power of the sponsors was substantial. At the global level, they had saved the International Olympic Committee in the 1980s when the very future of the movement was in doubt. At the organisation level, they constituted a third of our revenue. The Games would not happen without them. In the end, 44 companies signed up as domestic sponsors, in addition to the international or 'TOP' sponsors that maintained a relationship with the

International Olympic Committee. The sponsors ranged from long-standing Olympic partners such as Coca-Cola (supporter since the 1928 Amsterdam Games) and McDonald's to new partners such as Dow Chemical Company and British Airways. Each corporation had its own reasons for association – and association was expensive. They were therefore determined (in the most part) to maximise their relationship to their own commercial advantage. When an organisation has paid £80 million ($120 million) for domestic or worldwide marketing rights, they are understandably rather sensitive to anyone infringing those rights.

That presented a conundrum for those who wanted to create 'Everyone's 2012' by offering association to worthwhile non-profit, charitable and third sector organisations. LOCOG joined several employer forums and we allied ourselves with various charities. For a charity to come along and ask for association for nothing (or even for us to pay them) is therefore a delicate balancing act.

The lobby groups

We joined Stonewall,[7] Europe's largest lesbian and gay rights charity. It was hard for us not to quite frankly, given that I was Workplace Director there and established the programme we joined, the Diversity Champions programme. We joined Race for Opportunity[8] and Opportunity Now,[9] the ethnicity and gender initiatives of the UK's Business in the Community. We were also active with Business Disability Forum.[10] I used to have regular breakfast with their wonderful but slightly terrifying Chief Executive Susan Scott-Parker. She would arrive in a whirl of business officiousness, we would talk intensely for an hour, and then she would depart pulling her ever-present carry-on wheelie case and I would pick up the bill. Susan kept me on my toes.

There was the Employers Forum on Age and the Employers Forum on Belief (both of which we joined). They then merged to become the Employers Network on Equality and Inclusion[11] (which we transferred into). The breakaway 'Inclusive Employers'[12] we also joined, but the irony of a splinter group on inclusion was not lost on us. We also joined Family Friendly employers run by the Family and Parenting institute.[13] Of all the initiatives this went down best with the sceptics internally because most people could relate to the challenges of working on the Games and bringing up a family. We were a founding signatory to this campaign. We signed the Fawcett

Charter, challenging the objectification of women at work.[14] We signed the Women into Science, Engineering and Construction (WISE) Charter aimed at progressing the participation of Women in Science, Technology, Engineering and Maths (STEM).[15] We also signed and supported the Changing Faces charter challenging facial disfigurement[16] and were founder signatories to the Charter countering homophobia in sport.[17]

In all of these interactions, the message we tried to convey was the same. Don't lobby us assuming we're bad. Work with us assuming we're good and tell us what we can do in the next four years that will help you once we've gone. Some, like the Family Friendly scheme, got it. They wanted us as a founding signatory; it looked good to have us on board and demonstrated our confidence in their plans, helping their growth and future new business. We signposted a lot of new business their way.

Such cooperation and foresight was not universally present, however. There was an assumption in many quarters that with the brand assets of the Olympic rings and the Paralympic agitos alongside the perceived mission of the Games, Diversity and Inclusion was a *fait accompli*. Such assumptions came from people who had never worked with sports' governing bodies.

The world of sport

Removed from standard commercial pressures, distanced from dynamic consumers, often monopolies in their own sports, enjoying (ironically) little competition, sports governing bodies are in many ways challenged by Diversity and Inclusion. In 2004 UK Sport and the four Home Country Sports Councils established a programme called the Equality Standard for Sport.[18] It was designed as a framework to help sports governing bodies progress towards becoming more dynamic, merit based and open organisations. It was established in four levels, each demanding more progress in terms of widening access to sport and increasing the participation and involvement from minority groups. The business case was that greater diversity in sport would enlarge the future talent pool, helping future-proof performance. Most performance directors, the real power in sport governing bodies, did not see it that way. They knew where their future medallists were coming from (often dedicated, small, elite tracks) and it was more efficient for them to reinforce success there than to engage in new 'outreach'.

The Standard was designed to assist organisations in improving inclusion within their structures by developing the organisation and services. In many ways this was free consulting for sports bodies that commercial organisations had to pay for. There was also a strong correlation between their lack of commercial imperative and their level of inclusion competence vis-à-vis other commercial organisations who were much more consumer led and dynamic.

In order to intervene with these bodies, LOCOG worked to achieve the first stage of the Equality Standard, Foundation, in March 2009, demonstrating our commitment to Diversity and Inclusion through our basic policies and procedures. The assessors commented, 'LOCOG has a very strong commitment to their equality work. This commitment is throughout the organisation from Board to Officer level and the Diversity Action team ensures all staff have the opportunity to be involved in equality.'

Three months later, we had achieved the second stage, Preliminary, by demonstrating, through our action plans and early results, our intent to make a difference. It should be noted that most organisations that had supposedly been on this journey since 2004 had not yet reached Preliminary level. We achieved in three months what they had failed to achieve in five years. The assessors said, 'This is one of the most comprehensive Equality Standard Assessments reports I have had the privilege to read and should be held up as a model or template of best practice for others to follow.'

Three months later in September 2009, we achieved the third level, Intermediate. As only the third organisation in the country to do so, having started only that year, it begged the question, what had the other 100-plus sports been doing for the last five years? The principal work that helped us achieve this level were our three recruitment programmes: access now; action on inclusion; and attitude over age, as well as our LOCOG Overlay Access File for spectators, athletes and the Olympic and Paralympic Family.[19]

In December 2010, LOCOG became the first organisation ever to attain the Advanced Level of the Equality Standard. The delay was largely due to them having to invent the assessment method. Even though it had existed on paper for a number of years, since no one was in danger of achieving it, they hadn't needed to worry about it. By demonstrating how Diversity and Inclusion were fully embedded in all LOCOG's operations and culture, particularly through the Everyone's 22 projects,[20] LOCOG was congratulated for breaking new ground and delivering inclusion in a tangible way. Liz Nicholl, the Chief Executive of UK Sport said at a reception, alongside LOCOG Chief Executive Paul Deighton, 'LOCOG are to be congratulated on this significant achievement. In reaching the Advanced Equality Standard for Sport, they have shown commitment to embedding equality throughout the organisation and all of their work streams, which will prove fundamental to making London 2012 a truly inclusive Games.'

The reality was, however, confirmed by her second point:

This is also an important milestone in the history of the Equality Standard for Sport. We are delighted that LOCOG has found this to be a valuable tool to use to drive their equality agenda, as we support all Olympic and Paralympic sports and other UK Sport funded bodies to do so. I hope LOCOG will continue to share best practice in this area with their partners in British sport as we all aspire to embed equality throughout out work.

The sports bodies had been completely overtaken by a private sector new kid on the block, with less resources and less time. We didn't have an 'equalities' agenda, we had one agenda, a business mission, which was to stage the best Games we could. Diversity and Inclusion either added value to that goal or the programme didn't exist. A separate agenda was the antithesis of our approach. Many colleagues instinctively recoiled at the equalities word. Not because they were ardent right-wingers but because it positioned Diversity and Inclusion as static and anti business, a burdensome initiative to bear, rather than something that could add value.

The reason we had done this was not to self-congratulate. It was, with credibility, to benchmark the remaining sports bodies, especially the 26 Olympic and 20 Paralympic sports bodies on their own progress in the standard. We did not have the time or resources to invent some new benchmarking system, but we did like the benchmarking idea. So rather than undermine the Standard, we reinforced it, demonstrated it could be achieved and then gave it greater validity for the rest to follow. By showing we could go from zero to the first ever Advanced level in under two years, it focused attention on why the other better-resourced sports could not do so in a much more lax timeframe. As I have argued elsewhere, it is perhaps because of the lack of time that we did do much better and a little sense of urgency would not go amiss in some of these cosy monopolies.

Of course there was much resistance. But it came from the most unlikely quarters. When Debbie Jevans, our Sports Director, presented at a quarterly briefing on LOCOG's results and our desire now to see other Olympic and Paralympic sports progress through the Standard, she received a cool reception. The Wheelchair Basketball Federation, in particular, was very against. This was ironic, to say the least. In order to protect Debbie's relationships, and to avoid LOCOG being shot down, we partnered with allies who could deflect the heat; UK Sport (who actually ran the Standard) as well as government ministers.

Hugh Robertson, the Conservative ex-military Sports Minister was a surprising and enthusiastic supporter. At a Home Office summit, he focused right down on the key leverage point; 'If they don't do it, withdraw their funding'.[21] And with that, UK Sport made advancement in the Standard a requirement of continued capital support from the UK taxpayer. It made sense. Everyone was funding these organisations, yet they remained often exclusive clubs. In order to receive public money, open up. Some of the better sports followed suit, especially swimming. However, many sports, especially those furthest from commercial realities, languished at the bottom of the benchmarking system. Only the funding threat and LOCOG's intervention spurred activity. Media interest, scrutiny and government benchmarking is the way to ensure continued progress in this area.[22]

The conservatism of the sports movement can be seen in the 2013 appointment of two white middle-aged men to lead UK Sport and Sport England. Not only did they replace two extremely capable women, their appointment was also at the expense of Tanni Grey-Thompson, one of Britain's greatest ever Paralympians (and most capable in all senses). She was widely regarded as the best person for the job. As leading sports commentator Alan Hubbard said:

> By not appointing Tanni Sport England miss out on acquiring a much-needed inspirational figurehead who would have lifted a worthy but anonymous organisation from public indifference... This could be interpreted as a snub not only for Tanni but also for the advancement of women in sport and Paralympic sport. With the exit of Baroness Campbell from UK Sport, we now have both Government sports quangos headed by able-bodied men. And where were the black candidates we wonder?[23]

Outside the LOCOG tent was a diverse place. Stakeholders ranged from extremely commercially focused corporations who were funding the Games, to some inward-looking monopolies that carried outdated attitudes to inclusion. At the global scale, the International Paralympic Committee and International Olympic Committee came with their own histories and cultures. At the national scale, competing factions fought over the essence of the Games and what the legacy should be. At a local level, different London Boroughs competed for resources. This is the space in which Diversity and Inclusion were played out.

Diversity and Inclusion were therefore operating in an extremely fluid and often volatile environment where the techniques required would vary from organisation to organisation, meeting to meeting, and person to person. Over time, operational considerations would trump all else, understandably so, and therefore it was critical that we built the infrastructure and developed strong alliances early – and made Diversity and Inclusion integral to the operational reality that was coming down the track at 100 miles per hour.

Takeaways – outside the tent: the Olympic and Paralympic movements

1 A change process within an organisation is always dependent on the wider system within which the organisation is operating. That system can be harnessed to aid the change programme, or it could be a major factor in limiting it.

2 External relationships are crucial in building allies that have an effect within the organisation. To challenge deeply held beliefs is hard.

3 Diversity is infinite. In addition to the colliding world-views within an organisation, there are also factions outside the organisation. Again, these can be harnessed to aid the change programme.

Notes

1 For a comprehensive and simple explanation of the social and medical models of disability, see The Open University's pages http://www.open.ac.uk/inclusiveteaching/pages/understanding-and-awareness/social-model.php.

2 Conversation with Tanni Grey-Thompson, Paralympian and Member of the House of Lords, 13 July 2013.

3 The Russian government passed a law prohibitng 'propaganda' for 'alternative lifestyles', in a similar fashion to some African governments attempting to outlaw homosexuality as a valid human condition.

4 Seb Coe interview http://tribune.com.pk/story/424810/london-prepares-for-welcome-again/ *The Express Tribune* 23 August 2012.

5 See note 2 in Chapter 1, p 26 re FOI requirements.

6 Civil servants such as Shaun Cove, for example, were important in this respect.

7 http://www.stonewall.org.uk/at_work/.

8 http://raceforopportunity.bitc.org.uk/.

9 http://opportunitynow.bitc.org.uk/.

10 http://businessdisabilityforum.org.uk/.

11 http://www.enei.org.uk/.

12 http://www.inclusiveemployers.co.uk/.

13 http://www.familyandparenting.org/.

14 http://www.fawcettsociety.org.uk/.

15 http://www.wisecampaign.org.uk/.

16 https://www.changingfaces.org.uk/Home.

17 https://www.gov.uk/government/news/fight-against-homophobia-and-transphobia-in-sport.

18 http://www.equalityinsport.org/.

19 See Chapters 10 and 19.

20 See p 175 for full explanation of the 22 projects and how they were derived/delivered.

21 Summit Against Homophobia, Home Office, London 2011.

22 The Equality Standard for Sport can be viewed online at http://www.equality-standard.org.uk/. It is noteworthy (and ironic) how the league table of which organisations have achieved which level has now been hidden. For a full set of benchmarks, see Appendix p 317.

23 Alan Hubbard, Inside the Rings http://www.insidethegames.biz/blogs/1013910-alan-hubbard-cameron-must-shoulder-the-blame-for-the-baroness-tanni-grey-thompson-debacle 23 April 2013.

Re-defining Diversity and Inclusion

03

Every successful organisation has a purpose. The purpose of an organisation creates its value, and to that extent the purpose is sacred. To add any other programme into the mix, it must support that purpose, or else be of limited success. Many diversity programmes to date have been either detached from the purpose, and have therefore failed, or have been 'on message' but of such indeterminable added value that they are emasculated.

Let's define terms. What do Diversity and Inclusion really mean? To date, there has been either a superficial understanding, and subsequently a superficial response, or an overly academic approach too removed from fast-changing real-world realities. To come up with a different approach, it is first necessary to go back to basics.

Diversity

According to the *Oxford Dictionary*, the word 'diversity' originates from the Middle English and Old French *diversite*, or from the Latin *diversitas*. In the singular, it simply means a 'range of different things'. The example they give is 'newspapers were obliged to allow a diversity of views to be printed'. In Old French, diversity also had the distinct honour of meaning 'repugnant', which is how some people still view it.

Diversity is about difference, and in our context we are focusing on the differences between people. Diversity can occur easily, because the world is diverse. US cities, for example, are the proverbial 'melting pot' of waves of immigrants from a range of cultural, ethnic and religious backgrounds. Throw in sexuality, gender, disability and age dimensions and you can find some of the most diverse places on earth. Many of us view this as

TABLE 3.1 Real versus superficial inclusion

Type of Inclusion	Definition	Detail
Superficial inclusion	Including token diversity	Including homogeneous groups or minimal aspects of diversity, usually limited aspects of demographic identity only, eg race, gender
Real inclusion	Embracing infinite diversity	Including fuller aspects of diversity, such as ability (IQ, cognition, skills), experiences (cumulative life events, coming out, hidden disabilities) as well as demographic identity

intrinsically good. In other words, we like diverse places. When Londoners are asked what they love about living in London, one of the first responses given is its 'diversity'. A key aspect of the London bid for the 2012 Games was the city's diversity. New York City uses its diversity as a key part of its inbound tourism campaign.

But is diversity an end in itself? How inclusive are US cities? How inclusive is London? It's easy to be diverse, without being inclusive. US cities are often divided on ethnic as well as economic lines. Much concern has been expressed over recent housing policy changes, which could mean poorer Londoners moving to even poorer areas, furthering the social and geographic segregation increasingly evident in the so-called melting pot.

There is a vast literature on 'types' of diversity.[1] For the purposes of practicality and application to the organisation this book simplifies them to aid the practitioner with Table 3.1 above.

Real and superficial inclusion

The *Oxford Dictionary* definition of inclusion is 'the action or state of including or of being included within a group or structure' and the example the *Oxford Dictionary* provides is 'they have been selected for inclusion in the scheme'. Inclusion, again in our context, is about including people.

Superficial inclusion can be easy to achieve. Take France, for example. There is a very strong sense of national identity – among *most* French. The national motto is *liberte, egalite, fraternite* and it has a strong sense of territorial integrity, *les limites naturelles*. Or take Fortune 500 boardrooms. They are often very superficially inclusive; male, sensible and, in the main, intelligent.

But is superficial inclusion an end in itself? How does France really manage its diversity, from the *banlieues* suburbs in its major cities to its overseas territories that lie outside *les limites naturelles*? How diverse are Fortune 500 boardrooms? It's easy to be inclusive, without being diverse. By definition, it is easier to include people if the views/needs/characteristics are more closely aligned, because that necessitates less work. It's easy to be inclusive with a homogenous group. *Superficial inclusion*, as opposed to real inclusion, exists because people take the path of least resistance, associating with similar people. Many people don't want to be challenged by different people with different perspectives, especially when they already have a challenging 'to-do' list.

If diversity is difference, and inclusion is bringing those differences together, then both Diversity and Inclusion are required in order to move forwards as an organisation and as a wider society. Either in isolation simply won't do, not just because they are easily attainable independently, but also because independently they do not create value-added change. Superficial inclusion is about including token diversity or relatively homogeneous groups. But how valuable is that when the world is not homogeneous? Inclusion could instead be about embracing diversity in all its forms, including a range of talents, skills and life experiences. Beyond demographic differences, *real inclusion* is about true diversity – in thought as well as physical reality.

Real inclusion is hard to achieve. By definition, the more differences that exist, the more challenging it is to bring them together for a common purpose. But, without being trite, that's life. That is increasingly how organisations and their client/customer base are. And therein lies the work. That is the reality LOCOG had no choice but to confront. Other organisations can avoid this, by appointing a 'Diversity Officer' or some other position to engage in superficial inclusion, maintain the status quo, hire some token minorities and add some decorations to the tree. It may benefit the organisation in the short term, but they will lose out in the long run, as the heterogeneous world around them moves on and leaves them behind, stuck in their homogeneous cocoon.

It's important to realise that superficial inclusion is not something attributable only to the dominant group, for example, senior white males in Fortune 500 boardrooms. Superficial inclusion is unfortunately present among many minority groups too. How many minority groups do you know who keep themselves to themselves, talk to the already converted and still assume they are making progress?

The real point, post-definition, is that we should care about this. That's the 'so-what' question. Our world and our workforce is in fact diverse, becoming more so, and, as this book demonstrates, we can achieve so much more by bringing those differences together toward a common goal rather than letting them drift in isolation. Extreme real inclusion would actively seek out those differences in order to acquire new resources. What if recruitment focused on accessing niche talent that is currently under-represented in our talent pool through proactive outreach programmes? What if talent management then concentrated on developing that talent and gaining proportionately higher returns from individuals who have been ignored and under-developed for too long? What if customer services were geared towards diverse needs, intelligently informed by diverse talent on the supplier side?

Progress to date

Progress to date has been mixed, limited largely by the fact that diversity without inclusion doesn't work. I have attempted to summarise the main organisational diversity paradigms in Table 3.2. It is virtually impossible to propose a complete synopsis of organisational change/diversity programmes in the past two decades, but I believe the table below to be a fair summary, and hopefully recognisable to many existing practitioners. The terms will be explained as we progress through the chapter.

Diversity 101

'Diversity 101' programmes originate from the 1960s civil rights era, but can more recently be traced back to 1990s 'equal opportunities' programmes in the UK and 'affirmative action' programmes in North America. They tend to educate the general workforce in an organisation about the existence of diversity – usually gender and ethnicity. They were designed to raise awareness of difference, contribute to rectifying past injustices and in many contexts provided a useful window for employees into otherwise unknown minority worlds. In some ways, they are more watered-down affairs than equal opportunities and affirmative action programmes, designed to be less offensive to the status quo and in that sense not really challenge the existing paradigm. They offer a variety of initiatives anywhere on a scale of

TABLE 3.2 Diversity and Inclusion paradigms

Paradigm	Diversity 101	Diversity 2.0	Inclusion 3.0
	'Diversity for diversity's sake'	'Diversity for social responsibility'	'Diversity as business strategy'
Definition	Programmes designed to raise awareness of difference	Programmes designed to draw out the benefits of difference	Integrated systems designed to embed the benefits of difference
Education method	Diversity training, compliance-based business case	Diversity workshops, up-to-date business case	Structured conversations, original interventions, holistic business case
Leadership approach	Top down, authority led, compliance driven	Top down, authority led, auditing approach	Bottom up, top-level support, creative group leadership, peer review
Delivery mechanisms	Equalities team, equality impact assessments	Diversity team, needs assessments	Whole organisation, benchmarking and information sharing
Measurement	Quotas, legal reporting	Voluntary targets, Corporate Social Responsibility reporting/PR	Target zones, high frequency real-time reporting and individual accountability

action from awareness-raising of minority issues among the majority to actually creating opportunities for minorities in terms of jobs and training programmes.

Diversity 101 programmes are typically run by an 'Equalities Team' sitting somewhere in HR or the back office of an organisation. In many cases they are the 'office' for affirmative action programmes, government reporting and any outreach activities to minority groups. Mandated by the organisation to ensure compliance with legal requirements such as equal gender pay reporting, they can assist with employment tribunals and workforce equalities/legal compliance training. In many cases, they have an important role to play, and in many cases they were essential creatures of their time.

A recent 101 training programme I experienced talked a lot about language. It included, for example, a section on terminology and prohibited words or phrases including 'handicapped' and 'able-bodied'. Although I agree that 'handicapped' is disrespectful, 'able-bodied' is, in fact, how the majority of people identify. Even though I make a conscious effort to call 'able-bodied' people 'non-disabled' people, I know that hundreds of disabled people would prefer the language to not be a barrier to conversation and education – or a job. Language differs geographically too, for example *les handicapés*, is how we talk about disability in Francophone countries. And in the UK it is *disabled people*, whereas in the United States that is offensive and *people with a disability* is preferred. In other words, disrespectful language aside, people should be free to speak, communicate, connect and learn. Unfortunately Diversity 101 actually inhibits this more than it facilitates it.

Language can of course be incredibly important. 'Politically correct' language emerged in the 1960s as an understandable response to derogatory and downright dangerous language regarding minorities. However, political correctness, or 'PC', has subsequently acquired derogatory meaning itself, slammed by tabloid journalism for its supposed contribution to unjustified minority advancement and the limiting of free speech. And as Gary Younge of British newspaper *The Guardian* observed, PC has been attacked and misused by 'those who realize they are never going to win arguments about equality if they tackle their opponents head on'.[2] I am not advocating the death of political correctness, or total support of it. I am advocating a language that needs to be one the majority of people in the organisation understand, and not reinforcing of cliques, be they academic elites or a homogeneous crowd of diversity practitioners. In his discussion paper, Ziauddin Sardar concludes, 'The terminology used... needs to be accessible to the wider world and owned by the public.'[3]

Consider the widespread use of the terms 'male privilege' and 'white privilege' in US academic and professional circles. I am not for a minute denying that there is overwhelming theoretical and empirical data to support these terms, but how useful are they in practice? To label many straight white men 'privileged' is probably factually true, but does it lead to greater inclusion? Does it advance the 'cause'? I would argue it does the exact opposite on two counts. One, it probably offends and repels the more sensitive straight white men who might have been otherwise supportive of an inclusion programme. Two, it probably offends and further repels the diversity-disliking less-sensitive straight white men who are now running even further away from the tent. In London 2012, one of our key 'target groups' was white working-class young men who were fast becoming one of the lowest-achieving and hardest to reach groups. They were male, they were white, but they were far from privileged.

Diversity programmes, Diversity officers, Chief Executive speeches, websites and PR all point to the now widespread acceptance of the need to 'do something'. The problem remains that so many of these initiatives ignore the current realities within the organisational system, rendering most of them ineffective and possibly even counterproductive. In addition to a time and cost element, so many of the 101 diversity initiatives can make one cringe. What exactly makes one 'culturally competent' in a dynamic, devolved world anyway? There is of course an urgent need to learn about difference in order to effectively engage with it, but by the time an employee has been processed in a cultural competency 'training programme', 'culture' will have moved on. Unlike Diversity 101 training, culture is alive and dynamic. It all adds up to a poor platform for recruiting new advocates. As long as some white men are told that they are culturally incompetent, they will probably continue to refrain from listening.

Today, in many Western professional environments, Diversity 101 programmes are alive and well. Due to a fertile combination of increasing legislation and economic bounty in the 2000–08 period, there now exists a myriad of programmes and job positions. Training, diversity weeks, affinity groups, compliance questionnaires, equality impact statements and monitoring forms have become commonplace. Initiatives have sprung up and budgets have been allocated. According to Hansen $8 billion was spent annually on diversity training in US corporations in this period.[4] That's a lot of input. I am yet to be convinced of the output. As Frank Dobbin has concluded 'diversity training doesn't work'.[5] The fact that so much diversity infrastructure was scaled back post the 2008 economic crisis tells us a lot about the depth of these programmes and the organisational commitment behind them. They were discarded because a) they weren't really adding any value and b) they were seen as an opportunity cost in a zero-sum game when the budgets could be better allocated elsewhere.

Many corporations, governments and international organisations have rushed to develop 'diversity programmes' without really considering their relevance to the organisation other than pacifying government – and increasingly shareholder – reporting requirements. This is not a good starting point for actually adding value to the business. So many are poorly understood initiatives, just about sold in to sceptical Chief Executives, which have a cost requirement to them. This cost has to be small enough so as not to raise opposition, large enough to actually achieve something (usually an 'event' or 'training') but usually ends up being too small to make any significant impact.

Part of the Diversity 101 business case is that greater diversity will somehow lead to greater organisational talent. More diversity often does lead to better business outcomes (more on that later) but the crude approach offered here is to equate 'external' demographic characteristics (race, gender and so forth) with 'talent' characteristics such as IQ and skill sets. The danger of stereotyping here, based on superficial inclusion, is very real. It trivialises diversity and gives succour to opponents of change. Increased diversity does not necessarily increase the talent pool. Why would demographic diversity per se be a proxy for talent diversity? People's talents are not, as far as I am aware, perfectly correlated to their ethnicity or sexual orientation. I know black and gay people of varying intellects and abilities, and they are not all working in the music industry and interior design. The use of 'diversity' characteristics for 'talent' is worrying, lazy and potentially disastrous for future-proofing organisational capability.[6]

A question never addressed by Diversity 101 practitioners is 'Is diversity inevitably a good thing for an organisation and business performance?' Are 'diversity programmes' the best intervention we can make in order to try to improve the more negative aspects of organisational culture? There are negatives to diversity that are conveniently forgotten about by proponents of Diversity 101 and never asked about by the sceptics because they are disengaged from the whole programme in the first place.

Increased diversity can actually increase conflict. 'Relational demography' demonstrates that people like to associate with people like themselves.[7] Diversity 101 programmes can lead to lower motivation, commitment and happiness in the job. Other negative effects of diversity can include lower team cohesion, lowered likeability of each other and increased emotional conflict.[8] At a national scale it can include 'ethnic fractionalisation', which can actually undermine GDP growth.[9] Diversity 101 has nothing to say about this. For that reason alone I have never fully understood the notion of a 'Diversity Officer' in an organisation. It could be analogous to creating a 'Conflict Officer' or a 'Lower Growth Officer'. The absence of focus on inclusion is profound.

Another limitation of the 101 approach is to persist with a very West-centric point of view. What is a minority anyway? In South Africa, minorities ran the country for several decades. In Bahrain they still do. In organisations, the minority can control the direction of the organisation. When issues of power and hierarchy are addressed they are done so with a sledgehammer rather than a conversation. The result has been the alienation of those essential to the conversation.

Diversity 101's West-centrism also fails the *realpolitik* test. On a visit to Mozambique I deliberated the construction of the one major paved road in the entire country. It had been recently built by Chinese investors, in return for fishing rights off the Mozambique coast. When providing aid to Mozambique, a member of the British Commonwealth, the UK asks for statistics on gender diversity. It wants to do a Diversity 101 check on how the former Portuguese colony is complying with the UK's current version of reality. Do the Chinese investors ask for such box-ticking? Who got the fishing rights? This simplified example is made to illustrate a point; unless Diversity and Inclusion are systematised, they will remain an additional – and expendable – administrative burden.

Diversity 101 programmes are problematic on two counts. First, they don't really challenge the existing paradigm and therefore fail to impact the very injustices they purport to address. They are tolerated by authority precisely because they don't effectively challenge it. Second, they lack support and buy-in from the majority. Well-meaning attempts to support minority groups have unfortunately often led the majority of people who feel they do not fit into one of 'those groups' to run fast in the other direction. Furthermore, people often do not want to associate with those groups, even if they are defined as such. The real issue for many people outside the 'target groups' is that they feel Diversity 101 programmes are an intervention where non-merit-based selection criteria (ie demography, or superficial inclusion) trump ability and they feel that is intrinsically unfair. Advocates of Diversity 101 programmes have been unsuccessful in countering this claim. How often do you hear a Chief Executive proclaim their support 'for diversity' but not 'at the expense of quality'?

Diversity 101 policies fail because they are a superficial solution to what are in fact systemic problems. For example, the lack of women in senior positions is a systemic problem. Demand-side causes include male (and female) discrimination in hiring and promotion decisions, subconscious bias and implicit associations. Supply-side constraints include childcare, access to information and confidence levels. Yet the Diversity 101 policy response to date has been 'diversity training', which men, in particular, resist going to.

In defence of diversity practitioners and other professionals, many have realised the shortcomings of Diversity 101 approaches. Many have realised that pigeon-holing people and conducting 'Equality Impact Assessments' takes the work further away from the mainstream current in an organisation, rather than advance the cause of equality. It's analogous to poorly designed foreign aid programmes. No matter how many millions are spent on aid, they remain a fraction of the flows the other way from unequal terms of trade. Even the most well-designed diversity programme will fail to shift the trajectory of the organisation if it remains removed from where the real profit and loss incentives or other strategic levers of the organisation actually lie. It's time to stop the diversity aid programmes and focus instead on the terms of trade.

It is important to state the debt we all owe to many Diversity 101 practitioners. Many of these people are heroes and trailblazers hailing from the civil rights era and to whom we owe a great deal, for trying to make a difference rather than not, for caring rather than ignoring. This book is merely one example of many current interventions that are standing on the shoulders of giants. Without the work done by many Diversity 101 practitioners there would be no platform on which to build. However, the best legacy we can build on that platform is to remain relevant to today's realities. Diversity 101 has had its time and its place. With the exception of extreme discrimination cases, where compliance programmes are necessary, it's now time to move on.

Diversity 2.0

Diversity and Inclusion programmes have evolved to embrace other differences such as socio-economic or geographic, at national and international scales. These more recent programmes can be grouped into 'Diversity 2.0' programmes to reflect their better relation to current realities. Laura Liswood's book *The Loudest Duck*[10] is a move in this direction and critics have suggested it is on the road to becoming a more successful 'Diversity 2.0'. Diversity 2.0 programmes are better designed to draw out the actual benefits of difference, which are increasingly well documented. Rather than compliance-based training, soul destroying for many employees, Diversity 2.0 policies offer more 'workshop'-style events with an opportunity to ask (as well as be told) and a more up-to-date business case as to why a busy employee should sacrifice an hour of their day to learn about diversity.

Some more progressive companies have definitely moved on from Diversity 101 to embrace 2.0 policies and programmes. They use them in their PR and Corporate Social Responsibility reporting. They use them in their graduate recruitment, mindful that they are now competing with new kids on the block such as Facebook and Google for talent that is increasingly mobile. There are needs assessments (responding to business requirements) rather than 'equality impact assessments' and audits and there may even be a genuine desire at the top of the organisation to make Diversity 2.0 a part of their brand, marketing or overall Corporate Responsibility programme.

However, Diversity 2.0 is still a linear progression from Diversity 101. Although 2.0 programmes acknowledge many of the shortcomings of the 101 approaches, they are still defined and constrained by them. They still make their employees attend training, costing substantial amounts of money for unquantifiable results. The approach is still top-down – practitioners go to bed each night praying for the day the 'top team get it' and diversity receives an appropriate mention in the Chief Executive's speech. Worse still, Diversity 2.0 programmes are seductive for the busy Chief Executive wanting easy results, a couple of paragraphs for the annual report and to avoid changing the current strategy at all costs. Although there are now a plethora of online statements from leading corporations proclaiming their embracing of all things diverse, we know that this is often still far from the reality within those same organisations.

Mentoring

Diversity 2.0 talks a lot about mentoring. As discussed in Sheryl Sandberg's book *Lean In*[11] mentoring can be a great initiative, focused on cracking the unwritten code, and helping minorities advance. Dasgupta has written of the need to increase visibility of successful females in organisations, and to increase the prevalence of mentoring relationships.[12] This can be worthwhile, but when mentoring becomes about helping minorities 'blend in' we are left wondering what happened to leveraging the benefits of diversity and different perspectives. Making women learn more stereotypically male traits actually reduces diversity, which is a somewhat ironic goal for a diversity programme. At a recent World Economic Forum seminar I witnessed a female Chief Executive behaving in a more stereotypically 'male' fashion than her male counterparts on the panel. There persists a 'uniform' of shoulder pads and pearls, which still seems more appropriate to many than women simply being themselves. Of course, if people want to wear shoulder pads and pearls, or genuinely feel it is professionally appropriate to do so, then fantastic. But if they are doing so under duress, consciously or subconsciously, I think this is unfortunate.

Quotas

Diversity 2.0 practitioners are currently wrestling with the issue of quotas. Their frustration is understandable. Ignoring the business case completely, organisations have made excruciatingly slow progress towards including minorities, especially in senior positions. It is not surprising now, therefore, that the largest and most powerful 'minority' group of all has had enough. 'Women on company boards' is now a hot topic everywhere in Western professional life. Lobbyists have mobilised, alliances have been formed and the race is underway. But the race for what?

The '20% by 2020 Women on Boards' group proposes 20 per cent of board places for women.[13] Viviane Reding, EU Commissioner, proposes 40 per cent of board places by 2020.[14] Norway, outside the EU, has already imposed 40 per cent as a requirement for board composition among its top firms.[15] Quotas are in many ways a rearguard action, a crude, insensitive intervention and another barrier to the free flow of talent. They can also introduce uncertainty into promotion decisions and bring into question whether a promotion was merit-based or quota-based. This can undermine genuinely merit-based promotions and new hires. Unsurprisingly, many talented 'minority' candidates are therefore among the fiercest opponents of quotas. Quotas can actually further the stereotype that might be preferable to combat,[16] remove goodwill or individual agency in colleagues, and nullify the competitive process evident in merit-based selection.

However, how 'merit-based' is merit-based selection in practice? The literature on subconscious bias and implicit association is vast and growing. It is now widely known, for example, that, *ceteris paribus*, a competent assertive woman would be viewed as 'bossy and aggressive', whereas a man exhibiting the same traits would be viewed as 'normal'. Furthermore, the man would be rewarded for acting to stereotype, whereas the woman would be penalised for stepping outside her norm.[17]

The argument in favour of quotas, rarely well made, is actually quite succinct. If we assume that IQ and talent is equally split among the sexes, and we have no reason or evidence to suggest otherwise,[18] then, in an ideal world, power and decision-making would be reflective of that talent. The fact that it is not, highlights the imperfections and malfunctions in the structures we have created to govern ourselves. Since the structures are imperfect, we need to remedy them through an intervention, namely quotas.

Take the example of women in the UK parliament. A century ago the parliament was 100 per cent male. In 1919 Nancy Astor became the first female member of parliament but even after women won the franchise in 1928 there were only 16 members of parliament elected in 1929 (about 2 per cent). It increased incredibly slowly until 1997 when the Labour Party under Tony Blair won a landslide election victory including the use of all-female shortlists to select its candidates in many constituencies. This policy was controversial, and denied many capable men the right to stand in certain constituencies, but the number of women in parliament doubled overnight from 60 to 120 (about 18 per cent). Today members of parliament are still about 75 per cent male, but the injection of a cohort of talented women has achieved tipping point, provided role models and improved the scope and quality of debate. Rachel Reeves, Shadow Secretary of State for Work and Pensions and herself a product of an all-women shortlist, is regarded as one of the finest politicians and economists of her generation. All eight Leeds MPs (Members of Parliament) were men from 1970–2010. She points out that not only would she have been denied opportunity without the Labour Party's policy, but also that half of the members of parliament under 30 are now women.[19] Change has indeed been initiated.

To the extent that quotas influence existing norms, or create new norms, they can be an effective short-term shock to correct a structural imbalance. They can create role models and help an organisation achieve 'tipping point'[20] sooner. We know that one of the main incentives for minority progression in organisations is the presence of other minorities at similar or more senior levels. The problems start when quotas are positioned as an alternative to the free flow of talent in the long run. They cannot be a long-term solution if we want to achieve that free flow of talent. Over time they become counterproductive, like subsidies, giving fuel to the enemies of diversity, and increasing superficial inclusion among minority groups whose career trajectory, and subsequently life chances, veer even further off course from that of the majority. Subsidies have a cost, and they are ultimately unsustainable.

Nudges

Interventions don't need to be as dramatic, or crude, as quotas. They can be very small and free of charge – as long as they are profound. Perhaps the most profound of all would be people being authentic – gay people 'coming out', or people revealing a hidden disability, for example. Often this not only increases the productivity of the individual concerned, it can effect positive change in the team around them.

At a base level, Thaler and Sunstein have developed a theory of nudges.[21] In a *Financial Times* article,[22] Iris Bohnet talked about how 'nudge theory' could be applied to closing the gender gap. We think we are objective when making decisions, but this is an illusion, because we always rely on our cumulative experiences to date, which are unique to ourselves and are therefore, by definition, biased. We rely on heuristics, such as stereotypes, rather than the facts – the facts are often hidden underneath the veneer we put on things to act as a cognitive shortcut.

In a recent Harvard Kennedy School study[23] a more diverse recruitment resulted when candidates were presented in groups, rather than relying on traditional 1–1 interviews. The group effect decreases the effect of individual subconscious bias, meaning that when women were judged 1–1 (by male or female interviewers) they were judged with a strong gender stereotype. When they were judged alongside men, 'factual' things in past performance dominated. The 'nudge' increased the objectivity of the process and produced a more merit-based (and diverse) result.

'Diversity' as self-interest

One of the biggest problems with existing diversity 'initiatives' to date is that they seem self-interested. They care, or appear to care, more about the group that stands to directly benefit, rather than the greater good. Take the gender debate, for example. I am a feminist, like many people, both men and women. Like many others I am so because I believe that a world in which women have greater self-actualisation will be a better world for everyone. More women in positions of authority, and more men involved with childcare, will lead to better decision-making, as well as contribute to a more just world. However, the exclusion of race, sexuality, disability and other diversity characteristics from the discourse advocated by so many women leads many others wondering what their real motive is. Worse still, sometimes 'other causes' such as race or disability can often be viewed as competing for airtime with the main programme. Does it really come down to a zero-sum game of female advancement at the expense of others?

I was struck by an intervention at graduate school 10 years ago when the women in class, fed up of male-dominated conversation, decided to present together at the front of the room. They had emailed each other in advance of class and were ready to go up to the front as one group. However, they had forgotten about the one woman who was a wheelchair user and who could not 'go up' the steps to the front of the room. This female wheelchair user had even been excluded from the preparatory emails, suggesting that the ignorance was present from the beginning. Did the other women not see a female wheelchair user as a 'woman'?

We could learn from history. The Suffragette movement is rightly celebrated as an example of successful positive social change. However, the negative experience for black women is conveniently forgotten in the retrospective historical analysis. While white women in the United States won the vote in 1920, black women did not fully gain the right until 1965. Does that invalidate the Suffragette movement? No, because a movement has to make progress, but it should be progress that does not harm another human's ability to make similar progress, even if it is justice delayed, so long as it is not justice denied. The challenge is to identify what builds rather than what diverts. To walk the line between the strategic and the tactical with a preference for the former whenever possible.[24]

The reality remains; most professional people roll their eyes at the mention of Diversity and Inclusion, let alone practice. It is not seen as important, relevant, or useful to them. Marty Linsky, who teaches leadership at Harvard, is a friend and big supporter of Diversity and Inclusion, and says that he still hears too many senior executives reacting to Diversity 101 and 2.0 with, 'Why in the world would I care about that?'[25] Worse, often when Diversity and Inclusion are a recognised intervention and get people's attention, they get their attention for the wrong reasons. In a recent Harvard University Leadership class, I witnessed the Professor play loud tribal music to make a point about group dynamics.[26] It made the room uncomfortable. After less than two minutes someone had written on the board 'Who wants it to stop?' Groups have a very low tolerance for programmes they consider to be unhelpful and outside the legitimate remit of the group. Even when diversity programmes overcome this hurdle, they are then so watered down and meaningless as to be inoffensive to the majority of the customer base. End result? They are ineffective.

Real inclusion (Inclusion 3.0)

I argue for a very different Diversity and Inclusion. Where instead of additional programmes, with associated additional costs, we focus instead on the removal of barriers that already exist – subtracting, rather than adding 'stuff'. It is about removal of barriers to allow a more efficient functioning of the market for talent. It is about setting people free, not lumbering them with more protocol that adds little value and that many resent, diverting them from the day job and often lowering morale in the process. You don't need to sugar coat Diversity 101 policies or 2.0 programmes to achieve change. It's as much about the barriers you remove, as about the decorations you add.

It is about permission to have a sense of humour, one of the defining characteristics of a fun life and productive and happy employees. It is about a scientific basis to the work, rather than a political agenda masquerading with a patched up PowerPoint business case. It is based on a definition of Diversity and Inclusion that is honest and contextualised. I call it *Inclusion 3.0 or real inclusion* strategies, those that depart from a linear and historical trajectory from Diversity 101 and start in a different place. Strategies that start from the core purpose of the organisation and work towards paradigm shift, not emasculation. Strategies born from the real world, fast-paced and agile, not from 1970s reading lists born out of Berkeley.

Real Inclusion strategies integrate diversity considerations into existing infrastructure. This not only costs less than creating new (often ineffective) infrastructure, it actually embeds the benefits of difference where the decisions are made, through the line, in the hands of middle management. This can be seen in the results of the 'Everyone's 2012' projects we developed, detailed in Part Three. Inclusion 3.0 strategies do away with training, saving money and gaining goodwill. The answer lies not in failing to change individual value sets, but by changing the system. So, to take an earlier example, rather than 'diversity train' individuals, use the nudge of group interviews.[27]

Inclusion 3.0 starts from the premise that people want to do 'the right thing', they just need some practical tools, rather than to be lectured at. Granted, people do like to associate with people like themselves, and often shirk people they perceive to be different from themselves, but when they are working alongside difference everyday and it is part of business as usual, people adapt. That adaptive process is messy and it can be painful. But it is a reality check-in with the world outside. Ultimately, it is a necessary adaptation for survival.

Inclusion 3.0 strategies permit conversations, including difficult and seemingly facile conversations, such as how disabled colleagues go to the toilet or survive a business trip, or how Muslim colleagues can attend team drinks in a bar. 3.0 programmes offer original interventions such as guest presenters, celebrities, events, competitions and rewards and allow mass participation rather than limited participation in a top-down training programme. One of the most liberating, and effective, strategies employed in 3.0 organisations is the power of peer review.[28] Nothing affects individual professional behaviour more than reputation among colleagues. Peer review is a far more powerful tool for encouraging 'the right thing' than any training session. By sharing information, gaining the curiosity of colleagues, and positioning Diversity and Inclusion as a desirable goal, people can actually take up the baton willingly.

3.0 strategies are real time and relevant, rather than textbook and historical. With high frequency, near-real-time reporting, people can gain up-to-date information which they find both interesting and useful.[29] When this is coupled with individual accountability, it can produce focused behaviour, strong enough to counter the effects of subconscious bias and implicit association. There may be a resource constraint to the frequency and depth of this information sharing, but it can be integrated with existing systems in recruitment, procurement and customer databases. What gets measured gets actioned, but in the past there was no consensus to support the measurement in the first place.

To sceptics, who intrinsically recoil at the word 'diversity' I would suggest changing the language to something else, yet retaining the new Inclusion 3.0 meaning. We simply used 'Everyone's 2012'. People like to live in diverse societies, but people also like to associate with people like themselves. It's rather like Californians voting Democratic at the Federal level in order to have Barack Obama as their president, but voting Republican locally in order to enjoy lower taxes.[30] If people were less transfixed on language and more transfixed on including difference, perhaps more people would support Diversity and Inclusion, without even realising it.

Inclusion is not about inter-personal conflicts, individual demography or individual psychology as much as it is about understanding and then working with the existing power structures, status and hierarchies evident within an organisation. The challenge for leaders is to improve collective intelligence and hence improve overall group performance. It is necessary to have an honest and insightful understanding of the current dynamics – more diversity could be a threat, real or perceived, to the status quo. It doesn't matter how many women's leadership programmes you have, if men don't want women leaders because they perceive them as a threat in a zero-sum game, then diversity initiatives will be unsuccessful. It's about the system, it's not personal. A dose of *realpolitik* is required.

Zero-sum games and enlarging the pie

A conversation with a Harvard colleague was illuminating. She had heard the Diversity 101 business case for diversity a thousand times and remained cynical about change. Her argument was that men do not want to relinquish power and share with women. No matter how good the business case, it was meaningless if men were not prepared to give something up. My response to this is not to always position Diversity and Inclusion as a zero-sum game where one faction wins and one faction loses. Although that can be true, it is not always so. Assuming guilt in colleagues, before they can prove their innocence, has been characteristic of diversity programmes being rebuffed by the status quo to date.

So how do we remove the perception among the majority that it is always a zero-sum game? I remember when my former geography tutor at Oxford, Patricia Daley, told me how upon being appointed to Jesus College she entered the Senior Common Room. The other (white, male) professors assumed she was one of the staff serving drinks rather than the new tutor with a distinguished academic record. This wasn't just about ignorance, it was about comfort levels. It is simply harder work to engage people who are different from you. But how was her presence taking away from them? They still had their tenured positions, tea at 4 o'clock, generous pension allowance and stimulating students in class every week. Patricia Daley was the new African Studies Professor, a new role, a new resource for the college and its students and a breath of fresh air in the Senior Common Room.

Of course it's not always that straightforward. At Oxford, some of the dynamics of discrimination were obvious and inexcusable, but what about more nuanced situations? What about a male colleague losing out on a promotion to a female colleague? That sounds like a zero-sum game – for her to be promoted he has to forgo the promotion. If she is more qualified than the male counterpart, then it's a case of merit-based selection, as in the case of Rachel Reeves. If she is less qualified than the male colleague, then it's a case of positive discrimination and unsupported by Inclusion 3.0 theory. If, however, this is a successful company, growing, adapting, progressive, diverse and inclusive, there may well be multiple opportunities for both parties to seek promotion in the near future.

What about when people do need to sustain loss? What about when a majority group does have to concede ground? If and when they give something up, we need to work hard to articulate how they get more in return. The framing of the conversation is crucial. Again, the above example of women in parliament is instructive. A controversial policy still only resulted in a *quarter* of members of parliament being women – women were not taking over, they were catching up. The UK now has a new perspective, a new resource, and in the case of male members of parliament, maybe even a new friend and colleague they can learn from. With this window ajar, it is then the responsibility of the practitioner to advance a more intelligent coherent argument for inclusion, such that the status quo may even start to listen. It is the responsibility of the practitioner to emphasise change, which is hard but palatable, over loss, which will be rejected. Deutsche Telekom has set clear gender diversity targets for 2020. In achieving them, it is highly probable that very capable men will lose out in promotion. At an individual scale, we don't have an answer. Only by taking a holistic approach can we evaluate the wider benefits. Moving the conversation from 'zero sum' to 'enlarging the pie' is the responsibility of the inclusive leader.

Gay rights and religion are often positioned as a zero-sum game. Same-sex relationships are often positioned as running counter to religious teaching. Charles Radcliffe, of the UN Office for Human Rights says:

> In this case, the conflict between the rights of LGBT people on the one hand and culture, tradition and religion on the other is a false one. Protection of one need not be at the expense of the other. The key is to bring the debate back to the rights of individuals including the right to define their own beliefs, values and culture for themselves.[31]

In other words, religion is 'not monolithic, nor can they override individual freedoms'.[32]

Consider the example of inclusive design in enlarging the pie for everyone. For no additional cost, it is possible for architects to design venues accessible to all. Ramps instead of steps, lower urinals in the men's bathroom, automatic doors that are energy efficient to boot. Facilities that work not just for disabled people, but also for mums and dads with buggies, older people, younger people, 'able-bodied' people who temporarily broke their leg skiing, operational people who have to move equipment around and prefer level access. This is real inclusion, when everyone benefits, when people understand it doesn't always have to be a zero-sum game.

People are human, fallible and want to have fun

Police in the UK still know 20 words they are not allowed to use for Diversity 101 reasons and they are walking on created eggshells, resenting the imposition of training. Imagine if people could be themselves. We know that people perform better when they can be themselves. Think of the conversations, the infinite creativity unleashed. Inclusion 3.0 is liberating. Of course there is a requirement and a necessity for professional standards, I am not advocating otherwise. But we are adults, and we know the rules. If you don't know the rules, then perhaps now would be the time to put this book down. Otherwise, read on.

People like to have fun at work, which is understandable given how long many spend there and the impact it can have on their life. Prince Philip of the UK, famous for his inappropriate remarks, understands this. He is the most unlikely Inclusion 3.0 advocate in training, and he understands the importance of humour. I am not condoning his comments, but they make me laugh, they raise the issues and expose the elephant in the room. I appreciate them and the way he connects royalty with the millions of men and women at the opposite end of the social class spectrum.

'You look like you're ready for bed!' he said to the President of Nigeria, who was wearing traditional dress.[33] This caused consternation in the British Foreign Office, as it would in the US State Department. Actually, the President may have found it funny, and it provoked a conversation about cultural dress and traditions that might have otherwise been missed. It is in some ways mimicking the child who is the only person in the room who will ask a wheelchair user if and how they go to the toilet. Ask any wheelchair user and I guarantee you, nine times out of ten, they will be glad the child asked them and slaughtered the proverbial elephant.

In some ways, adults consciously and subconsciously work against inclusion. From the end of childhood onwards we collect baggage that we assume is the 'right way' to conduct ourselves in professional life. However, while maintaining respect, it might be helpful for us to revert to childhood curiosity in order to better engage with people who are different from us. Genuine curiosity is to be welcomed, encouraged and celebrated. Clearly and intentionally disrespectful behaviour is not. The corollary is that those who perceive themselves to be in the minority and the target of the alleged discrimination need to distinguish between decent intent and outright offence. That is an individual responsibility, not something taught in the classroom.

We all have implicit association biases and prejudices. That is natural and normal. For example, when I am tested on an implicit association test I tend to have a slight discrimination in favour of heterosexual people and against gay people, despite being gay myself. We all exhibit subconscious bias. We will tend to hire people in our own image because they seem a 'good fit' or they 'get it'. In one sense, we cannot fight human nature. People want to associate with people like themselves. After two decades of Diversity 101 and 2.0 policies, many are more convinced of this than ever before.

However, it is increasingly a precondition of successful modern life that we do exactly the opposite. Diversity 101 policies have failed us because they are compliance driven and repel more people than they convince. Diversity 2.0 programmes have failed us because they are relatively superficial and fail to deal with what are, in fact, systemic problems. 2.0 companies increasingly believe their own hyperbole. As the next chapter demonstrates, there is an overwhelming body of new evidence to suggest that new Inclusion 3.0 strategies are not only value adding, but are in many cases the key differentiator in competitive situations and the new way for organisations to achieve real inclusion. It is now time to intellectually and emotionally engage with a new way of seeing inclusion in business, for the sake of business, as well as society at large.

Takeaways – re-defining Diversity and Inclusion

1 Diversity is about infinite difference and real inclusion is about bringing those differences together to add value. Superficial inclusion is about bringing token diversity together, intervening at a personal scale, and assuming the work is done. This is true for minority groups who stick together and ignore the challenge, as well as for majority groups who maintain the status quo.

2 Diversity and Inclusion are both necessary in order to add value to the purpose of an organisation. Real inclusion involves strategies designed to add value by embedding infinite diversity in existing infrastructure, intervening at a systemic level, where decisions are actually made. That is in some ways harder work, but essential for real value to be harnessed.

3 Diversity 101 and 2.0 have offered contributions to empowering different groups but now offer largely superficial solutions to systemic problems, and are stuck in a zero-sum game world. Real Inclusion strategies start in a different place and focus on achieving systemic change, and enlarging the pie, to add value for everyone.

Notes

1 They are well summarised in Scott Page's book *The Difference* (Princeton University Press, 2007: 13–14), for example.

2 Gary Younge, The badness of words, *The Guardian* newspaper, 14 February 2000.

3 Ziauddin Sardar, *The Language of Equality* (Equality and Human Rights Commission, 2008).

4 Hansen, F (2003) Diversity's business case doesn't add up, *Workforce* April: 28–32.

5 Prof Frank Dobbin, as cited in http://donaldclarkplanb.blogspot.co.uk/ search?q=Dobbin and also quoted to me by Victoria Budson, Executive Director of Women and Public Policy Program at Harvard Kennedy School on 17 April 2013. Victoria Budson also reminded me, while we were discussing the limitations of diversity training, that Martin Luther King said 'I have a dream', not 'I have a gripe'. Diversity training seems to be mired in the gripe/moan/ blame/compliance culture that is self-defeating. Compliance will only ever create the minimum.

6 Scott Page, *The Difference* (Princeton University Press, 2007). See section on identity diversity as a proxy: p 13.

7 See for example, Christine M Riordan, Relational demography within groups: past developments, contradictions, and new directions, *Research in Personnel and Human Resources Management*, Vol 19 (2000): 131–73 (Emerald Group Publishing, 2000).

8 See for example, Elizabeth Mannix and Margaret A Neale, What differences make a difference? The promise and reality of diverse teams in organisations, *Psychological Science in the Public Interest*, 6(2) (2005): 31–55. Or D van Knippenberg, D and MC Schippers, Work group diversity, *Annual Review of Psychology*, 58: 515–41.

9 Katherine Phillips, 14 February 2013 'Can Female Leaders Mitigate Negative Effects of Diversity?: The Case of National Leaders', Women and Public Policy Program Seminar, Cambridge MA.

10 Laura Liswood, *The Loudest Duck* (Wiley, 2010).

11 Sheryl Sandberg, *Lean In* (A A Knopf, 2013), especially the sections on career jungles, as opposed to career ladders.

12 Nilanjana Dasgupta, 18 April 2013 'Thriving Despite Negative Stereotypes: How In-group Experts and Peers Act As Social Vaccines to Inoculate Women's Self concept and Achievement', WAPPP Seminar, Cambridge MA.

13 20% by 2020: http://www.2020wob.com/learn/why-gender-diversity-matters.

14 Viviane Reding, European Commissioner for Justice, Fundamental Rights and Citizenship, conversation at Davos meeting January 2012.

15 Norway passed a law in 2006 requiring 40 per cent of boardroom seats to go to women (or men in the rare cases that women are in the majority).

16 Mona Lena Crook researched the issues of quotas in political life. She concluded that they too often act as a fix for more structural problems. For example 'gender quota policies result in the election of more women, but only those who will reinforce rather than challenge the status quo'. As I discussed above with reference to 101 superficial inclusion, the idea that women can only represent 'women's issues' is worrying. Men are seen as advocates of general issues – why not women or other minorities? Women and minorities are diverse within groups as well as between groups. Crook, Mona Lena (2008) Quota laws for women in politics: implications for feminist practice, *Social Politics*, 15(3): 345–68. http://crook.wustl.edu/pdf/social_politics_2008.pdf.

17 Conversation with Iris Bohnet, March 2013.

18 This quotas example is based on gender but other minorities could be applied. A recent controversial article by an HKS doctoral student suggested that IQ was in fact different among different ethnic groups. IQ varies between and within groups according to a multitude of factors but for the purposes of this book the differences are statistically insignificant, as well as morally debatable.

19 Conversation with Rachel Reeves at her home, while on maternity leave, 24 May 2013.

20 Malcolm Gladwell, *The Tipping Point* (Little, Brown and Company, 2000).

21 Richard H Thaler and Cass R Sunstein, *Nudge: Improving decisions about health, wealth, and happiness* (Yale University Press, 2008).

22 Iris Bohnet, 13 October 2010 *Financial Times*, http://www.ft.com/intl/cms/s/0/59d7d2f6-d6a7-11df-98a9-00144feabdc0.html#axzz2Twnzq0YI.

23 Iris Bohnet, Alexandra van Geen and Max Bazerman, When Performance Dominates Gender Bias: Joint vs Separate Evaluation, Harvard Kennedy School, 2010.

24 Another example would be gay marriage vs civil partnership.

25 Conversation with the author, Kennedy School Forum, February 2013.

26 Dean Williams Leadership Class, Harvard Kennedy School, Spring semester 2013.

27 For an explanation of group interviews see Chapter 24, The Tools.

28 For more information on peer review see Chapter 24, The Tools.

29 See note 28.

30 The US Republican Party is also a great example of Diversity 101 or possibly 2.0. It has understood the need to decorate the tree but the embracing of diversity remains superficial and un-systemic. Until it adopts systemic, real inclusion it will fail to catch up with the changing demographics of the United States.

31 Charles Radcliffe, OHR UN video, 22 March 2013, http://www.youtube.com/watch?v=iupj5ns6s8w [accessed 11 October 2013].

32 Tradition and religion have been used in the past to justify some savage practices from slavery to child marriage, denial of property and inheritance rights to women and female genital mutilation. Sexual orientation has not yet been used to justify anything like this. That's why opposition to it requires strong statements, as espoused by the former British defence minister Sir Gerald Howarth. Regarding the UK government's plans for equal marriage, he said there were plenty of people 'in the aggressive homosexual community who see this as but a stepping stone to something even further'. In the absence of facts, people resort to hypothecation about what they fear might happen. It is my own view, therefore, that most professionals and organisations, and I suspect many religious people too, already know which way this debate is headed. We just continue to (sometimes violently) argue en route.

33 Prince Philip quotes: Relive 90 classic gaffes to mark his 90th birthday [online] http://www.mirror.co.uk/news/uk-news/princephilip-quotes-relive-90-133848

The real business case for action

Inclusion 3.0 is a call to action. This is not a business case for Diversity 101 or even Diversity 2.0. They can be found all over the internet and you can be the judge of how compelling they are. This is a business case for effective Inclusion 3.0 programmes, the type that was trialed at LOCOG. I have tried to take a more holistic approach from a systems perspective and offer five arguments based on customers, employees, growth, mathematics and ethics.

In Figure 4.1[1] we can see how the diversity paradigms play out in terms of creating shared value. Michael Porter of Harvard Business School says that shared value 'involves creating economic value in a way that also creates value for society by addressing its needs and challenges'.[2] Shared value is value that is created by organisations for themselves (profit, return on investment, shareholder value and so forth) as well as value for wider society (such as growth, social structure and new environmental solutions).

Diversity 101 would sit in the bottom-left quadrant. It is based on compliance and codes of conduct. It would create the least amount of shareholder value (which is expected, and not a problem for many proponents) but it also adds minimal *social* value. Diversity 2.0 is an improvement on this situation and can be found in the top-left quadrant, involving community investment, employee volunteering and other forms of charitable endeavour. However, it does not add any significant shareholder value, predominantly because it is comprised of a series of net cost initiatives. Only Inclusion 3.0 can credibly sit in the upper-right quadrant, with a systemic, value-adding approach benefiting both the organisation and wider society. That's why real inclusion is an imperative – for business and for society.

FIGURE 4.1 Approaches to creating shared value

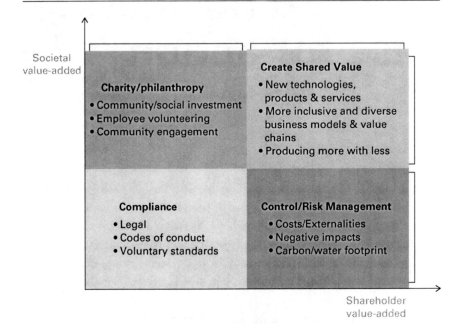

Adapted from Nelson, Jane (1998) *Building Competitiveness and Communities: How World Class Companies are creating shareholder value and societal value*, IBLF in collaboration with the World Bank and UNDP; and Nelson, Jane (2000) *The Business of Peace: The private sector as a partner in conflict prevention and resolution*, International Alert, Council on Economic Priorities and IBLF.

Real inclusion – for customer growth and retention

The world outside the organisation is changing faster than the world within the organisation. Without radically reflecting that world, the organisation will fail to connect with its customers, may lose market share, and die.

The best example of this is the Olympic movement. The baby boomers who watched Seb Coe win Gold in the 1980 and 1984 Games were still watching him and the Olympics in Beijing in 2008 – but the new generation, X, Y and the Millennials, was not.[3] The Olympics fan base was ageing. The younger, more diverse, more global generation, empowered by technology was not engaged. The most recognised brand in the world was slowly dying. It was in this context that London offered to reconnect the Olympic movement with a new, diverse customer base. That's why, 'in a world of many distractions', London offered to inspire young people to choose sport.[4] The movement chose Diversity and Inclusion, perhaps without even realising it.

Many current organisations are completely unprepared for the next few years. China will soon be the largest English-speaking country in the world. The top quarter of India's population as measured by IQ is greater in number than the entire population of the United States.[5] Facebook has a billion users, is available in 70 languages and would be the third-biggest country behind India and China. There are 31 billion searches on Google every month, up from 2.7 billion in 2006. The idea that existing marketing departments full of relatively homogeneous staff can handle this new reality is non-plausible.

In a very real sense, therefore, organisations are struggling to catch up with the world around them. Antonio Simoes, the dynamic Chief Executive of HSBC in the UK, articulates his organisational challenge as having to deal with 'being behind society'.[6] 'The tone from the top is right and focused on meritocracy but the challenge is to make sure 260,000 people globally behave that way.' As a global bank, with the widest possible range of customers and the most diverse marketing campaign of any major financial institution, Antonio has identified that his customers are still outpacing him. The external factors within which HSBC are operating are dynamic – the challenge is to instil them in the internal dynamics too. To open up, and bring them inside the tent. To add value to HSBC by embedding some of that external, infinite diversity in the internal infrastructure where decisions relating to customers are actually made. At the moment, in many organisations, those decisions are being made in a relative vacuum.

The Greek philosopher Heraclitus forewarned us 'change is the only constant'.[7] Indeed, right now the pace of economic and technological change is unprecedented. Commentators have labelled current times 'punctuated equilibrium'.[8] In this phase of transition, from homogeneous cultures to heterogeneous ones, from local communities to global ones, from neoclassical economics to complex systems, many organisations are increasingly looking like dinosaurs shortly before they started to die off. Complex system analysis shows us the effects of demographic change, changing consumer tastes and globalisation. How many managers understand diversity as a tool in their organisational armour to help up-skill the organisation to deal with this new reality?

If you spend five minutes online and watch the video 'Did you know?' on YouTube you may start to question your current organisation. I would go further and suggest that the very idea homogeneous and comparatively static organisations can keep up with rapidly changing consumer tastes, market developments and methods of interaction is frankly laughable.

Of course it varies from industry to industry and place to place. I am not talking here about an organisation such as a traditional furniture-carving business whose very core mission is to maintain 'traditions' often in the face of change. Or an antiques dealer whose value may actually increase in the face of change and people's dislike of it. I am talking here about the majority of organisations who are being outpaced by their customers in the same way teachers are being outpaced by the children in their classroom.

To reach a market audience of 50 million took radio 38 years. To reach the same audience took television 13 years, the internet four years, the iPod three years and Facebook a mere two years.[9] How does traditional market segmentation data work in this new exponential reality? How does an organisation know how different communities view them in real time via social media? How can its traditional recruitment practices run by people educated in a different era possibly keep up with developments that threaten the very survival of the business?

L'Oréal had a rude awakening to this new reality. The world's largest cosmetics and beauty company, it faced a 2005 Supreme Court of California ruling relating to Jack Wiswall, then general manager for designer fragrances. He allegedly told a colleague to fire a dark-skinned sales associate despite the associate's good performance, pointing to a 'sexy' blonde-haired woman and said 'God damn it, get me one that looks like that.'[10] Wiswall retired as president of the luxury products division of L'Oréal USA at the end of 2006. L'Oréal were also prosecuted, along with their recruitment partner (Adecco) a few years ago after a 10-year legal battle over recruiting *Les Bleus* – or French people that looked 'French'.[11] In July 2007, the Garnier division and an external employment agency were fined €30,000 for recruitment practices that intentionally excluded non-white women from promoting its shampoo, 'Fructis Style'.[12]

I am not suggesting a token 'employ black person, serve black person' mentality, but I am suggesting that a homogeneous workforce is less prepared, or able, to deal with diverse markets than a diverse workforce. I am suggesting that Jack Wiswall may have been challenged more if he was surrounded by diversity. Homogeneous teams are simply not having the internal conversations that a more reflective, heterogeneous team would do. A diverse workforce can fast-forward relationship building with new markets and it can solidify an organisation's citizenship in more communities than might otherwise be the case. It can be a cost-effective way of building collective organisational intelligence.

An article in the *Financial Times* highlighted the case of Italy and its stalling growth. Entitled 'Italy's clubby system needs fresh blood', and acknowledging its potential ageism on the one hand, it goes on to state 'Power networks spanning Telecom Italia, Mediobanca, Pirelli... and RCS Mediagroup... are running out of steam and need new ideas to survive in the face of globalisation and decline.'[13] It suggests that part of the cause of failure is the cross-shareholdings structure that conferred 'clubby power' on some of Italy's largest financial institutions and companies. The change needed takes the form of younger men (and even women) reaching the boardrooms of Italy's organisations, such as Generali, the insurance company. Here, the new Chief Executive Mario Greco, 53, has started to reduce its cross-shareholdings. Shares in the insurer, Europe's third largest by premiums, have 'ticked up by a third'. But Italy is still the country of septuagenarian politician Silvio Berlusconi, accused of sex with a minor,[14] and octogenarian chairman Giovanni Bazoli of Intesa Sanpaolo, Italy's largest retail bank in terms of assets. In April 2013, he was confirmed chairman for another four years.

Real inclusion helps create the right employer brand and reputation

In February 2013 I spoke with a class of Harvard undergraduates who were about to graduate. They were seeking career advice. My supposition going into the meeting was that I would offer some thoughts from my career and answer their concerns about the 'real world'. The reality was that they were much more in touch with aspects of the real world than I was. They had tracked various companies on social media (and not only through their 'official' sites). They were up-to-date on how various minority groups viewed the different organisations and what they said about working there. Having experienced diversity during the college years, they are loath to now give it up. The new reality is that the many graduates will actively seek 'diverse' organisations because they associate them with creativity, stimulation and fun. They are therefore initiating a virtuous circle of talent and diversity, which firms need to tap into if they want to hire them.

Klaus Schwab, Founder of the World Economic Forum, has spoken of the move from capitalism to 'talentism'.[15] Demographic shifts mean that the best talent doesn't necessarily look like it used to – if an organisation is not appealing to diversity then it will lose out. The talent pool is increasingly international and increasingly diverse. The Corporate Leadership Council has undertaken research on the Employee Value Proposition (EVP) and found that with a strong EVP, companies can avoid paying a premium to attract the right talent. When most of the new entrants into labour markets in North America and Europe are minorities, the EVP needs to be diverse. Generation Y, for example, wants 40 days' holiday per year.[16] Generation X is more concerned with medical coverage. And since recruitment happens overwhelmingly online now, through LinkedIn, apps and tagging, it's personal. Since people are infinitely diverse, diversity is in the ascendancy now, irrespective of whether recruiters are switched on, like it or 'get it'.

As well as the personalisation of recruitment, the same dynamics apply to retention. Employees want an 'effective ecosystem'.[17] As well as safety and security, people want to participate in a fulfilling career, to do 'something more than the individual'.[18] In this sense, real inclusion becomes critical in terms of employee engagement. If we are seeking to recruit and retain the best talent, we need to appeal to the individual (infinite) diversity characteristics of individual employees. Through adopting real inclusion policies LOCOG achieved employee engagement scores among minority groups that exceeded the average for all employees (which were already very high). This was captured in the regular YourSay staff survey and based on 20 diagnostic questions broken down by diversity monitoring. The fact that employees who identified with a minority group and who 'traditionally' would score less on equivalent surveys scored higher on this one strongly suggests LOCOG was effective in capturing discretionary effort.[19]

Real inclusion is good for employee recruitment and retention. Consider the market for talent, which is in flux as never before; the top 10 in-demand jobs in 2010 did not even exist in 2004.[20] The US Department of Labor estimates that the average current student will have 10–14 jobs by the time they are 38 years old. One in four current workers has been with their employer for less than one year.[21] In this mobile market staid organisations will not be able to attract or retain the right talent. Ten years ago, a top bank, law firm or government agency had to compete among themselves for the best and the brightest, as they perceived them. Today, the best talent is empowered by technology and information to enter different sectors (technology being the obvious one), to be more discerning in their choices, or to start up their own business. Why would a talented young person choose a discriminating, or even just homogeneous, environment when they have all these other options to choose from where they can be themselves?

The consulting firm McKinsey launched their now seminal 'War for talent' report in 1997.[22] It positioned increasing competition among organisations for talent as a key driver of organisational success or failure. As *The Economist* noted in 2006,[23] many in HR are unclear about the definition of talent, but it is clear that in increasingly global, increasingly flexible labour markets, diversity is emerging as a key differentiator in attracting such talent.[24] The recruiter Ann Marie Dixon Barrow has evaluated new research based on evolutionary ecosystems that suggests that diversity is essential for future success.[25] If evolution is the result of two forces – variation (diversity) and selection – then diversity (or choice) is a prerequisite of growth. Without choice, the best cannot be selected and therefore growth (amplification) is limited. We are in a time of 'punctuation', when the world is changing rapidly and survival depends on being able to adapt. Variation, selection and adaptation are critical to success.

One of the insights in Laura Liswood's book *The Loudest Duck* (2010) is that many corporations seek to build a 'Noah's Ark' of diversity, with two of every kind represented to check all the boxes. Savvy jobseekers see through that now. Whereas Diversity 101 or 2.0 programmes may recruit said 'couples', if they are the only ones in the Ark they may well feel isolated and non-included and leave. Real inclusion is about throwing open the doors beyond token recruitment efforts, or segregated 'initiatives' to systematise the recruitment machine. Only then will a minority have more chance of finding they are not the only one in the house and the tipping point is reached sooner and more comprehensively. Real inclusion is not only a transparent way to recruit diversity; it is also a risk-mitigating way to retain people. Real inclusion can help attract, retain and motivate employees effectively as well as ensuring that all talent pools are aware of the organisation and no talent self-selects out, without the organisation even knowing.

So in order to maximise customer market penetration and to maximise talent recruitment and retention, organisations should consider adopting Inclusion 3.0 programmes. The third reason to do so is for quality economic growth.

Real inclusion, for productivity and growth

The immortal line from Bill Clinton's 1992 presidential campaign, 'It's the Economy, stupid', is as true today as it was then. But in the new digital, information and knowledge economy, human capital replaces natural resources as the basis for growth. Technology is replacing lower-skilled jobs. The threat to growth comes from a shortage of high-skilled talent – and from people being able to be themselves and operate to their true potential. In a situation of resource scarcity it is vital that we maximise the productivity of the resource we do have – our people. Diversity 101 and 2.0

programmes are predominantly 'initiatives' which have a time and financial opportunity cost to growth. However, Inclusion 3.0 programmes instead focus on removing barriers to growth.

Barriers to enhanced quality economic growth and productivity are not just inflexible labour markets and taxes; they are also subconscious bias, implicit associations and sexist and homophobic attitudes that are deeply inefficient, as well as distasteful. In order to compete, an organisation needs everyone working to his or her individual optimum. Gay people kept in the closet, women suffering from glass ceilings and disabled people facing inaccessible environments are all inefficient barriers to more-productive employees. In fact, the combined effect of these micro inequities is estimated to cost $64 billion per year in the United States alone.[26] That amount represents the annual estimated cost of losing and replacing more than 2 million US workers who leave their jobs each year due to unfairness and discrimination.

Most of us would accept growth as essential to improving global human welfare. As Porter and Kramer assert in their paper 'Capitalism is an unparalleled vehicle for meeting human needs'.[27] The 1987 Brundtland Commission report Our Common Future defined growth in terms of sustainable development, 'development that meets the needs of the present without compromising the ability of future generations to meet their own needs'.[28] At the 2005 World Summit it was acknowledged that 'quality growth' requires the reconciliation of complex social and economic demands as well as environmental limitations; the oft quoted 'three pillars' of sustainability.

However, after several decades of relative consensus on these definitions 'the capitalist system is (in fact) under siege'.[29] Stakeholders are unhappy with the way many firms are pursuing growth and people do not believe that growth is improving their quality of life. This is in part because existing definitions of growth fail to sufficiently account for our most precious resource of all – people. Rather than people being the problem, how can we better utilise our human resources to ensure more quality growth?

Business men and women the world over focus on gaining value from the margin. The proportionately higher returns that come from engaging a new market, a new product, a new insight compared with existing ones. If this is true for markets, why is it not true for people? In increasingly competitive markets, value comes from the margin, from difference – a new way of enlarging the pie for everyone, therefore, is by reaching out to include more people in the pie in the first place.

We need to leverage people's differences in order to extract their marginal value. Therefore a real inclusion strategy, rather than being an 'add-on' or something we think about in terms of Corporate Social Responsibility, should actually be core to a firm/government/economy if that said organisation wants to maximise its human and growth potential.

One example of this would be how we (don't) include disabled people. Most disabled people's talents are under-utilised. For example, because they can't commute to work or the office is inaccessible. Or it may be a less tangible reason, such as lacking self-confidence after years of struggling to defy the stereotype of disabled people in non-disabled people's eyes. There is a cost to failing to unlock the potential of millions of people who could otherwise bring substantial discretionary effort into the workplace. Disabled people with PhDs remain at home because public transport is inaccessible. The wasted potential is infinitely more than the investment required to bring that talent into the fold through a taxi or homework solution.

Another example would be how we treat lesbian and gay staff. If people feel able to be themselves, they are far more likely to deploy discretionary effort and work harder.[30] One of the reasons thousands of global gay professionals choose to work in London or New York, for example, is because they have equality legislation to protect them and open cultures to allow them to be themselves. This costs the respective cities nothing, but results in significant added income and resource. When gay people remain in the closet they are 10 per cent less productive than when they feel able to be themselves.[31] One recent seminar advocated a 30 per cent productivity increase for LGBT people that could be 'out at work'.[32] Yet 41 per cent of American LGBT workers remain closeted in the office.[33] The amount of energy wasted concealing their identity and making excuses about what they did at the weekend is at the expense of focusing fully on the job.

Eiko Shinotsuka of the National Personnel Authority of Japan said that the 'insufficient utilisation of women as human resources, particularly in their intellectual resources' was a factor in Japan's slow growth.[34] More women attend college in Latin America than men.[35] This is not, however, reflected in the talent deployment across Latin American companies. Of the artworks auctioned over $1 million last year, only 3 per cent were by women.[36] In the Tate Modern gallery, London, only 4 per cent of the exhibited artists are women. Women received 45 per cent of the PhDs in science in Europe in 2006 yet occupy only 18 per cent of senior research positions.[37]

Fortune 500 companies in the top quartile for female board representation outperform those in the lowest quartile by at least 53 per cent return on equity.[38] Colombia Business School and University of Maryland studied the S&P Indexed firms over 15 years and found a gender dividend of

1.6 per cent or \$35 million on average.[39] Joe Keefe, Chief Executive of PAX World Mutual Funds, now insists on gender parity at all levels of his organisation from the top team down.

If the above examples of gender, sexual orientation and disability were replicated on a larger scale, unblocking barriers to quality growth such as racism and xenophobia, think of the efficiencies that could result. People perform better when they can be themselves. The problem is, in most organisations people are not able to be themselves. 'Company culture' often thwarts individual personality and, with it, the discretionary effort each individual could otherwise contribute. Even at Facebook, there is an obsession with 'fit' – if HR people continue to search for people who 'fit' with the existing culture, then real inclusion will never be realised.

Engagement, discretionary effort and innovation are a feature of people's informal relationships and feelings. They do not come from diversity training. Instead of unfairness and discrimination we can engage people's discretionary effort, marginal productivity (and innovation) through releasing them to be themselves. Indeed, the MD (Managing Director) of HireRight Steve Girdler talks about the need to 'kill corporate culture, not individual personality'.[40]

Of course, for many HR professionals, this is a big shift in approach from trying to integrate people into an established culture. This approach is not easy. Yet in many ways, diversity is already present in the organisation – it is simply being inefficiently utilised. The discretionary effort each (diverse) person is capable of, capturing individual marginal productivity, is not being tapped into. By removing barriers such as tolerance of sexist language in meetings, fixed working schedules, alcohol-only Friday drinks, steps instead of ramps, and then by marketing that fact to the entire talent pool, stakeholder community and customer base, a great return is possible. Diversity 101 may have brought two of each of Noah's Ark into the organisation, but through the methods it has deployed it has created new barriers to their inclusion.

It is a simple, yet important, insight that rather than by constructing a whole host of new initiatives to 'build' a Diversity and Inclusion programme, we should focus instead on what barriers we can remove to the potential already present. There are barriers to market growth such as L'Oréal and Italian firms experienced. There are barriers to employee productivity such as sexism and homophobia, and there are other kinds of barriers to suppliers including well intentioned but overly bureaucratic 'equalities' interventions such as 'equality impact assessments' or sloppy and repetitive monitoring when bidding for contracts and tenders. Real inclusion advocates their removal.

Real inclusion stimulates creativity, innovation and better decision-making

The latest research, based on mathematical models and social experiments, demonstrates how diversity can trump ability in group decision-making processes. In a nutshell, diversity reduces the average error in decisions. Scott Page of the University of Michigan developed the Diversity prediction theorem, whereby:

$$\text{Crowd error} = \text{average error} - \text{diversity}$$

or 'our collective ability is equal parts individual ability and collective difference'.[41] In other words, mathematics shows us that the more variation in the pool, the better the selective process. This is key to reducing 'group-think', the tendency of homogeneous groups to aggressively agree with each other and create a positive feedback loop that may in fact be based on shaky, irrational foundations.

We are all a function of our background and experiences to date. Talent and background carry more or less equal weight in predictive capability and therefore more variation in the current population will lead to a more robust future population in the face of change. As Darwin identified a century ago – if we select from difference, we adapt and innovate and we can subsequently not only survive, we can even thrive. It is intuitively logical that the more diverse the team, the more likely its predictive capability in the face of uncertainty. It seems obvious, yet many organisations still tend to recruit from the 'best' universities, ending up with a highly concentrated pool of highly capable people all with similar skill sets. So if we hire 'brilliant' people from three 'top' universities they may all excel at skills A, B and C. But without other people who did not go to the 'top' universities who may excel at skills D, E and F, the group lose out on an additional skill set, perspective and challenge to their prior assumptions.

There is a growing and authoritative body of literature on the benefits of diverse teams to decision-making and commercial success. McKinsey's ongoing study profiling gender diversity at board and senior level and demonstrating the correlation to financial performance is authoritative.[42] A Work Foundation report in 2006 'Rising to the Challenge of Diversity' demonstrated how diversity can lead to lowered groupthink and better ideas.[43] Research from Tufts University demonstrated how diverse groups perform better than homogenous groups using the example of juries and the legal process. They deployed 200 participants in 29 mock juries. They found that mixed panels of white people and black people performed better than only white or only black people.[44] Real inclusion is about creating 'constructive conflict' where 'diversity in teams creates a positive environment in which ideas synergistically resolve into higher-level outcomes than would be achievable in more homogenous teams'.[45]

Of course people are not even objective, let alone basing their decisions on mathematics. For example, people will justify not hiring capable women on the grounds that they 'lack experience'. In a study comparing decision-making processes with regard to a choice of two magazines, 92 per cent of male interviewees chose the sports magazine with the free swimwear issue (featuring scantily clad women).[46] They justified their choice by saying that the swimwear magazine had more articles and 'the number of articles per issue' was the most important factor in magazine choice. When the 'free swimwear issue' was changed to the other magazine, suddenly it was the 'number of sports covered' that was more important in determining the magazine choice. When there is a lack of diversity in the group context, these decisions are more likely to: a) be made in the first place; and b) go unchallenged. Behaviours tend to be self-reinforcing – they do it and therefore so do I. Even worse, when people cheat they feel smarter[47] and this self-deception works incredibly well for the individual in the short run. But it can be disastrous for the larger scale organisation in the long run.

The organisation cannot see its blind spots, and cannot understand what it fails to include. In order to meet the demands of rapidly evolving customers, organisations need to encourage a few of the outliers to come inside the tent and educate their existing 'experts'. We can think of these people as 'tempered radicals'[48] – creative and brilliant, yet 'tempered' in order to be able to interact productively with colleagues inside the tent rather than cause unproductive disharmony. However, 'company culture' deters them. Think about this for a moment. In an effort to be 'inclusive' of 'diversity' we create a company culture that actually repels the very diversity we are in need of.

So how does it play out with these tempered radicals? Well look at Wikipedia. Wikipedia is the ultimate example of what can happen when you encourage diversity and crowd source from diverse sources – you can build an encyclopedia.[49] Imagine if organisations adopted a similar approach to that of Wikipedia; Organisational dynamic encyclopedias capturing the ultimate marginal returns from outside the organisation. We need to nurture difference, and look after those tempered radicals. Unfortunately, as discussed earlier, most company culture does the exact opposite.

In an environment of real inclusion there is greater potential for internal crowd sourcing of ideas, challenging of ideas, and refining ideas in real time. Procter & Gamble's 'Connect and develop' tool increased Research and Development productivity by 60 per cent.[50] LOCOG's internal, online communication tool 'The Knowledge' saved me hours of research time by finding people with answers in real time. As we learned from *The Wisdom of Crowds* book[51] it is logical that individual life experience to date and bias will limit the ideas any one individual can come up with alone, but diversity improves collective intelligence. Irrespective of IQ to some degree, individual errors will be mitigated by a diverse portfolio, just like with stocks and shares. And, unlike a suite of Oxbridge economists, they are unlikely to all be the same error as you would find with a homogeneous group – those decisions can be catastrophic. The national airline of Switzerland, Swissair, was so financially solvent it became known as the 'Flying Bank'. One of the key reasons the airline failed is because they believed their own hyperbole, that they were infallible. The organisation was full of highly competent – and similar – people. By failing to challenge their own decisions and mismanagement, the airline eventually went bankrupt and the Swiss were left in shock. How could this have happened?

So having diverse teams can improve the quality of decision-making at all organisational levels, reduce groupthink and allow assumptions to be challenged more effectively. Heterogeneous teams are, on average, better than homogeneous teams on creative and complex problems.[52] They increase the number of perspectives, provide better understanding of customer needs and flex management approaches. However, diversity needs to be managed, in order to avert its negatives, especially unproductive group conflict. Inclusive leadership is required. Diversity and conflict management tools range from the simple Myers Briggs indicator, to the Thomas-Kilmann conflict mode instrument, to six-hat thinking.[53] These all equip teams with tools to manage difference. Even getting peoples names right would be a start.[54]

In 2013 a supercomputer was built that exceeded the computational ability of the human brain. Based on mathematical models, it might be an alternative to our biased minds – and a key aid to improving the decision-making capabilities of (male) boards. I would suggest until the computer becomes widespread, we invest in diversity in the meantime.

Ethics

There is a moral imperative to reach out and include diverse talent in order to ensure inclusivity, efficiency and optimum productivity in a time of increasingly fast-paced economic change.

In the United States, the richest 1 per cent of the population now holds 40 per cent of the nation's wealth while 80 per cent of Americans share only 7 per cent of the country's wealth.[55] Forty per cent of Americans hold only a negligible proportion. The widening gulf between 'haves' and 'have-nots', and the overburdened middle class, are destabilising economic as well as social forces. There is a moral case for action. Inequality is increasing, not just economically to disparate individuals, but socially to whole groups in our societies. This trend is worrying, not least because large chunks of our societies are being left behind, rather like a melting iceberg. At a global scale this has implications for migration and immigration, health programmes, aid and development, geopolitics and war. At a national scale it has implications for social security, infrastructure development, crime and disease. Even at the organisational level, this has implications for recruitment, retention, suppliers, customers and product development. It would be inconceivable in terms of its licence to operate that London 2012 would not have paid due regard to some of the most marginalised people and groups in society.

The fact that life chances are to a large degree determined by where you are born, not your intrinsic worth, is a subject worthy of ethical consideration. The fact that some people were born into privilege and have been able to maintain that social status throughout their life at minimal effort whereas some people, with equal intrinsic worth as a fellow human being, have remained in the comparative gutter is an issue of pressing ethical concern. One in four children in the UK now grows up in poverty.[56] Joseph Stiglitz said, 'with inequality at its highest level since before the Depression, a robust recovery will be difficult in the short term, and the American dream – a good life in exchange for hard work – is slowly dying'.[57] Rising inequality and slow or negative growth are in fact 'intertwined'. *The Economist* magazine ran a special feature in its October 2012 edition detailing how inequality is a serious threat facing the United States.[58] Stiglitz offers four reasons for this: the middle class not spending; the middle class being 'hollowed out' and not investing in future capability such as education; declining tax receipts; and increasing boom and bust, extremities of the economic cycle.

Ethics has an emotional dimension too. To be clear, emotion has intrinsic worth: to have compassion, to care and to be human. But in addition, emotion is not just an end in itself; emotion is also a business case because through emotion we can reach the parts of our consciousness that a qualitative or commercial argument alone cannot. Advertising uses emotion every day in order to sell us stuff. Stories, rather than numbers, are sometimes far more effective at raising consciousness, providing inspiration and contributing to action.

Consider the graduation speech of a friend of mine, Brooke Ellison. She is the first quadriplegic person to graduate from Harvard. She said, 'It is only by way of the work that others do that my paralysis becomes not the totality of my existence, but only a part'.[59] She went on to remind the assembled class of 2004 that we are all paralysed to various degrees:

There is paralysis of the spirit, which leaves some discouraged in the face of obstacles before them and powerless to make the necessary changes in their lives. There is paralysis of the mind, which leaves some ignorant to new ways of understanding people and nature of their conditions. And there is paralysis of the heart, manifested in fear or uncertainty, which keeps some stagnant despite all that needs to be done.

I encourage contemplation on that point. Brooke went on to say 'the possibilities that await are only significant to the extent that we can view them as collective, and not individual opportunities... just like I am unable to move without the assistance of others, the world cannot move forward without our cooperation'. Ten years later I can unequivocally say that I have learnt more from Brooke over the past decade than she has ever learnt from me. We are all paralysed to some extent, and by thinking about real inclusion we can begin to cure those paralyses. As Brooke concluded, 'For the spirit there is the potential for hope, for the mind there is understanding, and for the heart there is love.'

Future proof your organisation for the world to come

There will always be a million other priorities that, in many minds, will always come before Diversity and Inclusion work. In the same way that economic planning is not as 'sexy' as disaster relief, or how action on climate change seems intangible compared with saving an endangered species this year, Diversity and Inclusion seems abstract in comparison with live organisational and personnel issues right here, today. The reactive impulse triumphs over the preemptive intention, even though the latter may in fact be more courageous, more creative and more useful. Yet we ignore the importance and relevance of inclusion at our own future cost. Inclusive organisations are, by definition, future proofing themselves for the diverse world that is emerging around us.

This book is designed to inspire courage, to provoke creativity and to promote talent, whatever it looks like. All three ingredients are essential in order to bring about real inclusion. That is what our increasingly diverse world needs its organisations to now do. When there is no or minimal cost to systematising inclusion, or even cost savings to be gained, then the main barrier to implementation becomes attitude. Whereas additional 101 or 2.0 initiatives require a degree of tolerance, embedding inclusion in existing systems becomes an intellectual and very practical operational challenge. The organisation is one part of life we can control to great personal and societal benefit. It is an area where with leadership you can make a significant contribution to the greater good. With arguments such as those advanced above, the choice to act upon our better instincts comes down in the final analysis to courage and willingness to make a difference.

Sir Tim Berners-Lee, inventor of the World Wide Web (and cast member of the London 2012 Opening Ceremony) said 'we need diversity of thought in the world to face the new challenges'.[60] The framing of the challenge is of crucial importance. It will determine how it is perceived by the organisation, as well as suggest the motivation of the practitioner. Assuming we are proposing intelligent, contextualised Inclusion 3.0 work, which adds value to the organisation, the question before us is not therefore why should we engage in such work, but rather why wouldn't we?

Takeaways – the real business case for action

1   There are five compelling reasons for organisations to engage with Inclusion 3.0 programmes based on customer relevance, employee attraction, removing barriers to growth, better decision-making and ethics.

2   The first four reasons for real inclusion have substantial empirical evidence behind them to make a case for both (at minimum) correlation, and, in many cases, causality too. Regardless of whether individuals 'believe' in inclusion or 'feel' it's important, data makes a case of debatable, but measurable, evidence.

3   For other individual practitioners and participants, a case for and question of ethics may be the compelling factor towards the Inclusion Imperative. As with elements of attitude, passion and courage, the weight placed upon ethics will exist to differing degrees among individuals. Often stories and inspiration are better than numbers in order to motivate this group.

4 Diversity is a reality. Inclusion is a choice. Inclusive leadership is required to help us acknowledge current reality and frame the conversation in such a way that people can choose to act on the inclusion imperative.

Notes

1 Jane Nelson, Senior Fellow and Director of Corporate Social Responsibility Initiative Mossavar-Rahmani Center for Business and Government, kindly shared this diagram with me following a conversation in her office at Harvard in April 2013. She is author of many books and articles on this subject, the latest of which is *Corporate Responsibility Coalitions: The Past, Present and Future of Alliances for Sustainable Capitalism* by David Grayson and Jane Nelson (January 2013, Stanford University Press).

2 Michael Porter and Mark Kramer, Creating Shared Value, *Harvard Business Review*, January 2011: http://hbr.org/2011/01/the-big-idea-creating-shared-value.

3 There are five diverse generations in the current workforce:

Traditionalists, born before 1943

Baby boomers, born 1943–64

Generation X, born 1965–77

Generation Y, (millenials), born 1978–97

Digital natives, who will change the world, born since 1998.

4 Seb Coe speech, Singapore 6 July 2005.

5 http://www.youtube.com/watch?v=YmwwrGV_aiE. Karl Fisch, a Colorado teacher, produced this superb video for his high-school class. There have since been several updates – and rip-offs.

6 Conversation with author, Cambridge MA, April 2013.

7 http://en.wikiquote.org/wiki/Heraclitus.

8 Stephen Jay Gould https://en.wikipedia.org/wiki/Punctuated_equilibrium.

9 See note 5.

10 Wikipedia ref: http://en.wikipedia.org/wiki/L'Oréal#Advertising.

11 Conversation with Steve Girdler 16 July 2013.

12 See note 11.

13 *Financial Times*, http://www.ft.com/intl/cms/s/0/7ef79b48-adaf-11e2-a2c7-00144feabdc0.html#axzz2ZyAImxDI.

14 Bunga Bunga Trial: Silvio Berlusconi Guilty, Sky News – The former Italian prime minister is sentenced to seven years in jail for paying for sex with an underage prostitute: http://news.sky.com/story/1107593/bunga-bunga-trial-silvio-berlusconi-guilty.

15 Klaus Schwab, conversation in Nai Pyi Taw, Burma June 2013 in response to question from Fellow Young Global Leader Lucian Tarnowski.

16 In the future workplace, hierarchy is falling down, and crowd sourcing is on the rise. We will swarm a team to solve a problem. People will rate the Chief Executive online. Traditional performance reviews will fall short when Generation Y wants instant feedback.

A good comparison is Google and Cisco. Google is a generation X company, Cisco is a baby boomer company. By allowing 82 per cent of its people to homework, Cisco is attempting to compete.

17 Jennifer Brown, 'Future 2020 Workplace workshop' at Workplace Forum on Inclusion, Minneapolis 11 April 2013.

18 See note 17.

19 For more information see Chapter 13.

20 See note 5.

21 See note 5.

22 See Ed Michaels, Helen Handfield-Jones and Beth Axelrod, *The War for Talent* (Harvard Business Press, 2001).

23 Adrian Wooldridge, A survey of talent: The battle for brainpower, *The Economist* 5 October 2006.

24 Danny Kalman conversation, September 2013.

25 Ann Marie conversation, August 2013.

26 http://www.americanprogress.org/issues/lgbt/report/2012/03/22/11234/the-costly-business-of-discrimination/ [accessed 11 October 2013].

27 Michael Porter and Mark Kramer, Creating Shared Value, *Harvard Business Review*, January 2011: http://hbr.org/2011/01/the-big-idea-creating-shared-value.

28 Brundtland Commission Report (1987) Our Common Future http://consent.n7/pdf/Our/_Common_Future-Bruntland_Report_1987.pdf [accessed 11 October 2013]

29 See note 27.

30 Kirk Snyder, *Lavender Road to Success: The career guide for the gay community* (Ten Speed Press, 2004).

31 See note 30.

32 Goldman Sachs presentation at The Conference Board, New York City 26 June 2013.

33 'The Power of Out 2.0: LGBT in the workplace', Center for Talent Innovation, New York City, 2013.

34 Greg Pellegrino, Sally D'Amato and Anne Weisberg *The Gender Dividend: Making the case for investing in women* (Deloitte, 2011).

35 Carmen Pages and Claudia Priras, *The Gender Dividend: Capitalizing on womens' work* (Inter American Development Bank, 2010).

36 Drue Kataoka, Fellow Young Global Leader and award-winning artist, conversation in Myanmar, June 2013.

37 John Hagel, John Seeley Broan and Lang Davidson *Measuring the Forces of Long-term Change: The 2009 shift index* (Deloitte Development, 2009).

38 Lois Joy, Nancy M Carter, Harvey M Wagner and Sriram Narayanan. *The Bottom Line: Corporate performance and women's representation on corporate boards* (Catalyst, 2007).

39 David Ross, Some Research on the Business Case for Diversity and the Attitudes of Male Executives, The Sandford C Bernstein & Co Center for Leadership and Ethics at Colombia Business School Symposium on Diversity at the Top, 10 December 2010.

40 Conversation with the author.

41 Scott Page. *The Difference* (Princeton University Press, 2004).

42 See note 22.

43 Alexandra Jones, Rising to the Challenge of Diversity, Work Foundation report (2006), http://www.theworkfoundation.com/Reports/178/Rising-to-the-challenge-of-diversity [accessed 11 October 2013]

44 Tufts University: http://www.ase.tufts.edu/psychology/sommerslab/documents/raceRealSommersEllsworth2001.pdf [accessed 11 October 2013]

45 Fons Trompenaars and Charles Hampden Turner, *Riding the Waves of Innovation* (McGraw Hill, 2012), pp 74–75.

46 Michael Norton, Justifying and Rationalizing Questionable Behavior, 7 February 2013, Seminar at Harvard Kennedy School, Cambridge, MA. People lie in 30 per cent of all social interactions.

47 Michael Norton, Justifying and Rationalizing Questionable Behavior 7 February 2013, Seminar at Harvard Kennedy School, Cambridge, MA. There is a significant silent majority of people who find it difficult to talk about ethnicity or demographic issues seen for example in the playing of the game 'Guess Who?' Almost no one identifies the characters by their ethnicity – no one will say 'is he black?' Younger children tend to beat adults at 'Guess Who?' because they more readily talk about obvious demographic characteristics. At LOCOG we had to 'liberate' people to allow them to say 'Black' for example.

48 Marie Danziger, conversation with the author in Cambridge, MA, March 2013.

49 http://bits.blogs.nytimes.com/2009/03/30/microsoft-encarta-dies-after-long-battle-with-wikipedia/.

50 Mary Martinez, 16 March 2012 London Vanguard Seminar.

51 James Surowiecki, *The Wisdom of Crowds: Why the many are smarter than the few and how collective wisdom shapes business, economies, societies and nations* (Knopf Doubleday, 2004).

52 Hoffman and Triandis in: http://hec.unil.ch/docs/files/83/655/wiersema_bantel_1992_top_management_team_demography_and_corporate_strategic_change.pdf [accessed 11 October 2013].

53 For more information see http://www.mindtools.com/pages/article/newTED_07.htm [accessed 11 October 2013].

54 http://laughingsquid.com/bad-with-names-a-comic-about-forgetting-peoples-names-by-doghouse-diaries/.

55 There is a compelling video online that illustrates this: www.youtube.com/watch?v=QpkkQnijnsm

56 http://www.cpag.org.uk/child-poverty-facts-and-figures.

57 Joseph Stiglitz, 'Inequality is holding back the recovery', http://opinionator.blogs.nytimes.com/2013/01/19/inequality-is-holding-back-the-recovery/*New York Times* article above and book: *The Price of Inequality* (WW Norton and Company, 2013).

58 For Richer, for Poorer *The Economist* [online] http:www.economist.com/node/21564414

59 Brooke Ellison, Graduation Speech, Class Day May 2004, Harvard

60 Sir Tim Berners Lee [online] http://blogs.fco.gov.uk/ianhughes/2012/10/04/we-need-diversity-of-thought-in-the-world-to-face-the-new-challenges-tim-berners-lee-the-british-inventor-of-the-world-wide-web

PART TWO
Creativity

Introduction to Part Two

How to achieve real inclusion

If courage has its roots in Ancient Greece, creativity is a relatively new concept. It can be traced back to the Renaissance, when 'creation' began to be perceived as having originated from the abilities of individual humans, and not from God. Only in the Age of Enlightenment did creativity as a concept become mainstream. For example, in the writing of Thomas Hobbes imagination was argued to be a key element of human cognition. Creativity became a topic of serious debate in the late 19th century when there was an increased interest in individual differences inspired by the arrival of Darwinism. As we heard in the business case in Chapter 4, a useful analogy can be made between evolutionary ecosystems and the talent pipelines of organisations. Diversity is the key ingredient in creating creativity.

Creativity is of central importance to achieving real inclusion, and thus of key interest to the practitioner: how did we do it? Here I explain the framework for the change process (understand, lead and deliver) as well as the areas in which we would intervene (workforce, procurement and service delivery). This simple articulation of quite complex phenomena could be easily and naturally articulated by our senior leadership and easily understood by all staff. Its simplicity was key to its success.

Creativity, in the context of achieving inclusion, is about being entrepreneurial. Many people expect you to fall into role, based on their experience of Diversity 101 or 2.0 to date. Many dread what they perceive is coming down the line – training, audits and so forth. Creativity is about challenging those expectations, even surprising and delighting people so that they actually pay attention. Creativity is being able to articulate 'change' as distinct from 'loss' in the minds of the audience. They may not like change, but they can bear it, especially if it surprises them. Furthermore, change may actually be in their interests too. That depends on the ability of the practitioner to articulate the vision clearly enough. It also depends on the work of enlarging the pie for everyone rather than falling into the typical diversity trap of a zero-sum game when the dominant group will always resist change because they feel it to be at the expense of them losing ground to the minority.

We were fortunate at LOCOG because to some degree we had a blank canvas and so could experiment more easily than many organisations that come with their existing baggage, policies and procedures. We were also a growth company, enlarging the pie every day. However, the Olympic and Paralympic movements also come with their baggage and it is quite heavy. We had to manage some extremely conservative forces, strongly wedded to 'tradition'. Credit goes to the LOCOG leadership, especially the Chief Executive, who had the courage to allow experimentation on his watch. To permit failure, to encourage 'asking for forgiveness, not for permission', to tolerate a degree of risk. Pie enlargement is not solely dependent on growth. The pie can be enlarged creatively, through inclusive leadership and through actionable inspiration: read on.

The creativity comes in part from individual and collective courage. It also comes from working the system. At LOCOG, like many organisations, we had complex internal and external systems, but with a little courage, they could be our creative playground as we attempted to build 'Everyone's 2012'.

The diagram below summarises the creative process we established. It summarises the process of understanding, leadership and delivery. It articulates the three areas of intervention, namely workforce, procurement and service delivery. This was an iterative process. Successes and failures were fed back in real time. That evidence informed better understanding and subsequent leadership and delivery. That evidence also galvanised new recruits, as LOCOG's change programme became ever more deeply embedded in the project.

FIGURE 5.1 Achieving real inclusion complex system map

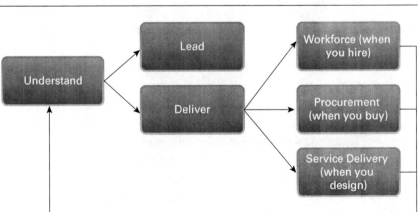

The process

05

This book aims to take the reader on a journey in 300 pages equivalent to the journey undertaken by the LOCOG team over five years. That process is defined as 'understand, lead and deliver' the simple and effective way we communicated the change programme to every man and woman involved in the project.

Table 5.1 summarises that process. In the upper half of the table the theoretical approach is laid out, demonstrating how we turned much existing orthodoxy on its head. For example, by acting as internal consultants who actually offered to help colleagues, rather than internal auditors who were there solely to ensure compliance, we were welcomed by colleagues and came to be seen as a resource. We were able to build trust and intervene deeply, rather than superficially, into the business. The lower half of the table details some of the tools we used in the process, to embed understanding, to encourage leadership and to instil a culture of delivery. They will be explained in each of the following chapters.

Understand

We needed staff to understand Diversity and Inclusion, what it was, and what it was not. We needed to give real inclusion a chance and not have its acceptance threatened by people assuming we were still in Diversity 101- or 2.0-land. That redefinition of Diversity and Inclusion was accompanied by a compelling business case and a reframing of the conversation. Understanding would not be created through training programmes, but by structured conversations.

It started with knocking on doors and getting face time with people who had never been challenged to really engage with inclusion before. This was on occasion terrifying, as it seemed at the time a never-ending process of putting your ideas up to scrutiny by every director, every head of department and every colleague, every day. But by listening, by getting them to

TABLE 5.1 Real inclusion process journey

Understand	Lead	Deliver
Redefine Diversity and Inclusion: Inclusion 3.0 > Diversity 101/2.0	Leadership versus management: Adaptive > Technical	Real time results: Competition > Quotas
Rediscover the real business case: Inspiration > Compliance	Information sharing: Transparency > Confidentiality	Letting go: Devolved > Centralized
Reframe the conversation: Consulting > Auditing	Not a solo heroic endeavour: Group > Individual	Point accountability and responsibility: Individual > Group
Tools used at each stage		
Role models – Mandela, Tutu, sporting heroes	Role model behaviour	Regular information sharing, monitoring and benchmarking
Surprising people	Leadership Pledge	Recruitment Action Plans
Structured conversations	Sponsors Forum	Talent pool
Internal marketing	Diversity Board	Guaranteed Interview Scheme (GIS)
Inclusive design	Group interviews	Test Events
Personalised customer service	Online procurement Legacy Evaluation Group	Awards and recognition Immovable deadline

talk about what inclusion meant to them, by reassuring them that we were not embarking on a Diversity 101 training programme and that we were in fact really about making the Games better, we won people over. It's amazing how much better a conversation can go when you approach it expecting to listen more than talk.

The main risk of this approach is the potential for the 'worst offenders' to be let off the hook as they come to realise this is not an auditing-led programme. Were we naive? With the knowledge that they will not be vetted as they may have been in the past there is the potential for many of the 'worst offenders' to revert to type. It's necessary to conduct a cost benefit analysis and weigh that risk against the upside of unleashed discretionary effort at the other end of the scale. Compliance rarely creates best practice. By definition, compliance encourages the minimum. By opening the Pandora's box of diversity and empowering people to lead, we were setting no upper limit.

In Seb Coe's winning 2005 Singapore speech he talked about 'a world of distractions' and why sport still mattered. The same is true of inclusion. For any professional, faced with real and challenging profit and loss situations, line management issues, board meetings, reviews, takeovers, mergers, office politics, childcare and relationship maintenance, how does a 'soft' topic like inclusion make it onto the 'to-do' list? The only way is to integrate it; on its own it will never be more important to individual decision makers than real-time issues that have more immediate impact on their career. It was therefore never a separate item on the list, but integrated in each bullet point.

We were trying to instigate a change programme that would become one of the defining differentiators of the London Games. Yet most people, if they were honest, still viewed Diversity and Inclusion as at best a low priority, at worst as irrelevant or even harmful to what they really cared about. So how to proceed from there?

We had to focus on what people did care about. We had to be creative and contextual. In LOCOG, about a third of the staff were receptive to the moral argument, point five of the real business case. That is, this wasn't just another job, this wasn't just another event, and we had a moral responsibility to include people in this opportunity of a lifetime. About a third of the staff were receptive more to the first four business arguments and the fact that the way we were positioning Diversity and Inclusion was extremely cost effective and this could be a great-value way to make the Games better – and secure a worthy legacy. But about a third of the staff were at first non-receptive or only receptive for political reasons, if they had to do it from a compliance perspective, or if they felt it could somehow advance their own agenda or profile.

Of course, I oversimplify for the purpose of analysis. Most people at different times were a combination of all three factors. And there were more factors, determined by the individual personalities, profiles, agendas, office politics and stakeholder interests at varying times over the course of the journey.

The key learning from the Diversity and Inclusion perspective was that we had to offer all these groups a non-offensive, palatable programme that they could support, or at least not oppose. We had to position the Diversity and Inclusion programme carefully, as a minimal cost (or even cost reducing, as we were later able to achieve) value-adding programme that would make the Games better.

The core purpose of the organisation was to deliver a great Games. We managed to get enough people to understand that Diversity and Inclusion would help make the Games better. It had something of the moral, as we were reaching out and genuinely changing people's lives. It had something of the cost-effectiveness factor, as the lifetime budget was £1.3 million and the procurement savings alone, which Diversity and Inclusion contributed to, were nearly one hundred times that. Most of all, it had something of the political factor, which individuals could take to use for their own agendas at convenient times.

This is not supposed to sound as Machiavellian as it might. Most people were good people and were doing it at least partially for 'the right reasons'. The starting assumption of Diversity and Inclusion at LOCOG was that most people wanted to do the right thing. Our job was to: a) give them the easy, cost-effective toolkit to do it; and b) not give them reasons for disengagement by screwing up. To that end, we made it as easy as possible, and we enacted the age-old KISS rule: keep it simple, stupid.

Lead

We needed staff to take personal responsibility for Diversity and Inclusion and lead on it, no matter what their level, grade or role. This was important, and an important distinction from 'manage', as discussed in Chapter 7. By encouraging transparency and working against confidentiality, information sharing gave people a wider sense of how we were all doing with the inclusion programme, rather than it being something that was done 'to' them. Importantly, this was group work, not an individual heroic crusade. As a group process it decreased the fear factor of being the only one to put the neck above the parapet. I, or any one, couldn't do it all, and the results would be worse if I did.

This echoes the point made in Chapter 1, namely the technical versus adaptive challenge. Delivering the Games was the ultimate technical test. At first, Diversity and Inclusion was seen as little more than the 'conscience' of the organisation. I had more than one director tell me that they wanted me to 'keep them honest' during the journey. We were able to move beyond this social insurance policy to being a value-adding programme that unlocked potential in hitherto undiscovered places.

By making it easy to 'do' Diversity and Inclusion we repositioned the question Marty Linsky posed 'Why on earth would I do this?' to 'Why on earth would I *not* do this?' In every talk, meeting, conversation where it was appropriate we would articulate time and time again the opportunity that was before people. There would never be enough time, there would never be enough resources, but one thing that was in infinite supply, free of charge and wholly within an individual's control, was their own capacity for leadership. And we were asking people to lead on Diversity and Inclusion. It was a message that worked.

People needed to believe that we understood their situation. The venue manager who was responsible for thousands of staff and customers and felt under-resourced. The commercial guy who needed to land a deal in order to secure revenue that actually paid for the Games and didn't need any 'tricky' clauses in the contract. The HR manager who wanted to hire 'diversely' but happened to have the very best candidate in front of them and he was white, straight and male.

The Diversity and Inclusion interventions needed to be targeted to reflect the realities of people under pressure. It was no good theorising about the moral rectitude of the programme to the staff member who had been up 24 hours straight finishing a commercial deal. So we employed a range of methods and created a flexible toolkit, both of which could be adapted by an individual to actually help them, rather than burden them.

An example would be the volunteer programme. Recruiting, training and deploying 70,000 volunteers when anything from 10,000 to over 1 million might apply was a daunting task. We positioned Diversity and Inclusion as helpful, rather than burdensome, because by knowing the diversity of the recruits, it would be easier to ensure language and cultural skills, for example, were adequately captured and the workforce would work for a global client base. Lauren, on the Diversity and Inclusion team, also became an integral part of the volunteer team and a key conduit in terms of recruitment and advice.

Another example would be the Torch Relay, where knowing the access requirements of an individual ahead of time was crucial in securing a cost-effective range of adapted torch carrying mechanisms, planning the route in terms of accessibility, and avoiding potentially embarrassing PR. Of course, an argument could be made that it would have been cheaper still to exclude disabled people altogether. As the real business case tries to make clear, ethics are an individual choice and, to many, a personal responsibility.

People rarely act in isolation. Any leadership they execute is in the context of a group. Their peers influence them more than they realise. People have surprisingly little influence over their own behaviour. Therefore we had to capture the group system narrative and make inclusion part of it. I knew we had reached a milestone when a previously hostile director was espousing verbatim what the Chief Executive had said at a management meeting earlier in the week about Diversity and Inclusion being a personal passion of his. Suddenly it was a personal passion of this director too. New norms can be created.

Deliver

In the same way that we could not afford to miss technical deadlines, we could not afford to miss Diversity and Inclusion goals through theoretical procrastination at the expense of concrete delivery. One of the important factors here was individual accountability. Whereas leadership was a group process, with whatever support was required offered, delivery was an individual accountability, with no hiding behind the group. Benchmarking and competition were important motivators, akin to the information sharing mentioned above. The constant drumbeat of results was the best way we converted the sceptics.

Several times we came under pressure from the Equality and Human Rights Commission, the Commission for a Sustainable London 2012 (CSL) and various lobby groups to adopt a more 101 approach, to ensure a more compliance-based strategy. I remain firmly of the view that such an approach would have at best achieved far less success than we did, at worst been a complete failure. Adopting such an approach would have been business as usual and if ever there was a time in professional life to experiment, this was it. That was, however, my view. Others subscribing to the technical challenge approach would have taken the exact opposite view; that now was precisely the time to avoid any risk and to focus on the massive technical challenge of staging the Games, and only that.

Trying to instil a change programme in a constantly moving organisation is hard. Trying to instil it with minimal resources in an organisation of unprecedented momentum, growing from 50 people to 200,000 personnel focused purely on delivery for a defined exercise in a defined period of time with an immovable deadline was simply daunting. To wade through this complexity, as outlined in earlier chapters, we had to be as focused as

FIGURE 5.2 Real inclusion process cycle

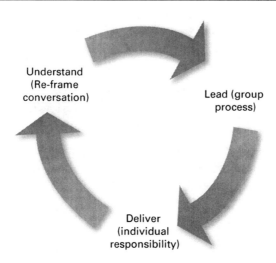

possible, as simple as possible, and as concise as possible. Anything else and we would not achieve the necessary cut-through and traction required to get people in the right mindset for delivery.

When this process was enacted, the important thing for us to remember, and against every natural instinct of those of us who designed it, was to remember to let go. 'Letting go' is the idea that individuals delivering to their optimum within a framework would be messier but ultimately more productive and effective than trying to do it all top-down. Not only was it physically impossible for a small team to be in every meeting, be involved in every decision and give advice in every situation, it was also a bad idea. Inclusive leadership is about empowering others, not offering all the answers. That is not only a self-survival strategy, it is a more effective way of creating creativity. Give people the framework and direction and let them create. It does require an appetite for risk and it does require courage as well as creativity. But the results prove it can be a far better strategy than top-down control.

The process outlined above was iterative and ongoing, not simply linear. It was a framework for people to lead their own work. You can't do it all, and the results would be worse if you did. The real value of the 2012 experience was in answering the question 'how do you create change'. 'Set them free' is not far from the truth. Let's now look at the three process stages in more depth.

Takeaways – the process

1 In defining the process for change, the overarching requirement was to make adoption as easy as possible. Only then would busy people be able to engage: the key word is KISS: keep it simple, stupid.

2 The process is defined as Understand, Lead, Deliver: respectively, a redefinition of Diversity and Inclusion (Inclusion 3.0); group leadership; and individual accountability.

3 The process is a framework that is used to empower people to lead their own work around Diversity and Inclusion. You can't do it all, and the results would be worse if you did.

Understand

06

For too long, diversity has been seen as the 'other', largely by a comfortable homogenous group of decision makers who are running the show. Critically, many of the 'minorities' that constitute 'the other' define themselves in this sense too and thus partake in their own exclusion. Scholars such as Michel Foucault and Simone de Beauvoir have written extensively on the concept of the other. The idea was popularised by Edward Said in his book *Orientalism*[1] using the example of Imperial Britain and its increasing understanding of self in relation to its colonies around the world. A person's definition of the 'other' is a key part of what defines their own being. Thus, white men understandably think their way of doing things is 'normal' and minorities accept it as so. In each sense, their understanding of the other side reinforces their own situation.

In many Western societies, when a white male commits an atrocity, such as Timothy McVeigh and the 1995 Oklahoma bomb, or Adam Lanza and the school shooting at Newton in 2012, they are labelled 'crazy guys'. When a Muslim male commits an atrocity, such as the Tsaernaev brothers in Boston 2013 or the two men who hacked a British soldier to death in London 2013, they are labelled 'terrorists'. In some ways a *white* terrorist would be the most disturbing of all for the majority, acting completely outside the constructed norm, which is why we call them 'crazy people' instead. There was a male Member of the LOCOG Board who made a couple of homophobic comments that I overheard. I observed how he was far more comfortable with a 'camp' gay head of department (conforming to norm) than he was with a 'masculine' gay head of department (challenging his perception of gay people). Norms and stereotypes are key determinants not only of our behaviour, but also of our beliefs.

Take socio-economic situations, or 'class', for example. This is a 'strand' of diversity that is often ignored by 101 and 2.0 practitioners. Many lower socio-economic groups, or 'working class' individuals will purposely self-limit in order to avoid feeling uncomfortable. My mum is a classic example of this. Even though she is very intelligent, has worked hard, becoming the first person in her family to reach university, and became a professional teacher, she is still bound by her working-class roots. When she was offered an upgrade on a recent flight, she turned it down because she would feel 'more comfortable' in the main cabin. When she was strongly encouraged to use the business class lounge by a sympathetic British Airways employee (breaking the rules, but exhibiting inclusive leadership) she quietly asked another sympathetic-looking woman where she had to pay for her food.

As long as diversity remained 'the other' it was doomed. The decision-making powers and associated resources would never be focused on it. So diversity had to be brought back into the realm of the current and present. As explained in Chapter 3, it is easy to be diverse without being inclusive and easy to be inclusive without being diverse. We had to articulate the value to individuals in LOCOG in truly embracing infinite diversity, Inclusion 3.0 style.

Sarojini Sahoo, an Indian feminist writer, builds on the work of De Beauvoir, by asserting that women can achieve self-actualisation by 'thinking, taking action, working, creating, on the same terms as men; instead of seeking to disparage them, she declares herself their equal'.[2] In this very sense, we positioned acceptance of diversity as a given and focused efforts on inclusion. Many would argue this was a betrayal of diversity, but this was not superficial inclusion, this was real inclusion, the embracing of infinite diversity.

Starting the conversation

We started the conversation inside the tent with a staff meeting. It was one of only two occasions that I addressed all staff, the idea being to de-personalise the message and have a diverse array of messengers delivering the same message, rather than the same messenger again and again – otherwise the messenger becomes the message. We posed the question to people directly about what they understood Diversity and Inclusion to be. Most people articulated Diversity 101 and 2.0 ideas, in the main based on their previous corporate experience.

We responded with the basics, starting with the winning London bid campaign. In Singapore Sebastian Coe said that we would create a Games for everyone, where people from all backgrounds, races, creeds, religions would be welcomed and encouraged to take part. There was a clear difference evident in Singapore between the French bid team, and the London bid team. The French had showcased technical excellence, *gigantisme* with air shows and the entire Champs-Elysées turned into a running track, but their presenters were all old white men. They represented the past.

We attempted to be as creative as possible in providing illustrative and famous examples to challenge people to think again about their current understanding. London's bid had comprised 30 per cent children and young people from East London, technical competence and a very compelling idea. Simply put, the Olympic fan base was ageing and the movement was not recruiting at the younger end of the spectrum. So the Olympic movement faced a real risk of becoming increasingly irrelevant to modern-day youth, society and culture. London positioned itself as a solution, offering to reconnect an increasingly conservative movement with the next generation, to save it from itself.

In the same way, we positioned Diversity and Inclusion as a solution for the Organising Committee, connecting the London Games with its customer and stakeholder base. We used Mandela and other global icons that were inspirational. But we also used more familiar, popular and respected role models who people could relate to in the context of their everyday work, such as Tanni Grey-Thompson, Paralympian and member of the House of Lords. Tanni represented 'actionable inspiration'. She could eloquently articulate how inclusion would make the Games better for athletes. She also said she would rather stick her seven-year-old child on a different bus than her racing chair.[3] It's important to have role models, especially female role models, who are not superstars who leave women feeling their achievements are unobtainable. That's why British Prime Minister Margaret Thatcher and black sports stars such as the Williams sisters are of limited use in this area.[4] Not all women can become Prime Minister or Wimbledon champion.

Research shows that women identify more with a subject when the authority figure is also female. For example, women identify more with Science Technology Engineering Maths (STEM) professions when the professor is female.[5] Whereas men were fine with either a male or female professor, female students were more negative towards mathematics with a male teacher. Whereas men already have a 'social vaccine inoculation', women felt more threatened when they were the only woman in a team. In other words, female managers matter, and are important in decreasing the gender gap.[6] LOCOG worked hard to profile its female directors and was successful in creating a culture where female leadership was the norm, not an oddity.

In the same way that we needed to move from bid campaign to practical delivery organisation, we needed to translate inclusion understanding into visibility and action. This was essential not simply for its own sake, but to gain and maintain credibility and keep the momentum going. With the bid won, it would be all too easy for the operations to be taken over by the usual suspects of competent technical white men who found the bid commitments an annoyance.

Guardian-reader syndrome

LOCOG suffered from '*Guardian*-reader syndrome', a term I invented and weaved into the induction at work. This is tongue-in-cheek – some of my best friends are *Guardian* readers and it is one of the best newspapers around. I hope they (and it) will permit a little self-deprecation for the purpose of explaining how to achieve real inclusion. *The Guardian* is a progressive/ centre-left newspaper in the UK. A lot of people at LOCOG read it, or were associated with people who read it. But in any case, it was a metaphor. Think New York Times limousine liberal, gauche caviar, cocktail parties masquerading as fundraising events for a very worthwhile cause.[7] These were good people, who had gay friends, black friends, probably not disabled friends but there might be 'someone in the family'. But when pushed to see how they would feel if their *own* son was gay, rather than someone else's son, or if their *own* daughter was dating a black man, rather than a white man or just having a black friend, the limits of progressiveness and niceness were tested. This is where LOCOG, and I suspect many more Western organisations, was at.

I know hundreds of people in 'liberal' and 'progressive' professions with similar outlooks who are absolutely convinced they are colour blind, that they 'don't discriminate', that they treat everyone 'the same'. Lateef Martin, a video-game designer from Montreal, put it brilliantly when he said 'saying you don't see colour is a lazy way to see the world. It exempts you from putting yourself in someone else's shoes'.[8] The fact is we all have biases, and the world is not a level playing field. Saying you treat all people the 'same' is a misnomer when people are intrinsically different – treating different people 'the same' leads to inequitable outcomes. The notion that you can 'be objective' is non-plausible.

Good people thought that reading *The Guardian* was sufficient, they were doing their 'bit'. This climate of seeming acceptance and tolerance was seductive and dangerous. We had to appropriately call out the fact that thinking and feeling was not enough. It was *doing* that produced results. There were no medals simply for having 'gay best friends'. The cold hard fact is that a 'better world' does not 'just happen'. People make it happen. And the appalling silence (or inaction)[9] of the good people can actually prevent it happening.

When there has been an obvious 'problem', such as discrimination against gay people in the military, there has been an intentional focus on correction.

But in supposed 'liberal' sectors such as the media and arts, there remains a great deal of complacency, and they remain a long way from real inclusion. This is the exact opposite of what many people in those sectors believe.

But you do have to believe that most people want to do the right thing most of the time. Otherwise, you can become terribly depressed and/or resort to 101 or 2.0 strategies to police adults like children. Again, you could argue we were naive. However, this return to childlike curiosity worked. Good people, who are naturally biased, responded better to consulting than auditing. People suffering from *Guardian*-reader syndrome responded better to 'why wouldn't you?' and 'how can I help?' rather than 'you need to'. People responded better to being asked a question rather than told an answer. And we didn't have all the answers in any case.

Knocking on doors

We had to sequence the education process. We worked top-down, directors, heads of department and then all staff. Directors took the form of 1–1 private discussions behind closed doors where they could be honest about their true feelings, and misgivings, and also talk freely, including on occasion the hilariously bad use of language to describe certain groups and individuals. I had multiple 1–1s with every director and every head of department. A little 1–1 intense focused education became a critical early win in this area. Rejecting the typical hierarchy, we also had key conversations with the key influencers and connectors in the organisation. The people who were most active on social media, organising staff ski trips, parties and other events. In this way we covered the people we were 'expected' to cover as well as those people who were role models in a peer sense.

As the conversation got underway, we reminded all staff that anyone at any level could access the Diversity and Inclusion team at any time. At the first director management meeting I presented 'Diversity – the opportunity and the risk' and asked for feedback on which way they thought we should go. We came up with a phrase in the early days, 'WADI', or 'what about Diversity and Inclusion?' This was translated to 'when I hire, buy or design' in the Leadership Pledge.

With the staff conversation underway, and some wind in the sails, it was time to look up, venture outside the tent and talk to our bosses in Lausanne and Bonn. Although Diversity and Inclusion were actually core to Olympism and Paralympism in action, that had not been terribly cognisant in conversations with the International Olympic Committee and International

Paralympic Committee thus far. While the Olympic values are excellence, friendship and respect, and the Paralympic values are determination, courage, inspiration and equality, this was the first time a Diversity and Inclusion programme had ever been undertaken in an organising committee.

It doesn't just happen

We had meetings with the International Olympic Committee and International Paralympic Committee on regular occasions, from the formal 'Coordination Commission' meetings to the less formal 'Project Reviews'. At the latter meeting in March 2009 we had a meeting with Gilbert Felli, the International Olympic Committee Executive Director and his male colleagues, mostly Swiss. On the other (LOCOG) side of the table was Paul Deighton, Chief Executive, Jean Tomlin, our black female HR Director, Sue Hunt, our female Strategy Director, Debbie Jevans, the first female Sports Director of any Summer Organising Committee, Terry Miller, the female General Counsel, and me, the Head of Diversity and Inclusion. After an introduction from Paul, the female directors presented our Diversity and Inclusion strategy, without notes, loosely based on PowerPoint, but mainly based on conversations we had had to date and their own personal feelings on the subject.

At the end of the presentation, Gilbert Felli looked at us, looked at his colleagues and replied, 'It doesn't just happen'. Paul replied, 'It doesn't just happen'. My job was safe for the moment and we had understanding from the International Olympic Committee of the process we wanted to instil in the organisation of the Games. I was extremely proud of the directors who had intellectually and emotionally 'got it'.

We repeated the same exercise with the International Paralympic Committee and Xavier Gonzalez, their Chief Executive, had the same reaction – 'It doesn't just happen'. The International Olympic Committee and the International Paralympic Committee were beginning to understand Diversity and Inclusion and in the case of both, it was a first for them. In a professional and appropriate way, it challenged their *modus operandi* to date. The usual relationship between franchisor and franchisee is a power relationship top-down. Here was London 2012 offering a thought leadership policy bottom-up. And it was being listened to.

In the case of the Paralympics, there was a compelling case that bizarrely had never been articulated. There are 10 million disabled people in the UK of which 6.8 million are of working age and at least 1 million want to work.[10] There are 8.6 million with a hearing impairment and 1.2 million have a learning disability. One in seven of the population experience mental health issues and one in three disabled people have been refused service or turned away from a public place. Fifty per cent of disabled people feel they are not listened to and only 8 per cent of secondary schools are accessible. If ever there was work to do, and ever an excuse needed, this was it.

Building the conversation

With the conversation underway with the International Olympic Committee and International Paralympic Committee we could accelerate the conversation back inside the tent with the staff. We began a circular education process involving LOCOG staff, the International Olympic Committee, International Paralympic Committee, stakeholders, and yet more LOCOG staff as they joined the growing organisation. If there was one message we kept repeating, and which others picked up and repeated themselves, it was 'It doesn't just happen'.

We had to paint a picture of what success looked like. We had to offer colleagues the 10-second 'elevator pitch'. So we used the England football team. Specifically, we used an image of supporters from every country in the world all wearing the same shirt, to represent diversity (people from every country in the world) and inclusion (them all wearing the same shirt). In an information-overloaded, crowded world, in a world of many distractions, we reminded people in the simplest way possible why inclusion mattered. This was their opportunity to lead on what mattered to them.

We followed up with two images of the sight lines from the VIP seats at the Indoor National Gymnasium in Beijing. This had been a key venue in the Beijing Paralympic Games. The first image was my view of the action, which was a perfect sight line. The second image was my colleague Dave's view of the action. He was a wheelchair user. Here we were in the best seats in the house at the Paralympic Games, and his view was obstructed by the ledge and some flowers. The architects got it – it didn't just happen.

A film we often played back to the International Olympic Committee was their own film *Giants*. This featured Jesse Owens, the inspirational US black athlete who won gold in Hitler's Berlin in the 1936 Games. Muhammad Ali was featured lighting the flame at Atlanta in 1996. Greg Louganis was featured at the 1988 Seoul Olympics. Most famous for banging his head on the board on his ninth dive, only Greg and his coach knew at the time that he was HIV positive and therefore why he was so upset at the resulting blood in the water. The concentration of chlorine ensured there was never a risk to other athletes but without knowing this, and being under unbelievable pressure, he had to compose himself, take his tenth and final dive and went on to take Gold (Louganis, 2006). When framed in the context of Diversity and Inclusion, this film demonstrated how diversity had been a key part of the history of the Games. It had been a natural occurrence, but it had never been leveraged – until now.

Creating a circular conversation

We took the conversation to other stakeholders now, further outside the tent and into key players in the system, the Olympic Delivery Authority, Greater London Authority, Government Olympic Executive and sponsors. We partnered extensively with hundreds of community organisations. Often this was difficult, on occasion torturous, but with hindsight it was an essential move for two reasons. One, we engaged people who desperately wanted to be listened to, felt they had been ignored too long and here was the biggest event in the world asking their opinion. Two, it was free consultancy, saving us thousands, if not millions of pounds, in advice. By working with the communities who had themselves experienced discrimination or exclusion we were achieving the double whammy: happy stakeholders and genuinely cost-effective input.

In order to embed understanding among our colleagues and stakeholders, we undertook a series of 'Diversity weeks'. At first, these terms make me cringe, rather like 'diversity training' and other Diversity 101 initiatives that are ineffective time and cost sinks. They start from the supposition that for the 51 weeks of the year when it's not 'diversity week' we are somehow homogeneous. It is analogous to the way that diversity training is required as some kind of belated social education to tell us all how to be nice to black, disabled and gay people. I kid you not, in the British pub, the standing joke is 'black, lesbian woman in a wheelchair'. We should have called them 'Inclusion focused weeks' or something far snappier than I can think of.

While we jettisoned the 'diversity training' we persisted with the diversity weeks, emphasising that they were a celebration of everyone (including straight white men) and simply providing a forum for staff to showcase their work and receive recognition. It was a risk, because holding diversity weeks in some ways went against our overall philosophy. But the diversity weeks did help us to synthesise work that had been taking place across the organisation and give it profile. In the end, we renamed them 'Everyone's 2012 week' to emphasise that everyone was included (we especially wanted to see the sceptics) and we held them in March 2009, 2010 and 2011.

In 2009 we held a launch conference with the Chief Executive, directors and other stakeholders presenting. Partners, sponsors and community organisations invited. We had a very democratic structure, which was a mistake because it was hijacked by the more extreme community activists who used it as a showboat exercise to peddle their own (narrow) agendas. However, we were able to hold summits, for example concerning homophobia in sport, and in so doing promote London 2012 as at the forefront of Diversity and Inclusion thinking and action and confound many of the sceptics. Internally we had a poster campaign with statements designed to provoke the 'why wouldn't you do inclusion?' sentiment. Examples ranged from 'A homosexual cannot do the job of a footballer' (Luciano Moggi, former manager of Italian football club *Juventus*, April 2008) to 'Spanish football fans still chant monkey noises when a black player passes the ball', to 'Only 1 of the 26 International Sport Federations we work with has a woman in charge'. In each case, the statement was followed up by: 'Let's use the power of the Games to inspire change' Diversity week 9–13 March, find out more on the Knowledge (the LOCOG intranet).

In 2010 we were less democratic with the conference but more so in terms of the community events we supported. We wanted to be on the front foot, post our major intervention (see next chapter) and maintain momentum. We profiled women's boxing (back in the Games for the first time since 1904) and Boccia (the least well known Paralympic sport) held in conjunction with an Accessibility summit where we canvassed the views of 100 disabled people and disability experts in the design of our venues. A dedicated career day in Mile End Park pavilion was attended by 500 mainly black Londoners from the local neighbourhoods in the East End. We did this because we were getting poor attendances at career days in Canary Wharf and the feedback was that local people don't go there. Unlike our front door in Canary Wharf, they knew where Mile End Park pavilion was. They had the opportunity to interact directly with 40 LOCOG staff who had given up their day to come and meet our potential recruits face to face.

I remember pre LOCOG having had aspirations to get involved in the bids with Manchester and then London early on and being constantly frustrated by the perceived infallibility of the wall that surrounded the organisation. Once inside, I frequently said to colleagues 'remember how it felt when you were on the outside? Well that is how these guys feel, so now you are on the inside, break down the wall'. The 500 mainly black Londoners career event was a turning point, a tipping point if you will, in terms of getting diversity into the LOCOG recruitment pipeline. It needed an event of that scale to reach the tipping point in the time we had available.

In 2011 we held another launch conference and a follow-up accessibility summit, finalising approvals and engagements for our accessibility work on all the venues and accounting for the varied needs of disabled people. We also held fast-track group interviews for candidates against a generic job description to maximise their choices and maximise the best role fit for them. We presented generic information about LOCOG, including advice on how to perform at selection, followed by a series of 30-minute interviews with same-day decision-making.

In March 2012 we held an Everyone's 2012 day, rather than week, in respect of everyone's time in the final run up and also to have a bigger media hit. We used the volunteer selection centre in ExCel, in London's docklands. Accessible, easily reached by public transport and, more importantly, free of charge since the volunteering team allowed us three days to bump in, host the day, then bump out. This was an important day to consolidate all the work that had been done by so many people to date, allow them to take pride in our collective achievements, gain media profile and set the tone among all our stakeholders that we were ready to host the most diverse and inclusive Game possible in a few months' time.

We used videos that had been produced over the years. We produced timelines showing how the work had developed from bid stage till the present day. Rather than a top-down conference, we invited guests to go on a guided pathway journey. They moved around the venue to experience as many of the 22 'Everyone's 2012' projects as possible, to witness some of the work that had been already accomplished and they had the opportunity to talk to the staff who had been directly involved. For example, meeting the ceremonies team and hearing about some of the plans for the Torch Relay, meeting the procurement team, meeting the sports teams and how we intended to present the sport in venue and on broadcast at Games time.[11]

Creating understanding was an iterative process. We started inside the tent, and then moved outside, first to the International Olympic Committee and International Paralympic Committee, then to our stakeholders, and then to the wider community. We created a self-reinforcing system where each would converse with the other about inclusion, so the discussion was not one way, but circular. We highlighted nothing more than existing reality to reframe the conversation in a more arresting way, designed to create 'actionable inspiration'. By building the understanding of inclusion in this manner, the message was not just coming from the Diversity and Inclusion team, or even just from LOCOG, but it was evolving as a group discussion, of which we were a key part.

If I had to summarise the understanding process, and sequence how we embedded learning, it would be something like this. In 2008, we wanted to be internally 'diversity confident', that real inclusion was an accepted part of our values. In 2009 we had ventured outside the tent and into the system with credibility: we were 'cutting it' and real inclusion was part of our brand. In 2010 we were perceived externally as 'leading edge', symbolised by participation in our conference. In 2011 the International Olympic Committee and International Paralympic Committee had recognised the value of this work to 'move the world forward'. Finally, in 2012, we would be able to host the most diverse and inclusive games ever.

Takeaways – understand

1 Redefine Diversity and Inclusion (Inclusion 3.0) and use real-world examples and icons to bring alive the diverse reality both inside and outside the organisation; actionable inspiration. Use history, stories and job descriptions to begin building an understanding of Diversity and Inclusion.

2 Rediscover the real business case for inclusion based on customers, employees, productivity, decision-making and ethics. It's about removing barriers, not decorating the tree. We didn't state it as such, we just lived it and called it 'Everyone's 2012'.

3 Reframe the conversation, away from 'compliance' and 'why you should', to 'challenge' and 'why would you not?' Challenge *Guardian*-reader syndrome through building a 360-degree marketing campaign that asks the questions allowing people to *themselves* come to the answers that create the new norm. People like being consulted, not audited, and asked, not told. This is doubly helpful since you don't necessarily have the answers yourself in any case.

Notes

1 Edward Said, *Orientalism* (Penguin, 2003).

2 Sajorini Sahoo – see, for example, *The Dark Adobe* (Indian Age Communication, 2009).

3 Conversation with the author 13 Jul 2013.

4 WAPPP seminar, 18 April 2013, Cambridge, MA.

5 Nilanjana Dasgupta, 18 April 2013 'Thriving Despite Negative Stereotypes: How In-group Experts and Peers Act as Social Vaccines to Inoculate Women's Self-concept and Achievement'. Women and Public Policy Program Seminar, Cambridge, MA.

6 Matt Huffman, 25 April 2013, 'Female Managers and Gender Inequality: Evidence from Private Sector Firms', WAPPP seminar, Cambridge, MA.

7 See, for example, the Woody Allen film *Everyone Says I Love You*, especially http://www.youtube.com/watch?v=kkwvygjvLcE [accessed 11 October 2013].

8 BBC online http://www.bbc.co.uk/news/magazine-22318657 [accessed 11 October 2013].

9 This echoes the famous Niemoller quote http://www.ushmm.org/wic/en/article.php?moduleId=10007392 [accessed 11 October 2013].

10 The statistics come from http://www.stem-e-and-d-toolkit.co.uk/thestrands-equality/disability-background and from http://www.papworth.org.uk/downloads/keyfactsaboutdisabilitynew_081103143956.pdf.

11 I came down from Yorkshire for the day and was present, but it was between my dad's sudden death and the funeral so I was not completely prioritising the day as I would otherwise have been. The result is testament to inclusive group leadership and the Diversity and Inclusion team, especially Tom Secker-Walker, stepping up.

Lead

07

There are approximately 86,166 books currently listed on Amazon pertaining to leadership. I know that 25 of them are very good, but I am not sure about the rest, and I am not sure how many actually deal with leadership.

Leadership is about getting groups to face up to real challenges and address them to benefit us all. It's distinct from management, in the sense that management is administration, a technical exercise, which can be often vital but is rarely transformative. The fact that MBAs are still called Masters of Business Administration seems strange to me, given what is most needed at this moment in time are not administrators, but leaders.

Leadership is not about ego, or power or authority, although a measure of all of these can sometimes help. Leadership is more about empowering others, empowering a team towards a collective goal or mission, the result of which is greater than the sum of its parts. Leadership is necessarily a group process, not an egotistical adventure. It is about seeking out the discretionary effort from each individual and combining it to some greater good. When people achieve self-actualisation, it not only benefits them, but the entire organisation, indeed all of us.

Exercising leadership can be dangerous. Anyone who wants a quiet life should avoid it at all costs, because by necessity you are upsetting the apple cart. With a high-stakes game such as the Olympics, you are confronting very real vested interests, histories and world-views. It is easy to forget that this was the first time any organising committee had ever undertaken Diversity and Inclusion. 'Understanding' was in its infancy and although the external view of the Olympic movement was a celebration of humanity, the internal reality was extremely conservative and resistant to change.

The Diversity and Inclusion team had to exercise leadership if they wanted to deliver. This was about keeping the adaptive challenge of 'Everyone's 2012' on the table when many would prefer to focus exclusively on the technical challenge of games delivery. It was about avoiding 'management' speak and administrative necessity clouding the bigger picture of strategic and systemic change. It was about rapidly finding and building allies, people we could partner with to do the work and avoid isolation. It was about up-skilling colleagues and then setting them free to lead on their own work, and them gaining due credit in the process, encouraging them to continue and achieve even more.

This was about standing solidly in your purpose, not in your role. If we had followed a 101 or 2.0 role we would have become predictable, we would have been kept in our role and we would have been departmentalised and ignored. A lot of Diversity 101 people don't seem to understand that adults react badly to being policed. Paul Deighton joked with me that his biggest challenge was not to interfere and mess up people otherwise doing their job. By standing in our purpose, we were trusting people to do the right thing and by monitoring the result, in 9/10 cases they will deliver a better result. In 10 per cent of cases you have to put out fires, but that's your job as an inclusive leader.

Leadership as defined above was an empowering concept, organic, bottom-up and liberating for employees who had previously been frog-marched into diversity training. But this was not motivated by benevolence. This was to empower people to do what we as a small team could not, namely create Everyone's 2012. The question was how to get people, of their own volition, to act on Diversity and Inclusion and deploy their own discretionary effort towards a greater goal.

We created a range of interventions to suit a diversity of people with different work styles.[1] But within the framework, we attempted to get them swimming in the same direction. A third would front crawl, some would backstroke and a few would doggy paddle.

Above all, we needed to have an attention-grabbing start, an effective intervention that would make people realise this was not business as usual. The intervention took a lot of preparation but came to fruition on 4 February 2010.

Desmond Tutu

Desmond Tutu was a childhood hero of mine. I had grown up listening to him as the voice of the anti-apartheid movement in South Africa. He was the reason why we didn't eat Cape apples and also why I later watched *Spitting Image*.[2] His laugh, his manner, his humanity were infectious and made me happy and optimistic. I wanted to bottle that.

Desmond Tutu, Archbishop Emeritus of Cape Town, represents the ultimate inclusive figure who would reach out and breach divides, bringing people together, inviting them to join in. He also embodies the humour essential to the success of the London 2012 Diversity and Inclusion programme, the ability to melt even the most sceptical of diversity critics with the revelation that inclusion is actually in their interests too.

He was also the most inclusive living icon I knew of – even more so now since Nelson Mandela's passing. Unlike other figures who to me symbolised diversity but not necessarily inclusion, here was a man who reached across the divide, who brought in 'the other', who engaged new audiences and who made people listen. Tutu said:

> As a South African, I know how much sport can help bring different people and different nations together. I feel strongly that the London 2012 Olympic and Paralympic Games will be a fantastic celebration of the many different communities and cultures which exist in London and the rest of the UK and will bring everyone together.[3]

Consider a surprising counterfactual example. I was invited to a lunch with the extraordinary American civil rights activist and Baptist Minister Jesse Jackson, hosted by the UK Member of Parliament and Chairman of the Home Affairs Select Committee Keith Vaz. It was to celebrate Jesse's work and leadership to date, especially in the run-up to the Olympics which people now knew of as 'Everyone's 2012'. In Jesse, here was an icon to millions, a hero to many and an impressive man. But the talk was aggressive; the talk was 'them-and-us', not 'we'. Keith Vaz, who did not know me at the time, also implied to the room that he did know me and accused me of personally betraying all the London 2012 bid promises, not least the budget. The way I was scapegoated as 'the other' made me feel completely excluded from what I had been promised was an inclusive lunch. Some of those present were happy to point the finger when the media coverage was negative (in this case, about the budget) but then claim credit for their part in bringing about the most inclusive Games ever. It was very Diversity 101 and very much the glorification of the uninvolved.

So Desmond Tutu was different from Jesse and Keith. He won the Nobel Peace Prize in 1984 for a reason, campaigning against apartheid division. Post apartheid, he was one of the principal advocates, alongside Nelson Mandela, for forgiveness and for an inclusive and tolerant South Africa, Chairing the Truth and Reconciliation Committee. He was a unifying figure who reached out to those who did not agree with him, rather than vilify them. It was a long shot, but I was on a cycling holiday with my now-late father in South Africa and I decided to stop by the Cathedral in Cape Town. I made enquiries, followed up and kept pestering. Eventually we made email contact, talked a bit, and eventually when I asked for his help, Archbishop Desmond Tutu readily agreed.

He was staying in a central London hotel with his nephew, and Paul Deighton kindly lent me his car and driver Andrew for the day. I joined 'Father' or 'Arch' as he insisted I call him, for breakfast, rather unexpectedly. As I tucked in to crumpets he quizzed me on some of the latest work. He was genuinely interested in how we were progressing with inclusion of different minorities, dealing with homophobia in sport, making venues accessible. His eyes were piercing and I felt I was being judged.

Nervously, we got in the car and Andrew drove us to the London 2012 Headquarters in Canary Wharf. The whole journey was in silence as Arch insisted on his quiet prayer and contemplation time. I broke the silence only to point out a billboard for the newly released film *Invictus*, of which he approved. I only realised the value of that silent time in the car later in the day after non-stop questioning, cameras flashing and general activity.

The lack of communication in the car, and my failure to steer the conversation at breakfast, being somewhat in awe of my hero, had left the Archbishop non-briefed as he entered 2012 headquarters. While I was fretting at the time, in retrospect he didn't need a briefing. He had, after all, been doing inclusion a lot longer than I had. He shook hands with everyone he met, including bemused door attendants, security guards and cleaning staff knocking off after the night shift. After a chance to have a cup of tea we made our way to the usual tour bus that took visitors around the Olympic Park.

We sat together at the front of the bus and the tour guide started his commentary, rather nervous at the guest on board, but the atmosphere was informal, relaxed and jovial. Arch was genuinely thrilled to see the transformation that was taking place. He had attended Kings College here and lived in London with his family for a number of years. London was also a key centre of anti-apartheid activism and he maintained regular contact with the city. To see the biggest transformation of that city since World War Two was, I believe, genuinely intriguing him. He said, 'Well, we've spent some time in London and it's just fantastic to see the transformation that's taking place here.'[4]

We met local schoolchildren and did some photo shoots and, again completely unscripted/briefed, he chatted with the children and gave his thoughts to camera. Arch remarked, 'People are tending to pull apart. We need something that will say we are different not in order to be pulled apart but so that we should know our need of one another.' A local schoolgirl responded, 'He is so inspirational, the way he talks about how the Olympics is bringing us all together, it's amazing.'[5] Julie from the communications team had quite a challenge managing the requests for time with the Archbishop that were now coming in thick and fast.

We sped back to headquarters and crashed the LOCOG board meeting. As Chief of Staff to Paul I had been a regular attendee but now as Head of Diversity and Inclusion I needed an Archbishop to get in. It was interesting to note the behaviour of the board as he came in. The first to greet him was our Chair, Seb, who was genuinely pleased, but I am not sure the briefing had got through that he was coming. Still, Seb was a natural diplomat and a consummate ambassador. The board members all rose individually and took their place in line to greet the Archbishop. I was now sure that the briefing had either not made its way through or at least had not been read. Sir Charles Allen (now Lord Allen of Kensington)was another natural diplomat and Sir Philip Craven, President of the International Paralympic Committee, enjoyed talking to him immensely. The biggest greetings, however, were between Arch and Princess Anne, and they took off to the corner of the boardroom for a cup of tea and a gossip.

Extracting the Arch was always harder than immersing him. We managed to get him away for a little lunch and then, almost forgetting, had him sign the Leadership Pledge alongside Paul and Seb. We moved into a huge space we had hired across the street, the only auditorium in Canary Wharf big enough to fit our staff (all of whom signed up) so they could listen to the Archbishop together, a group experience.

It was called the Winter Garden and it was a suitably wintry day as the LOCOG staff downed tools to cram into the hallway of a shopping centre to hear the Arch. His message was inspiring: 'You have one of those rare opportunities in life, a quirk of fate bestowed upon you, to really make a difference, should you wish to take advantage of that opportunity.' Even the Finance Director was moved.

Watching the response of colleagues to Desmond Tutu that wintry day in London was one of the most moving experiences of my professional life. I eyeballed hundreds of colleagues, who were at various places on the diversity spectrum. There were the believers who were already on board and were eating this up. There were the cost-effectiveness folks, who were melting (and we had a cost-effective toolkit for them, ready for the after party). There were the politicians who were impressed that this had been pulled off and who could not fault the man, and wanted to have their picture taken with him.

There was a colleague in venues, a tough guy, unsupportive of Diversity and Inclusion at that point in time who met the Arch after his speech with a football shirt. He had played in his team at university and worn his lucky shirt 'Tutu' after the degree he was hoping to achieve (a 2:2, an average degree in UK universities). It was common parlance among university students to talk about 'being happy with a Tutu'. If that was the hook that worked for them, then fine by me. The guy was loving his moment with the Arch, had his photograph taken and signed the Leadership Pledge.

When I spoke to him afterwards, and asked him what he thought of Diversity and Inclusion his response stayed with me. To him, it didn't matter what you called it, he was willing to do the right thing if it didn't divert his time away from his principal goal of readying a venue for Games time. He agreed, indeed supported 'Everyone's 2012'. This was the target audience we had been after. This was the guy who had been (somewhat understandably) suspicious of 'Diversity and Inclusion' programmes in the past, but was willing to give this one a go if what was said by Arch and what was on offer at LOCOG would work for him.

I organised a separate session with the heads of departments, which was more intimate. There were about 60 colleagues, and these really were my peers. They were all there, again representing the full spectrum of warmth/antipathy toward Diversity and Inclusion, and they were all more attentive than I have ever seen them in any Monday or Tuesday morning management meeting.

This was an intervention that had to break some people out of their current mindset, if Diversity and Inclusion were to have any chance of being a central tenet of delivery, if it was to shine as a differentiating factor of London 2012. They had the opportunity to ask questions and then we had a group photograph. Extremely busy people queued up to sign the pledge and to have a moment with the Arch.

I felt guilty by this point that I had exhausted an elderly man and he let me know it was time to take a break. We had some down time before his final event of the day, the lecture at the Royal Society of Arts in central London.

This was an opportunity to reach beyond the staff body (although some were there, some seeing him talk for the third time that day). It was an opportunity to reach those critical stakeholders and allies/partners outside LOCOG who were essential to delivering inclusion as part of the Games. We had painstakingly researched people we wanted to be in the audience. It included colleagues from government, especially the Government Olympic Executive and key departments that could help us. It included key sponsors, from Panasonic to Adecco, from British Airways to Lloyds Banking Group. It included colleagues from the Olympic Delivery Authority, Greater London Authority, British Olympic Association and Paralympics Great Britain. It included influential people who were outside the Olympic Family but who could benefit from seeing Archbishop Tutu and help us in return.

Archbishop Tutu was well aware of all this. He kept asking how he was doing. It felt rather ludicrous for me to be telling Archbishop Tutu that he was 'doing brilliantly' as I briefed him on the hoof for the next event.

During his Royal Society of Arts address, he paused a few minutes in, and scolded me publicly. He recognised some faces in the audience who had been at his talk earlier in the day and complained he could now not make the same jokes. He blamed me for not forewarning him and told everyone he was going to 'fix me', but in a 'non-violent way'. Lest I had any doubts, he invited me to join him for dinner back at the hotel after what had been a physically and emotionally draining day. Sitting in the restaurant with Desmond Tutu and his nephew eating chicken with our hands and talking about gay rights was a memory that will stay with me forever. He asked me if I had a partner and I told him I did. He said that was good. He asked if we were going to get married and I explained that we couldn't. He said we'd have to fix that.

I left Father about 10.00 pm and joined a few close friends and colleagues in a nearby pub. I was exhausted and they had a beer waiting for me. Did that really just happen? They replied in unison, 'Steve, you should know by now, it doesn't just happen.'

I called the team to thank them and then got a few hours' sleep before we reconvened early the next morning. We had to strike while the window of opportunity existed. We sent out all staff emails from Seb and Paul, had a permanently manned desk for Leadership Pledge signing and questions and answers prepared. By the end of the day 96 per cent of our target audience had signed the Leadership Pledge. People were taking personal ownership for Diversity and Inclusion, and they were enjoying it, and feeling good about it. The follow up was tailored, allowing colleagues to choose how they wanted to lead on Diversity and Inclusion. We had several tools waiting for them.

The Leadership Pledge and follow-up tools

The Leadership pledge was an easy win for individuals to sign up to. It was designed to initiate leadership around the three areas of our intervention – workforce, procurement and service delivery, or simply when you hire, buy or design. See Chapter 9 for more information. It challenged hiring managers to check their subconscious bias in the interview room, and have at least one other colleague present, to benefit from a different perspective. When buying, they should look at minority suppliers and small businesses and when designing they should remember that picture of the Beijing Paralympics and the flowers blocking the view. It was a personal signing, in the presence of Archbishop Tutu (or at least his facsimiled signature) and aligned with the LOCOG values of team, open, respect, inspire, distinct and deliver. My cynical side dominated slightly whenever I remembered the LOCOG values by the acronym TORIDD. Some days were torrid, but not this one.

The Leadership Pledge was designed to raise awareness of Diversity and Inclusion within LOCOG and encourage people to 'push beyond their personal best' and take individual responsibility for making London 2012 the most diverse and inclusive Games ever. Signatories committed themselves to help deliver a memorable Games, with a lasting legacy, and take personal responsibility for an inclusive approach that is fully integrated into every business decision.[6]

The reason for its success was partly the open and transparent methods we deployed. Everyone could sign, it was voluntary and people displayed them on their desks, sharing something with Seb and Paul. It was the opposite of secrecy and confidentiality. The combination of group leadership coupled with individual accountability proved to be a winning combination. The pledge was so successful among our paid staff that we rolled it out to volunteers and so all 70,000 Games Makers were invited to sign a 'Personal Best Leadership Pledge' too and counter discrimination and create an inclusive environment at Games time.

We empowered even the most junior staff to lead on Diversity and Inclusion and act above their pay grade, instead of blindly following the orders of their line manager. Results ranged from organising the first ever Olympics involvement in a Gay Pride event to hosting the Professional Footballers Association 'Black List' Award Ceremony. These events were people's own desire for personal legacy. It was self-actualisation for many. In April 2013 I received an email from a colleague, now in the same role at a major UK-based global company. He was depressed. He felt he was undergoing the very opposite of his opportunity at LOCOG. When I asked him why, the first and principal reason given was the fact that he was supposed to manage–he was not allowed to lead.

The support infrastructure we created, to allow people to lead in their own way, included the Diversity Board, Management Committee Champions, the Diversity and Inclusion Sponsors Forum, the Access and Inclusion Integration group, the Diversity Action Team and Working groups. The vast majority of the toolkit we created was positive, carrot-led and inspirational. The only stick we created, and I have absolutely no regrets about this, was Functional Area (Departmental) benchmarking. This is detailed in Chapter 10. This is not as much 'infrastructure' as it might at first appear. In most cases, it was reinforcing, using or adapting existing processes and functions.

Management Committee Champions

We instituted Management Committee Director Champions, a creation to bring individual accountability into the system, as well as develop role models. We asked directors to champion a strand of diversity. This would involve leading on issues pertaining to that strand, ensuring that strand was visible and represented within LOCOG and that hiring was as inclusive as possible. For example, our General Counsel Terry Miller and Venues Director James Bulley championed disability, our Strategy Director Sue Hunt championed sexual orientation and our Marketing Director Greg Nugent and Commercial Negotiations Director Charlie Wijeratna championed race/ ethnicity. These champions had job descriptions and took up positions on the Diversity Board.[7] We also instituted a Youth Board, which was sold in as an opportunity to LOCOG board members to mentor a 'young person'. The reality was the opposite: the young people ended up mentoring the LOCOG board members and bringing them into the 21st century, with iPhones, music and the latest critical eye on effective youth engagement.

Diversity Board

We persuaded Paul to chair the Diversity Board[8] and his agreeing to do so, plus the time commitment involved sent a strong message to the rest of the organisation. The board met quarterly and was composed of the above-mentioned Director Champions plus Youth Board members Paul Ntullia, an inspirational young deaf man from Manchester and Barbara Soetan, the trailblazing 22-year-old Chief Executive of Elevation Networks, a social enterprise that seeks to develop the leadership potential of young people to increase their employability. They were joined by several key external figures, ranging from Baroness Tanni Grey-Thompson, one of Britain's greatest ever Paralympians, to John Amaechi, the first openly gay NBA basketball star. Also included were: Lord Rix; Mike Brace, former Chair of the British Para-lympic Association; Paul Elliot, the first black captain of Chelsea Football Club; Ayesha Qureshi, a local community activist and lawyer; and Baroness

Floella Benjamin, the former presenter of Children's TV Series *Playschool* and now a member of the House of Lords.

The purpose of the board was to review the work of LOCOG and advise where necessary, suggesting improvements or alterations to the work of the Diversity and Inclusion team and functional areas they were working with. This board was extra management work for the Diversity and Inclusion team, but it was essential in increasing the number of allies throughout the organisation and outside the organisation among key stakeholders, to build support for what we were trying to do. It also deflected the heat from a very small Diversity and Inclusion team that might otherwise get shot down. Paul challenged me once, after an average board meeting, on the effectiveness of the board. I replied that, even at its worst, it was still valuable in bringing functional areas to the table and those functional areas hearing from other people what they were hearing from me. This was about delivering the same, consistent message, via a different messenger, to achieve the desired outcome.

Most of the functional areas enjoyed the recognition that came with presenting their work to the board. Some did not always appreciate the review and adjustments requested by the board, but they understood the bigger picture and it was the senior people in the organisation plus senior stakeholders, and that authority worked. The best use of the board however, was in terms of recognition. Members of the Diversity and Inclusion team suggested that we launch a series of inclusion awards every quarter chosen by the Diversity Board. These became fêted prizes and when a department would receive an award for great work, we would make a big fuss, with a certificate being presented by the Chief Executive, photography, internal communications, the works.

External organisations, such as UK Sport and Diversity Works for London, and 'critical friends' such as the Commission for a Sustainable London 2012 (CSL) and even the Equality and Human Rights Commission were invited to Diversity Board meetings. This was a risky strategy, but effective, as it built credibility by offering external organisations a privileged insider view of how we were instilling our Diversity and Inclusion work and the conversations we were having. It worked well with the CSL as Shaun McCarthy, their Director, could see the genuine conversations we were having and the genuine dilemmas we faced. He was impressed at the seniority of staff present, the thoroughness of discussion and the way the functional areas would tweak their work in response to feedback. When Steve Girdler, Adecco Director, was invited to the board he was impressed with the thoroughness of discussion, the serious, if informal, tone of the meetings and felt the pressure of several Peers and VIPs quizzing him about outputs and expectations. There was a genuine sense of mission, which came across to all invitees.

It didn't work as well with the Equality and Human Rights Commission. I know of no other organisation in the UK that invited the regulator into their private meetings like we did. Remember in addition that we were a private company and had no compulsion to do this. The response was mixed. While we worked hard to develop great relationships with several key people within the regulator, one of their commissioners leaked a story that resulted in a full-page newspaper article proclaiming LOCOG's 'row' with its regulator on human rights.[9] I later spoke with the commissioner concerned and they apologised, but I remain disappointed that our vision and openness was not reciprocated on their side, even if it did ameliorate their criticism.

Stakeholder Forum

Not our own creation, but a useful stakeholder engagement tool, was the Greater London Authority-hosted Equality and Diversity Forum. This was an interesting arrangement. Established by Lee Jasper, Mayor Ken Livingstone's firebrand equalities supremo, it had been originally intended to give the private sector organising committee an interrogation on a regular basis. The logic was that, since LOCOG was not subject to the public sector equalities legislation, then the public sector had better create a mechanism to hound and vilify/push LOCOG as appropriate. I remember the first meeting where Paul Deighton (who had spent 22 years at Goldman Sachs) and Jean Tomlin (ex Marks and Spencer, egg and Prudential) and I (ex advertising and consulting) were placed opposite the inquisition. Jean and I were nervous. Paul was blissfully ignorant. The interrogation revolved around our inherent evilness as a private sector company and assumed guilt before any chance of innocence was allowed to be aired. Paul raised an eyebrow at me, Jean looked down and I looked up at the ceiling. We all left the meeting in a mood akin to having survived a corporate awayday at a slaughterhouse.

However, when Ken Livingstone lost to Boris Johnson, things changed. Not that it mattered regarding Lee Jasper. He had resigned owing to an alleged corruption affair. But with Boris in charge (who, while extremely likeable, did not convince me of his commitment to Diversity and Inclusion) Richard Barnes, Deputy Mayor, took over as Chair. He could not have been more different from Lee Jasper. He was still combative, still initially suspicious of LOCOG (which, by the way, was avowedly bipartisan), but Richard was a dyed-in-the-wool Conservative, not a Socialist like his predecessor. He became a key ally.[10] I will be forever impressed with Paul and Jean and the way they glided from being interrogated by a Socialist to being interrogated by a Tory. We managed to get on to issues of substance, from diverse volunteer recruitment to accessible transport, and, on occasion, there was genuinely value-adding input to LOCOG's work.

This Forum changed over the four years we attended from being a witch-hunt to actually being a forum for (in the main) friendly challenge and best-practice exchange. It had nothing to do with the party politics per se, but as it became clear the project would be a success, it was more about attaining a share of glory by being associated with the right people, rather than vilifying them. Besides LOCOG and the Olympic Delivery Authority, the Greater London Authority, Department for Culture, Media and Sport, Government Olympic Executive, Olympic Park Legacy Company and Equality and Human Rights Commission were represented at the Forum. It produced an annual report to demonstrate progress across stakeholders in the area of business, workforce, service delivery, communities and participants.

External Access Group

An adjunct to the Forum was the 'Access and Inclusion Integration Group'. This snappy-titled grouping met to focus specifically on the physical customer journey experience of people with accessibility requirements, ranging from disabled people to older people and parents with children. This was chaired by our General Counsel, Terry Miller, and was an interesting take on a private company holding largely public sector organisations to account for delivery of infrastructure. It was a reversal of the Lee Jasper situation.

Sponsors Forum

We brought together our sponsors at a LOCOG-chaired Diversity and Inclusion Sponsor Forum. This allowed Heads of Diversity and Inclusion and other senior managers from LOCOG's commercial partners to come together once a quarter to exchange ideas and good practice. There was also an unstated expectation that they *should* attend and tell us what they planned to do to help us bring about 'Everyone's 2012'. Many organisations were inspired by the work we, and they, were doing and it led to some partners activating around Diversity and Inclusion, for example Adecco with talent pools and BMW with adapted vehicles.[11] Leadership, as a group concept, lowered the individual fear factor here and organisations were constantly alive to what others were doing and not wanting to be seen as laggard. I don't know of any other organisation that did this, we just felt it was a good idea. It worked in terms of generating positive competition and achieving more than would have been the case otherwise. In this sense, it was a catalyst and an incubator of ideas, something other organisations could benefit from.[12]

Diversity Action Team

It was important that by Games time, all LOCOG staff had been offered ample opportunity to contribute to the diversity of the Games. All staff had the opportunity to input into the decision-making process via the Diversity Action Team (DAT), which was a staff-led forum that met monthly. Membership was open to any employee of whatever identity or seniority who wanted to help us achieve our vision. They received updates on the Diversity and Inclusion programme to date and opportunities to get more involved; for example volunteering on the Tutu visit. It was a wonderful mixture of the most junior and most senior staff. Due to time pressures towards the Games this was transferred to an email list serve. We would email the group in advance of everyone else with news and initiatives and so forth and they remained our strongest supporters to the end.

Staff networks

It was notable how many junior staff felt empowered to tell senior staff their ideas and opinions. Staff established a series of Working Groups. The Black, Asian and minority ethnic staff group and Lesbian, Gay, Bisexual and trans staff groups were the most popular and well attended/supported but there were other groupings such as a disability working group. The aim was to be a staff consultative forum and provide advice to the Diversity and Inclusion team and organisation in terms of making the Games better. They were particularly effective at quickly integrating new members of LOCOG into the organisation.

Recognition and momentum

It should be noted that all of these infrastructural elements – boards, champions and forums – are not 'results' because they are not outcomes that have created social change, they are purely enabling mechanisms. It is disappointing when many organisations trumpet their diversity 'results' as a collection of meetings and forums without demonstrating any real added value. The same is true of awards, of which we won a series. Awards were part of our leadership process work in creating 'Everyone's 2012' and only useful in establishing credibility and momentum to encourage others to follow suit.

We were first in the country to attain the Diversity Works Gold Award (see Chapter 11), first and fastest in country to gain the Equality standard for sport award (see Chapter 4) and a crusading organisation for the Two Ticks disability programme (see Chapter 10) when the Minister for Disabled People, Jonathan Shaw, presented LOCOG with an Award in December 2008. We won the Best Private Sector Innovation award in June 2010 from the Employers Forum on Age (EFA) and were an Age Positive Champion from the UK Department for Work and Pensions for highlighting the business benefits of an age-mixed workforce. We won many more awards, commendations and recognition that would become tedious to list here. Suffice to say, they helped maintain momentum and gave the Diversity and Inclusion programme added credibility in colleagues' minds.

The Diversity and Inclusion Team

The Diversity and Inclusion Team was very diverse. Paul and Jean initially decided to hire a Head of Diversity and Inclusion, and they deserve the credit for this 'inspired' move. However, it was my job to demonstrate the need for more than one person if we were to achieve our mission. The problem was that we didn't have the budget for any more staff. While I played the long game (it was all relative in LOCOG given the deadline), I launched a 'creative resourcing' strategy. I called all the recruiters I knew and asked them who was looking for work, was good and might want to volunteer their time and skills for free in the meantime. I had the pleasure to meet Tom Secker-Walker, a former estate agent who initially (and thankfully) knew nothing about Diversity and Inclusion but was superb with clients. His job was to market Diversity and Inclusion to people both around the organisation and externally and he did that with aplomb.

I called stakeholders and managed to persuade the Department for Work and Pensions (government) to loan me one of their hands-on managers, Jackie Parkin. She was tasked with integrating our plans with HR in terms of paid recruitment. Within a few months, I managed to hire Tom and formally second Jackie, who then brought another colleague over with her, Andrew Moncrieffe.

I managed to secure a paid position for an Accessibility Manager and recruited Mark Todd, the constant comedian and mobility scooter user from Manchester. I managed to persuade the Greater London Authority to loan me David Morris, their cult-like leader of all things access, inclusion and disability rights. He came over with his assistant and we established a formal secondment. The Royal National Institute of Blind People (RNIB) were persuaded to loan us Lauren Finnegan, a bright young woman who was frustrated in the charity world (I had been there) and who yearned for more responsibility. Internally, I stole Louise Oastler from her job in programme management. She was bored there and I gave her heaps of responsibility in terms of incorporating Diversity and Inclusion in all of the LOCOG reporting systems and Test Events.

By the end, we had Jackie and Andrew focused on paid staff, Lauren and her assistant focused on volunteers, Tom focused on procurement, Mark and Dave focused on service delivery and Lou helping me with the overall programme and measurement.

We also had a constant stream of volunteers, interns, secondees, anyone we could get for free that would add value. Ben Supple, Garima Jain, Jenn Choi, Laura Birkman, Joe Troedsen... I took on interns from local universities and colleges every summer who provided a fresh challenge to our thinking and work and kept us up to speed and switched on. We had Abdul and Kohinur from the local council. We had bankers and lawyers between jobs, unemployed due to the economic downturn, or who just found working with us more fulfilling than what they had been doing. We had friends, Lou's dad Bernie, stakeholders and volunteers. The parameters were all tightly controlled, but the day-to-day activity of the team was not. This allowed great innovation and heightened morale, but did mean I was putting out fires on more than one occasion.

The above leadership framework of intervention, pledges, boards, teams and staff-led projects allowed people to act upon their own motivations for contributing to Everyone's 2012. Based on understanding of real inclusion, they were empowered to lead within a framework that permitted discretionary effort to produce the most efficient marginal results possible. The single biggest resource, bar none, in achieving the Diversity and Inclusion results that we did for London 2012, was a team of talented, creative and brave people.

Brave people, inclusive leadership

These were people at all levels of the organisation who intellectually and practically believed in what we were trying to do. It was in the job description, but these are people who operated way beyond their job description, people who operated way beyond their pay grade, and people who worked far harder than many of their colleagues in partner organisations.

Rheiss Brown was one of the 'Get Ahead' school leaver graduates. He was from the South East of London, lived with his mum, played football, worked hard. He was the first to ask Desmond Tutu a question at his address at the Royal Society of Arts in February 2012. 'What advice do you have for a young man who has no resources but who wants to change the world?' Rheiss became an active member of the Diversity Action Team.

Pierre Louis Fayon wrote to me asking if he could intern on the Diversity and Inclusion team. Many people wrote in and we often didn't have the time to even reply, let alone engage. But he persisted and I was intrigued. Here was a young French man, wheelchair user, mad on sport, willing to give up university for as long as it took, to play his part in making London 2012 inclusive and accessible. So I gave him an internship. After travelling to London alone, finding an apartment alone, commuting around London, alone, all without a fluent grasp of English and all in a wheelchair, Pierre ended up gaining a permanent job in the Strategy team and went white-water rafting with them at a staff event.

Sinead, the female Venue Results Manager for Weightlifting, said:

> I thoroughly enjoy working here. I am very comfortable and am definitely able to be myself. I am completely 'out' for the first time in a job; this has been a great experience for me. I told my whole department about my engagement to my girlfriend. I was overwhelmed with the positive response and congratulations. It was pretty amazing to me that in my workplace I can do this and feel 100 per cent positive about it. Obviously for me the open and comfortable environment at LOCOG is very important.

Craig Beaumont worked in the Government Affairs team and was a workaholic. He took a call one day from a very irate supplier who was complaining about the Diversity and Inclusion requirements in the tender document. The supplier thought our Diversity and Inclusion requirements including, for example, stating the number of women employed at senior level in the organisation, was a joke and he could not believe his application had been returned on the grounds of non-completion. Craig in his characteristically brilliant way, refused to be bullied, refused to be intimidated by the usual threats of 'I'll talk to your boss' and politely and firmly reminded him of the benefits of the LOCOG Diversity and Inclusion policy.

Debbie Jevans was the first female Sports Director of any summer Games. At the outset she was, by her own admission, a Diversity and Inclusion sceptic, if not downright opposed to the idea. However, not only did Debs become the 'Age' champion, introducing, among other events, the 'Zimmers' rock concert with our oldest and youngest employees in attendance,[13] she also defended the LOCOG Diversity and Inclusion programme among the sceptical world of sport governing bodies. When we presented to the sports bodies and introduced the idea of benchmarking the Equality Standard for Sport and faced opposition from some National Governing Bodies of Sport and it would have been more convenient for her to drop Diversity and Inclusion, she held the line.

Paul Deighton joined me at a Home Office-sponsored round table on tackling homophobia in sport chaired by Theresa May, Home Secretary, and Lynne Featherstone, Minister for Equalities. This was a busy Chief Executive, and he didn't have to go, it was my job to go. Not only did Paul attend, he spoke with fluency about why he was there and what he wanted to achieve. The other Chief Executives of various sporting organisations were largely there under duress, not least because, unlike LOCOG, they were either publicly funded or publicly regulated and needed to impress the paymasters. At half time, many made their excuses and left. Paul stayed. He was one of the few senior people, outlasting virtually everyone else in the room, Ministers included, who remained to see the conclusion, a charter against homophobia and transphobia in sport.

Diversity and Inclusion are leadership issues because they do not have universal acceptance: they are leadership issues because whilst diversity is a reality, inclusion remains a choice. It is only through people exercising leadership, stressing real inclusion over token diversity, that thought becomes action. We were able to make this a subject that gained far wider acceptance than is the norm.

Whereas it is sometimes easier for individuals to debate more 'mainstream' issues such as gender and age than talk about 'controversial' issues such as sexuality or Islam, at LOCOG, everything was on the table. The table was initially set by the Diversity and Inclusion team, but the issues were kept there by a widening group of allies who saw the value in allowing people to discuss relevant issues, create an open environment and allow people to be themselves. Why? Because when people could be themselves, it made the Games better.

Leadership became a collective activity, inside and outside the tent. Literally thousands of people led on Diversity and Inclusion. They cannot all be named here but they know who they are and they saw the difference they made in the summer of 2012.

Takeaways – lead

1 Leadership is not management: the Leadership Pledge gave all people permission to lead, from any level. Failure is permitted, even encouraged, with support infrastructure in place to put out fires.

2 When practising inclusive leadership, transparency trumps confidentiality. Practise constant information sharing including monthly updates. Create new role models to increase the visibility and normalcy of minority groups. Practise rapid, real-time exchange of best practice and encouragement through award and recognition programmes.

3 Leadership is a group process, not an individual heroic enterprise. This reduces the fear factor that can otherwise hold people back; disproportionately minorities.

Notes

1 See Chapter 9.

2 *Spitting Image* – a popular British Comedy series using puppets to mock famous celebrities and politicians.

3 http://www.insidethegames.biz/olympics/summer-olympics/london-2012-news/8922-tutu-predicts-london-2012-will-leave-a-fantastic-legacy.

4 http://www.insidethegames.biz/olympics/summer-olympics/london-2012-news/8922-tutu-predicts-london-2012-will-leave-a-fantastic-legacy [accessed 11 October 2013].

5 London 2012 video of the visit played at Diversity week 2011.

6 For the full text, see Appendix, p 314.

7 Going forward, I would recommend interviewing for these positions. That is not to say our champions were in any way disappointing, quite the opposite, but in an organisation people generally have to be 'persuaded' to do this kind of championing role, when in fact it should be an honour. Interviewing

candidates starts from a position of success rather than a position of weakness, and gives the roles a better chance of being taken seriously and doing value-adding work.

8 See note 7.

9 Jamie Doward, *The Observer*, 19 December 2009, 'Sebastian Coe's London Olympics team in row with equality watchdog' http://www.guardian.co.uk/uk/2009/dec/20/coe-olympics-equality-row.

10 For example, Richard was very helpful in stressing the importance of the Lesbian and Gay Pride Pin from the Mayor's perspective, which was definitely noted within LOCOG.

11 See Chapter 11.

12 See 'Game changers' section, p 281.

13 See full description in employment section, p 146.

Deliver

08

When the pressure became too intense, Lauren Finnegan, Diversity and Inclusion team member, told me in no uncertain terms 'I can't do this'. One month later, in July 2012, she successfully and brilliantly retained 2,000 disabled people in Games time roles, an unprecedented result. Understanding and leadership had been, and continued to be, a group process, the support was there. But individual responsibility was key to successful delivery.

Being open

One of the forms this took was monthly information sharing. We created simple one-pagers for each work stream containing a simple red, amber or green (RAG) rating and key comments on current challenges, risks and next steps and milestones.[1] Their succinct nature, high frequency and wide sharing around the organisation allowed these reports to gain traction and credibility. They also allowed people to gain credit for great work but also to have the pressure of peer review for delivery. People disliked, and worked against, letting other people down.

We integrated Diversity and Inclusion reporting into the organisation-wide monthly risk register. We measured impact vs likelihood on all 22 key Diversity and Inclusion projects (see Chapter 9) and integrated them with the overall monthly reporting. So for example, Martin Green, Head of Ceremonies was accountable for the RAG status on ceremonies, not just from a technical perspective, but also from an 'Everyone's 2012' perspective. This approach applied with Deborah Hale on Torch Relay, Laurie Neville on procurement, Paul Nickson on arrivals and departures and so on. In all of these interactions, it was a cooperative, consultative approach between the business areas and the Diversity and Inclusion team, but the framework and the competitive dynamic were the key stimuli.

Quarterly Inclusive Awards were presented by the Chief Executive to the Volunteering team, Procurement team (twice), HR Recruitment team,

Ticketing team, Venues team, Technology team, and New Media team and on and on. It kept the momentum going, gave visibility to success and positioned us further away from 'compliance' in the minds of the wider team. These award nominees were shortlisted by members of the Diversity and Inclusion team on the basis of their work with the functional teams, and then presented to the Diversity Board for voting, so the result 'came from the top'.

Test events

Our real chance to test delivery, in advance of the Games came in July 2011, when LOCOG held 45 test events over three clusters. There were 42 sport events in 28 venues over 183 days of competition. Test events were our opportunity to test key Games time policies, procedures and venues and 350,000 spectators wanted in; 8,000 athletes from over 50 countries took part, as did over 25,000 workforce and 10,000 'Games Makers' volunteers.

The objectives were to identify whether we had achieved our critical success factors for each of our nine client groups. These are detailed in Table 8.1. Test Events were our opportunity to truly operationalise Diversity and Inclusion and to bring it alive for anyone who was still unsure what inclusion looked like. It was about reconfirming confidence in the work done to date, identifying particular areas/client groups that may require more focus or additional development, and maximising the opportunity to work with the venues teams building relationships that continued through to Games time.

Lou Oastler on the Diversity and Inclusion team did a great job of persuading Head of Test Events Mark Darbon to make Diversity and Inclusion an integral part of the LOCOG Test Event programme. We made Venue General Managers accountable for ensuring Diversity and Inclusion was addressed at their venues, both at Test Events and at Games time. At Test Events there was a non-blame culture, we wanted people to talk to us about things that went wrong while we still had time to help. Members of the Diversity and Inclusion team fulfilled operational roles predominantly in workforce but in terms of access and operations too.

The Diversity and Inclusion team ran a proactive programme throughout our Test Events, gathering learnings in Cluster 1 that were refined in Cluster 2 and finalised in Cluster 3. We undertook 'specific' Diversity and Inclusion test events analysing the 22 key Diversity and Inclusion work streams (see Chapter 9). For example, we tested accessibility[2] in all three Test Event

TABLE 8.1 Client groups and success in terms of inclusion

Client group	Success definition
Athletes and National Olympic and Paralympic Committee delegations	Diverse athletes receive an inclusive welcome – Faith, LGBT, Disability etc – an inclusive experience
Technical officials	Knowledge and application of London 2012 Diversity and Inclusion strategy
Media and Broadcast	Diverse and inclusive values as key differentiator of London 2012 – our story is told globally
Press	Diverse and inclusive values as key differentiator of London 2012 – our story is told nationally
Workforce	Every person is 'diversity confident'. Knowledge and application of London 2012 Diversity and Inclusion strategy, providing an inclusive welcome to all client groups
Spectator	Everyone feels able to attend and their experience exceeds expectations
Marketing Partners	Knowledge and understanding of London 2012 Diversity and Inclusion Strategy – contribute where appropriate
Olympic and Paralympic Family	Knowledge and understanding of London 2012 Diversity and Inclusion Strategy – contribute where appropriate
Public	Interpret diversity and inclusion as a key differentiator of the London 2012 Games. Experience exceeds expectations

clusters. We looked at distance from disabled parking to the entrances. We analysed the booking system for the Games mobility service. In terms of ticketing, we looked at how the allocations were implemented on the day, so if someone had requested an end of row seat were they allocated one? We invited wheelchair users to a basketball event in Cluster 1 and had some significant learnings to take on board. In the diving test event in Cluster 2 the same people were effusive in their praise for what we had improved beyond expectations; for example family groups being able to sit together where only some of the group were disabled people.

We also held 'integrated' Diversity and Inclusion tests events. For example, 'meet and greet' or catering services, as part of the overall LOCOG test-event structure. We recruited a team of volunteers who would provide us with confidential feedback about their experiences. These volunteers participated in three capacities – as spectators, as observers and as workforce. We focused them on the most relevant areas and they duly completed questionnaires benchmarked against the above client-success criteria. By using these volunteer mystery shoppers from across our stakeholder community, we were given a confidential heads-up from a client perspective, through detailed questionnaire feedback. For example, we tested the quality of commentators for audio description and how equipment was provided to visually impaired people.

After the first cluster of test events, we found a heap of positives. These ranged from extremely helpful and friendly staff to a diverse mix of spectators and workforce. The accessible viewing areas were good, paths and track ways generally smooth, spacious and level and the bus drivers polite and knowledgeable about accessibility. Commentary was lively and entertaining and there was a positive atmosphere throughout. Negatives included inconsistency in security checking, such as a failure to search wheelchair users, gaps in track way, speakers located at accessible viewing platforms, inaccessible toilets and high counter heights. The workforce was only addressing the non-disabled person, talking to the 'carer' and they were not yet 'diversity confident'.

Resourcing and politics

In developing our operational plans we considered delivery factors carefully. LOCOG's approach to Diversity and Inclusion was nothing if not pragmatic, with a real appreciation for the sensitivity that 'equality and diversity' issues can trigger, generating moral and political views from every sector of society. However, without apologising, and by focusing on tangible outputs and outcomes to an immovable deadline, we attempted to circumnavigate the views and vested interests that are part of the discussion in this area. Crucially, we avoided getting bogged down in non-productive conversations and activities. To aid delivery, we always asked 'Would it make the Games better?'

The resources allocated to Diversity and Inclusion were limited (which allows us with the luxury of hindsight to say 'carefully considered'), primarily because of the clear potential to ostracise such work from the main operational folks if they felt the opportunity cost was too high. To invest large amounts of money that on a relative scale the organisation perceived should have been allocated to other functional areas would have created a negative climate in a culture of resource scarcity. So we deliberately set out not to create a large Diversity 101-style structure. Instead we adopted an operational approach to ensure Diversity and Inclusion was incorporated in everything we did and delivered through the line with in-house expert consultancy support from the Diversity and Inclusion team to functional area leaders.

Jean Tomlin, HR Director, said 'having established a structure that relied heavily on the organisation to deliver it remained imperative to ensure that delivery focused on things that mattered to LOCOG and was not distracted by side bar issues related to why this function exists at all.'[3] Thus by creating a culture of aspiration and competition, rather than compliance, individual discretionary effort could be cultivated with no upper limit set.

Delivery was undeniably hard work. We had a work ethic of delivery. There were target zones and public statements that were widely known and we could be judged against. We took solace in group leadership, this being a collective experience. But delivery was an individual responsibility based on near-real-time feedback. We established role models and created an environment of constant information sharing, a journey that everyone was interested in.

Letting go

Perhaps more than anything else, we learned the importance of letting go. The people who designed this real inclusion system did not have all the information to execute it – we were therefore not best placed to make the detailed decisions that became necessary. The project was complicated from the start but as the complexity built, as each variable became interdependent with yet more variables from departments coming on stream or ramping up, it could seem overwhelming. In addition we had a small group of people and the organisation was growing daily. So with the framework set up, we had to trust people to operate within it and find their own solutions to challenges.

Through deep understanding of real inclusion, and ongoing group leadership, we could all find inspiration to deliver; we all want to be inspired. But sometimes the inspiration is so overwhelming that it feels too much and not actionable. We had to convert the understanding and the leadership into delivery. 'Actionable inspiration', if you will. Every organisation will claim it wants to deliver. But few had the immovable deadline and global audience we had. This would have been even more significant had we failed to deliver.

Takeaways – deliver

1 Delivery is an individual accountability, subsequent to group leadership. Individual point accountability does not only motivate, it rewards great work through recognition.

2 Competition and 'actionable inspiration' creates better results than compliance. Compliance rarely creates best practice because you are attaining a minimum; with competition there is no upper limit. Peer review is one of the most powerful and underused tools that works and which takes the heat off you.

3 The importance of letting go. With a clear framework, target zones, deadlines and other parameters, it is essential to allow people to lead their own work, find their own way to express. You can't do it all on your own and the result wouldn't be as good or sustainable if you did.

Notes

1 See Appendix, p 318.

2 For more information see Chapter 19 and also 20 on access.

3 Conversation with the author.

The interventions

09

In order to achieve systemic change in the project, rather than merely decorate the tree, we had to intervene in the business where the business decisions were actually made. To genuinely add value, and to truly make the Games better, there was no point being an external 'initiative', we had to be integral to existing work streams.

Due to limited time and resources, as well as the scaling up of the project to 200,000 people, we had to calmly and carefully evaluate how, when and where we would intervene. In the original strategy I wrote in 2008 we said, 'as LOCOG is only in business until September 2012 we have taken a strategic approach to Diversity and Inclusion to ensure that we can make the most impact in a relatively short period of time'. The force of circumstances led us to be systemic.

With a general understanding developing in the organisation, a willingness to lead and a hunger to deliver (the days were counting down), that good intent and energy had to be efficiently directed. How to intervene in a project of such depth and breadth? Of such complexity and risk? How to intervene and make a difference in such a short space of time with limited resources? Should we intervene in easier situations that were more or less guaranteed to get a result? Or should we tackle the 'high hanging' fruit and take greater risks to influence an outcome at great opportunity cost should we fail? Where was the precedent and, most of all, how did we create that 'actionable inspiration'?

The complexity and size of the project, not to mention pace of change and scrutiny, meant we had to ruthlessly prioritise. We designed the interventions to be systemic, working through existing infrastructure rather than creating additional bureaucracy. And we designed the interventions to be in three main areas, workforce, procurement and service delivery that were easily understood and easily articulated, as per Table 9.1.

TABLE 9.1 Interventions to create real inclusion

	Workforce *When you hire*	Procurement *When you buy*	Service Delivery *When you design*
Understand	We want a diverse workforce – Talent and diversity positively, not negatively, correlated	We want a diverse supply chain – Transparency and competition reduce costs and source innovation	We want to stage a Games for Everyone – Diversity and Inclusion can improve customer service
Lead	We will hire diverse talent – Check subconscious bias in interviews	We will make the supply chain transparent – Proactively search for innovative new companies	We will explore a range of client journeys – View diversity as a source of innovation
Deliver	I will be accountable for my hiring record – Aim for target zones and monthly benchmarking	I will be accountable for the goods and services I buy – Aim for cost reduction and monitor supplier mix	I will be accountable for client satisfaction – Complete RAG monthly peer review

These were important, a simple articulation of complex phenomena, a dissection of an organisation of 57 departments and various directors, heads of departments, egos, agendas and backgrounds: 57 departments were delivering 26 simultaneous world championships and then two weeks later delivering 20 more. The subject areas were vast ranging from food to security, transport, venues, sports presentation and ceremonies. Fifty-seven departments per se were too much for a handful of internal Diversity and Inclusion consultants, but nine client groups (detailed in the previous chapter) with a strategic plan were manageable. On top of that, we were constantly giving the work back to the business rather than providing all the answers for them and 'departmentalising' the issues.

Workforce

'Workforce' covered all HR operations related to paid, volunteer and contractor staff and is the most familiar area for existing Diversity and Inclusion practitioners. We determined that building an inclusive workforce was about hiring and integrating brilliant diverse talent, not affirmative action. The temptation was to stick to HR and focus everything on making a difference in the paid recruitment and workforce area. This was not a silly potential strategy. At this point there were only two people working on Diversity and Inclusion and 200,000 people to recruit. There was much existing data upon which to benchmark and plan a line of attack.

However, there were two problems with that approach. One was the poverty of limited expectations. This was the chance of a lifetime to demonstrate what could be done in a pressurised environment across the business. To look back in summer 2012 on a diverse workforce, but nothing else, would have felt half-complete. The other was practicality. While 8,000 of the workforce were paid, a further 70,000 were volunteers and a further 130,000 were contractors, so we would have to engage the procurement team besides the recruitment team if we wanted to influence this far larger recruitment. Suppose we had focused on the 8,000 paid recruitment but then procurement had progressed oblivious to Diversity and Inclusion? The 8,000 people would have been dwarfed by the 130,000 no matter how talented and diverse they were. This led to procurement, and an appreciation of its importance to the project.

Procurement

'Procurement' covered all aspects of the supply chain and supplier diversity, run by the LOCOG procurement team. There was interaction with HR in the realm of contractors in particular. Building an inclusive supply chain was about making all our opportunities available to all businesses and then creating shared value from those we worked with. Like the recruitment machine, the procurement machine was being designed and there was an opportunity to influence the strategy from the start with the right relationships and trust.

Besides the impact on recruitment, by influencing the procurement process we would be able to influence so much more, from the accessibility standards of venue procurement to the CSR policies of bus contractors.

Procurement is significantly under-rated as a mechanism for creating change, both inside and outside the organisation. If the UK government, for example, with their £236 billion supply chain, were to adopt some of the measures we took (which cost almost nothing or saved us money) then a seismic shift could occur in the economy, in terms of its ability to help all sections of society more than it does at present.

The challenge with deciding to intervene in procurement was the sheer breadth and depth of the supply chain coupled with lack of resources to effectively manage it. Unlike a simple business with a small supply chain, LOCOG's supply chain was literally a slice of the economy, from HR and financial services to physical goods, from seating to temporary toilets. However, this depth and breadth of complexity required us to emphasise building the right relationships with the procurement team to influence them to lead on the work. Which is, in the end, what happened.

Service delivery

The third area of intervention was perhaps the most complex of all, because it was seemingly infinite in scope in comparison with the size and resources of the Diversity and Inclusion team and because it was very new – Diversity 101 and 2.0 don't have much to say about how you create inclusion in customer service delivery. 'Service delivery' was the collective name for the majority of our 22 projects that directly affected one or more of our nine client groups. Building an inclusive customer experience was about creating a series of shared moments that were open to everyone. These moments became some of the defining legacies of the Games.

With Inclusion 3.0 we were attempting to influence not only the workforce and the supply chain but also the end product, the customer experience and how men, women and children would 'touch, taste, see, hear and smell London 2012'. We undertook a lot of work on the client journey. The brilliant Heather McGill led cross-functional teams on 'a day in the life' exercises putting us in the shoes of various diverse customers in order to see if the Games would exceed their expectations. It was a major learning experience for our people and critical in building cross-functional collaboration on inclusion, and furthering the conscious conversation.

By adopting the same principles used in workforce and procurement, namely understand, lead and deliver, we tackled the at times overwhelming series of LOCOG departments and projects in an attempt to influence the customer experience at Games time. 'Workforce, procurement and service delivery' became the responsibility to understand, lead and deliver on Diversity and Inclusion when you hire, when you buy or when you design. It was a simple articulation that worked and everyone, from the Chief Executive down used it in conversation. It was articulated not by the usual suspects, the diversity practitioners, but specifically by the people one might least assume to be talking about inclusion. This was critical to our success.

Takeaways – the interventions

1 The interventions had to be much simpler than the complex reality (KISS), easy to understand and easily articulated. We had to make 'the ask' (what we wanted people to do) as achievable and credible as possible.

2 The interventions were defined as 'Workforce, Procurement and Service delivery' or 'when you hire, buy or design', which everyone understood and which made the rather nebulous 'inclusion' very real and tangible. People had to know what inclusion looked like if they were to work towards it.

3 The interventions provided a framework for when people should be thinking about inclusion in their decision-making (such as when they procure a new contract), rather than a set of answers. People were free to pursue their own results rather than have them spelled out for them and this freedom unlocked far greater innovation than we possessed on our own.

Workforce

10

With 200,000 people to recruit, train and deploy, the workforce would literally be the face of the Games. We wanted that face to be as diverse and as inclusive as possible. This chapter details how we intervened in both the demand for labour, by influencing our colleagues, and in the supply of labour, by working with hundreds of stakeholders.

An additional challenge at LOCOG, besides the ramp-up and volume (from 50 people to 200,000 in five years), was that the profile of the Games tended to attract job applicants who were highly networked and who had previous 'Games experience'. This pool is even less diverse than the typical London/UK labour market. If we believe the relational demography research then, at core, we were trying to get people to hire against their gut instinct, a tall order in any circumstances.[1] Furthermore, we could not afford to make (many) mistakes with our hiring as we simply did not have time to re-hire to replace a wrong hire. We needed to be right first time – was inclusion a risk or, in fact, was it a risk mitigation tool?

Table 10.1 details the principal interventions we made, which will be explained as we progress through the chapter.

Outreach through finding recruitment partners

On the supply side for talent, we undertook unprecedented outreach and partnered with hundreds of community organisations. These ranged from the government's Job Centres and the host borough job brokerages to the East London Mosque, Elevation Networks and the Stephen Lawrence Trust, which seek to connect disadvantaged, talented young people with employment opportunities. They could reach talent quicker, more efficiently and more effectively than we could.

We took calculated risks, for example attending Friday prayers at local mosques and seeking permission from local Imams to hand out job flyers.

TABLE 10.1 Talent supply and demand determinants

Supply-side workforce interventions: decreasing barriers to people applying Goal = 'Become employer of choice'	Demand-side workforce interventions: decreasing barriers to hiring diversity Goal = 'Create the new norm'
1 Outreach and partnering	1 Coaching, inductions and job descriptions
2 Recruitment action plans	2 Leadership Pledge and supporting infrastructure: group understanding and leadership
3 CV workshops	3 Information sharing, target zones and high-frequency benchmarking/ tracking
4 Talent pools	4 Individual accountability
5 >access now	5 Role models and peer review
6 >attitude over age	6 Group interviews
7 >action on inclusion	7 Consultancy support and team work
8 Games Makers early start	8 Awards and recognition

That created an impact with the local Muslim community that was unprecedented for a 'corporation', let alone the Olympic Games. We were creative, partnering with local football clubs such as Charlton Athletic, who had resources and commitment, but lacked expertise.

Jack Hiett of the Stephen Lawrence Trust said they worked in partnership with LOCOG to 'ensure the Games embraced the diversity of London and delivered real training, skills and employment to inspire a new and diverse generation of young people from all backgrounds'.[2] Jacqueline Faulkner, Way to Work project manager at the London Muslim Centre said of LOCOG's approach, 'their commitment to ensuring that the workforce for the 2012 Games is diverse and inclusive of the many communities and cultures in the Olympic host boroughs is to be commended'.[3] In fact, it was born out of strategic desire, and Jacqueline deserves the credit for partnering with us.

Encouraging our recruitment partners to follow recruitment action plans

With many partners, we developed recruitment action plans (RAPs) to implement a detailed process for getting the people they knew to apply for jobs with LOCOG. This reversed the usual relationship between lobby group and organisation from one of lobbying the organisation to 'take' people, to requiring the lobby group to 'find and supply' people. It also allowed us to benchmark the effectiveness of our partnerships. Our recruitment team sent an updated list of current opportunities to these organisations every week. This listed upcoming vacancies to all our partners so they knew before jobs hit the website/open market. We developed 52 Recruitment Action Plans for paid positions and over 100 RAPs for the Volunteer programme.

We organised events in other organisations, or simply sent along a representative. This was a resource light, effective way of us continuing to reinforce our message that we were serious about attracting diverse local talent. We made use of existing networks rather than try to reinvent the wheel or, worse, undermine existing efforts in the name of a short-term labour market intervention that would then leave these organisations in a weaker position post 2012. We attended every job fair we could. We reinforced the power of association, to highlight our vacancies and to encourage applications.

Running CV workshops for target candidates

We ran local CV workshops to enable target candidates to up-skill in advance of interview. These encouraged local people to get involved with the Games when they otherwise didn't even know where the front door was. We had celebrities 'pop in' to generate excitement; Seb, athletes, role models. We began the workshops monthly, then stepped up to weekly as we accelerated our recruitment. These events were the perfect opportunity to advertise job vacancies, answer individual queries and rebuff any negative stereotypes in the most direct and honest way possible. Here was a human face to the enormity of the Olympic Games. These were staffed by 'normal' people who smiled. This early and consistent reinforcement of our image as an employer of choice that was serious about diversity was crucial to our success.

On 11 March 2011, as our ramp-up really started, we used 'diversity week' to interview more than 80 talented deaf and disabled people. Applicants had been sourced from the local job brokerages and matched against a generic job description. We presented a top-line view of the organisation and then followed this with interviews for those who wanted them. We gave feedback there and then, honest, and in real time. Working with our functional areas, we went on to hire over half of those people.

We still had the challenge of an extremely time limited ramp-up. How would we find the talent in such a short space of time? Did we have enough time to convince the doubters that they should apply? And how seriously would diversity be taken when the recruiters were under pressure? Would it drop off the list, the thinking? How could we ensure it would be integrated?

Building talent pools

To answer all this, we came up with the idea of talent pools. This came from the Diversity and Inclusion team and brought together the HR team, recruitment team and Adecco, our official recruitment services provider. The talent pool was to capture those people who had been through the process but been runner up in a job. Rather than let all that effort and preparation (and education on our part) go to waste, we invited the candidates to opt in to a talent pool. This allowed us then to stay in regular touch with the individual by email and send them weekly vacancy lists. To actively identify roles that would suit them and match their skill sets; to invite them to CV workshops, notify them of upcoming events and communicate inspiring news stories and case studies.

Moreover, besides helping them land a job, it was efficient for us, avoided repetition, and allowed us to fast-track pre-screened candidates to final-stage interviews. It was a critical method in not only fulfilling confidence in us that we were serious about inclusion, but also positioning Diversity and Inclusion to the HR team as a cost- and time-saving measure, rather than an additional burden.

We opened the talent pool programme to people who identified as disabled or having a long-term health condition, being an ethnic minority or a local resident. It was explicitly not positive discrimination or affirmative action because they had to pass the same interviews as everyone else. If you need a term, it would be 'positive action'. There was no lowering of standards, but there was significant efficient use of effort on the supply side to get people job-ready. It also allowed us to reward effort and to give a job to those people who showed persistence and determination, something not lost on the hiring managers. I have countless anecdotes of managers thanking us for introducing them to someone who was grateful to have a job, worked hard and who they would never have otherwise met from their existing social or professional circles.

There were, however, various legal hoops we had to jump through in collecting and storing the 'diversity data' and we had to proceed step by step and become best friends with our legal team. This was fully within the law, but definitely an area of professional development and thought leadership for our legal team who became genuinely quite interested. And in order to develop the technology and scale it up we had to convince Adecco, our recruitment partner, to come on board.

I started with Steve Girdler, their Director, who got it from early on and became a kindred spirit. We then tackled their Chief Executive together, with a few other folks around a table, and delivered a crash course in Diversity 101, 2.0 and 3.0. There were some alarming comments aired around the table concerning outdated, nay litigious, terms for various sections of society. There was an understandable, but at times overwhelming, focus on the bottom line and PR. But by positioning real inclusion as the value-for-money thought leadership that it really was, the eventual outcome (after many meetings, prep calls, beers and expletives) was that we managed to get Adecco over the fence. They not only helped us with the talent pools, but made Diversity and Inclusion the central pillar of their London 2012 sponsorship activation.

As with 'understand, lead, deliver', used internally, we had to design and articulate the outreach programmes required in a simple fashion externally. This was not only to be easily understood by applicant and hiring manager alike, it was also to debunk the myth of diversity being the antithesis of talent and make it quite clear we were asking for nothing other than merit-based hires.

Of the groups least likely to apply there were three in particular we wanted to develop programmes with. We launched three dedicated programmes, >*access now* for disabled people including a guaranteed interview scheme for paid positions and an early opening on volunteer applications, >*attitude over age* for older and younger applicants including our School Leaver programme 'Get Ahead' and >*action on inclusion* for ethnic minority and local candidates. We were not just trying to increase the supply of minority talent in the recruitment pipeline. We were aiming for a step change in diversity recruitment. We had to recruit 200,000 people and we had a limited time in which to do it, so these recruitment programmes had to be strong, scalable and easily understood.

>access now

Our first programme, to create a shift in the employment and career development of disabled people, was >access now. The name was designed to make it about accessibility, not disability. This was not about having to tick a box to say you were less able, this was about appealing to anyone who identified as disabled, or deaf, or having a long-term health condition. Many of these people had experienced discrimination and frustration with prior application processes. We had to convince them that we wanted them and we wanted them now. Time was of the essence and we were doing things differently. We handed out cards imprinted with Braille and easy read. They said 'join in' on one side on the reverse: '>access now: Apply to work with us and be part of the most inspirational event in the world'.

We launched it on 3 December 2008, International Disabled Person's day, with the Minister for Disabled people, Jonathan Shaw and our Chief Executive Paul Deighton. They were joined by General Counsel Terry Miller and Venues Director James Bulley who had chosen to act as Disability Champions in LOCOG. The programme comprised a guaranteed interview scheme for anyone who identified as disabled or having a long-term health condition. This definition (back to the importance of language) was important as many people, my sister included, refuse to tick the 'disability' box for fear of stigma or admitting to themselves that they were, in fact, disabled when they had previously been in denial. But they do recognise they have long-term health issues. We took people on good faith if they requested a guaranteed interview. There was remarkably little abuse of the system because most non-disabled people did not want to be thought of as disabled and there was even a stigma around long-term health condition. It would be pretty apparent when we asked them what their access requirements were if they were trying to pull a 'fast one'. In the 200,000 recruitments we did, I think we had only three or four individuals who tried to abuse the system.

It is important to stress again that we guaranteed an interview, not a job. It fast-tracked the supply side but not the demand (hiring) side (although the cumulative effect of seeing disabled people come into our offices every week for interviews undoubtedly made an impact on hiring managers). The interviews were all merit-based. We did use our talent pool system quite heavily here however. Many of the disabled people we interviewed were not quite job-ready. After, in some cases, years of professional neglect and poor experience with recruitment in general, some were 'rusty'. We identified the talent, encouraged them to join the talent pool and they then improved with every subsequent interview until they landed a job. By Games time, our talent pools were nearly empty, meaning that the pipelines we had built up were fully deployed. That is an efficient use of human capital, cost effective for us, and allowed as many disabled people as possible the opportunity to gain meaningful employment.

We guaranteed all new disabled employees would have whatever support they required in order to fulfil their job. This was not an HR cost as we took advantage of the government's 'two ticks' programme where the taxpayer covers all additional employment costs, and saves on welfare payments. Examples ranged from minor desk adjustments to taxis to work. The government had instigated this programme several years prior but no companies had ever systemically taken advantage of it. In the spirit of partnership we worked closely with government and advised that our ambition was to hire hundreds of disabled people and in order for this to work, and their system to be showcased as a model, we needed some support.

The government had publicly stated their intention to reduce the number of people claiming disability living allowance and they were very keen to transfer disabled people from social security into work. We agreed that we could have one dedicated advisor who would be our 'go to' person in government to expedite any expenses incurred in hiring a person with access requirements. This dedicated link proved vital as we saved infinite time avoiding government bureaucracy and processing hundreds of expenses quickly and efficiently. As we proved the worth of this arrangement, government increased it to two dedicated people. By interacting with government creatively, we were able to retain the loyalty of hiring managers that we were as good as our word when we guaranteed not one additional penny in hiring costs.

>action on inclusion

Ethnic minority folks were a majority in many parts of the East End of London. We called our outreach programme here >action on inclusion. It purposely wasn't diversity (difference) because we wanted all sides to meet half-way. This wasn't about us bending the rules to allow unqualified applicants to gain employment on their terms. But it wasn't about us remaining in our ivory tower content with our current connections either. Inclusion spoke to that. Action spoke to the need for a sense of urgency rather like >access now.

Not only were Black, Asian and Minority Ethnic (BAME) people underrepresented in employment generally, this was especially so in sports management/administration. We engaged in positive action to break down barriers about how we were perceived as an organisation. This was important, as many of the senior figureheads were white men – Jacques Rogge in Lausanne, Seb Coe and Paul Deighton in London. We used our Diversity Board and ethnic minority staff, as well as white staff to portray LOCOG as the diverse organisation we wanted it to be. As a white man, I happily presented to all-black audiences. Again, this was a two-way street and not about creating a Benetton advert that was detached from reality – it was highly possible that a new black recruit could end up in an all-white team (at least in the early days) and we wanted to be upfront and honest about that.

Following the success with disabled people, we extended the talent pool to BAME applicants if they wanted to opt in. Again, it would identify those people willing to persevere and continue to put in the effort to land a job. We held dedicated recruitment evenings for talent pool members and others during Diversity Week. We recruited 'recruitment ambassadors' who would be role models in their communities and promote LOCOG vacancies.

The link with the BAME LOCOG staff group became quite strong, with BAME staff members choosing to mentor applicants. Greg Nugent, our white male Marketing Director, took over from Charlie Wijeratna as the BAME Director Champion. He was great in challenging the group and focusing effort on initiatives that would actually add value, such as the mentoring programme and supporting the work of the Diversity and Inclusion team rather than establishing separate unsupported initiatives.

>attitude over age

>attitude over age was the most fun programme to launch because of how we did it. We deliberated 'what would most appeal to sceptical or worried hiring managers and be unlike anything they perceived 'diversity' to be?' We came up with the idea of a rock concert.

We invited the youngest staff member, Steven Burnham at the time, and the oldest staff member, Tony Sainsbury at the time, to join the Age Champion, Debbie Jevans, Chief Executive Paul Deighton and others alongside the rock group The Zimmers.

My friend Andrea had taken me to see a US older persons' group at the theatre in London a few years before and despite my initial scepticism, I had ended up in floods of tears as a bunch of 70-somethings sang *Forever Young*. Many had lost their partners, many had even contemplated suicide, and here they were singing as a group to paying audiences. I wanted to capture some of that and bring it into the Olympics to touch hearts as well as engage people with humour.

I contacted the manager of the band and explained that we were launching a programme called >attitude over age and I felt The Zimmers exemplified that sentiment better than anyone else I knew. Would they come and help us out? He said that for some of the band members, to be asked to perform for the Olympics was a dream come true. When they arrived at Canary Wharf on a spring evening in March 2009, Tom and I began a game of cat and mouse as we chased various band members around the building. Some had taken the service lift instead of the regular lift. Some had turned up on Barclays' trading floor and were cavorting with the traders. Barclays' security reprimanded us (we were always getting into trouble) as we had 'lost' several 'old people'. By this stage in our life cycle, it was just presumed any whacky guests were for 'the Olympics on floor 23'.

When we assembled the band together, they belted out such tracks as *Fight For Your Right to Party*, *Hey Jude* and *Wonderwall*. The lead singer Alf, was 92. The average age of the band was 75. When they sang my personal favourite, *Fake Plastic Trees* by Radiohead, everyone ended up in tears.

It was important for us to do this, not least because all our marketing was about inspiring youth to choose sport, next generation, and so forth. We wanted to make it clear that in our hiring practices we would not consider age as a barrier. In fact we were one of the first organisations to use '70+' in the monitoring forms. We did some media with Seb where he brilliantly articulated that 'we didn't believe in retirement' and again, we were ahead of the law as the default retirement age was only scrapped after we had already established the programme and recruited our first septuagenarian.

It was a fantastic opportunity for older and younger people to come together and to learn from one another. Our Age Champion, Debbie Jevans, was a self-confessed diversity sceptic. She loved it. And she championed this through to the end, including then going on to push support for the Equality Standard for Sport too. Like Terry and James with disability, and Charlie and Greg with ethnicity, Debs would come to Diversity Board meetings and see the big picture in terms of the Diversity and Inclusion programme. She went from sceptic to supporter in about a year.

We partnered with The Age and Employment Network (TAEN) and Employers Forum on Age (EFA), Job Centre Plus and other young and older persons' groups to source talent for the recruitment pipeline. We had dedicated recruitment evenings for older people. We worked with Adecco to benchmark recruitment agencies on the age of candidates to encourage greater diversity and of course we were benchmarking the internal functional areas on age diversity too.[4] We developed a buddy system whereby new young or old employees could partner with someone at the opposite end of the age spectrum to teach each other new tricks and help them in their role at LOCOG. This offered those leaving school or college the chance to gain a paid apprenticeship with the greatest show on earth. We used our Age Champion and Age Positive marks in all our recruitment materials, and gained best private sector innovation award in 2010 from the EFA.

The Volunteer programme and supply-side outreach

We swiftly progressed to the launch of the Volunteer programme. We could apply many of the lessons from the Paid recruitment experience to the recruitment, training and deployment of the 70,000 *Games Maker* workforce too. If we felt out of our depth with the paid programme, it was even more so with the volunteers. We had no certainty whether a million-plus people would apply for 70,000 positions or whether too few might. The modelling was, in any case, wrong.

We had to focus on the supply side to start with and help people self-select into the programme application route. It was important to remove all barriers to diverse talent applying. On the one hand, I thought it would have been less difficult to attract diverse talent to apply, as the job descriptions were less specific and technical, more generic and more sellable to communities. However, they weren't paid, and that was actually the biggest barrier for many target groups, especially in the East End minority ethnic communities where the concept of volunteering is not the same as it is in more middle-class, more affluent, white communities.

In order to not end up with a homogeneous cohort of people (who could afford the time and lack of payment to become 'volunteers') it was imperative that we launch a serious supply-side programme to outreach for diverse talent. The Volunteering functional area was totally in agreement with us, passionately believing that a more diverse volunteer cohort would make the Games better.

We opened the application window six weeks earlier for disabled people to allow them more time to prepare and submit their applications. Although this was criticised in the *Daily Mail*, most people understood that this was an early application, not an early offer. It was the strongest signal we could send that we meant to include everyone in this chance of a lifetime. We had adapted the uniforms, trained all the recruiters, and made all the venues accessible, now we just needed the talent.

The website was designed by the LOCOG New Media team to be fully accessible, in a range of formats, such as easy read,[5] and simple to navigate.

Again, this was not special adjustments for special groups, but adaptations that would make it easier for all groups, the Luddite yours truly, included. Subtitles benefited everyone, including those whose first language was not English. The website could be adapted to suit personal requirements. For example, too much contrast was generally bad for people with dyslexia, but too little contrast didn't work for visually impaired people. The New Media team understood infinite diversity and they delivered a really inclusive personalised website.

The Volunteering team ran a contact centre for anyone unable to use the internet or without online access. In addition we partnered with the Museums and Libraries archive to allow anyone to submit a free application online at any library or museum in the UK. Again, this required initiative on the part of the applicant but there were no apologies for that.

We partnered with hundreds of community organisations and of those that we worked with, we provided them with a code they could pass on to their clients when applying. This guaranteed nothing, except that we could track them in the system and therefore alert the community group of their members who had not finished their applications and so they could target their help and resources accordingly. Continuing the reversal of lobby group vs organisation, we benchmarked them on their supply of talent to us vis à vis the Recruitment Action Plan (RAP) they had previously submitted as well as vs other partners. We generated competition over the supply of diverse talent.

We advertised in dedicated magazines such as *Pride Life*, *Muslim Post* and up-weighted the campaign in the local host boroughs. The sell internally to functional areas was that we wanted local people, not simply for the moral case, but because it helped us mitigate risks such as transport failures or adverse weather. Local people were more likely to be able to get to work and ensure the Games began on time.

Reasonable and unreasonable adjustments

We produced information about the Games Maker programme in a range of languages, again to show intent, but stressed that English was a requirement for the position. In the application process we asked about accessibility requirements and made every possible adjustment at interview stage. We provided reasonable adjustments, such as meeting visually impaired candidates at the station and supporting them to the selection centre. Andrew Newman, one of our brilliant Volunteer Managers, recounted a story of an upset mother. Normally accustomed to 'mothering' her learning-disabled son, she was perplexed at our customer service that spoke directly to him, not to her. When she complained, I backed Andrew all the way for doing a brilliant job and delivering our inclusive approach superbly – we talked direct to the person, not about them to their 'carer'.[6]

Reasonable adjustments are what they imply. They are not, as some candidates or spectators requested, unreasonable adjustments. If it were unreasonable at the application process, it would probably be more so at Games time. I was made aware of one individual who was upset because they could not bring fizzy drinks into the park through security. Everyone knew the rules; as with airport security there was a 100 ml maximum liquid allowance. We provided a range of drinks and constant free water within the park. However, this person insisted they could only take their medicine with fizzy drinks, none of the ones we provided would do (even the fizzy drinks we provided were the wrong type). This was an example of being unreasonable. If a medical note had been produced we would have made allowances. None was forthcoming, and so we didn't. We made special arrangements for them to go to a specific vendor to buy a fizzy drink to take their medication.

Another annoyance was the attitude of some deaf people to sign language provision. We offered sign language interpreters to anyone who requested it, at our expense. When some people didn't have the courtesy to turn up for interview and it was too late for us to cancel the signer, we lost money, each and every time. A purist argument is that to allow equality, signers should be on hand at all times. A practical argument is that real inclusion is a two-way street. Many people were unfortunately stuck in a superficial inclusion world, preferring to disengage and complain, talking only to the already converted.

The selection centre we chose was an example of our procurement process best value criteria in action. A different venue was actually cheaper, on one criterion, but refused to put in place the accessibility requirements we would like to see to make it an inclusive centre and reduce our costs in the long run by abolishing the need for day-by-day adaptations to cope with interviewees with various access requirements. The *Daily Mail* picked up on this in a speech I gave in Toronto and lambasted LOCOG for 'pushing up costs in order to meet diversity targets'.[7] Needless to say, therefore, the venue had automatic doors, lower desks, and accessible transport on hand and thousands of disabled people were interviewed there without complaint.

Contractor workforce

During the Games, over 100,000 people delivered a variety of services such as catering, cleaning, security and transport. They formed the contractor workforce, and were not directly employed by LOCOG. The Diversity and

Inclusion team and the Contractor Workforce team asked each contractor organisation to complete the Diversity Works for London (DWFL) assessment within 30 days of contract award (see Chapter 11) and implement the Guaranteed Interview Scheme in the recruitment process (see p 144). In order to help residents of the six host boroughs, we also encouraged contractor organisations to develop plans for recruiting through the local job brokerages, especially people who were previously unemployed. We asked each contractor organisation to achieve, through their recruitment for Games-time roles, the same target zones as for our paid and volunteer workforce.

To ensure each contractor organisation's commitment, we implemented a monitoring process that required each organisation to report on the diversity of their workforce for the Olympic Games and Paralympic Games in 2012. This included their employees, workers, consultants, secondees and any staff or sub-contractors involved in the Games.

Contractor organisations were encouraged to use the diversity and inclusion process provided by LOCOG to collect the information. We also made sure this information was collected in a manner that maintained anonymity and was stored in compliance with data protection legislation.

Demand-side interventions

Besides the range of supply-side interventions, we analysed actions we could undertake on the demand-side for talent too. In the same way that supply-side interventions had been designed to decrease barriers to talent accessing opportunities, our demand-side interventions were designed to decrease barriers to managers hiring diverse talent. If the supply side was about creating a strong employer brand in a short space of time and making LOCOG an 'Employer of Choice', then our internal demand-side activity was about creating 'The new norm'. Not only were diversity and talent positively correlated, hiring diverse talent became business as usual at LOCOG.

Credible coaching, compulsory inductions and pithy Job Descriptions

It started with an analysis of the full recruitment cycle, and tracking interventions at each stage. We had to start by displaying inclusiveness, and our PR, communications and website were all geared to that end. We had messages from the Chief Executive, HR Director and others on the website alongside profiles of recent hires and role models. We displayed our awards, leadership philosophy and Management Committee Champions. We signposted our delivery partner websites and articles. It all added up to a credible and believable authentic display of who we were and what we stood for. As Gandhi said, *be the change you want to see in the world*. For us this wasn't trite, it was very real.

We challenged HR to improve the job descriptions. They were redesigned to focus on skills and competencies, not 'evidence of experience' which would be a subtle, often unconscious way, that diverse talent was otherwise filtered out of the process. It is incredible how recruiters are still seduced by certain triggers on a CV as opposed to the actual skill set and what the person can *do*. I see CVs from top universities that are very impressive, but they use unspoken code and associations to imply that they can do the job, irrespective of how much attention they have paid to the job description. I see CVs from 'non-traditional' backgrounds that have raw talent throughout them, presented poorly. We had to focus on what people could do, not simply how good they were at marketing themselves, hence the critical importance of our CV workshops.

We inculcated Diversity and Inclusion in the induction, which all new starters went through. They got to meet a member of the Diversity and Inclusion team in their first week and appreciate its importance from then on. We implemented a coaching programme tackling subconscious bias. As stated previously, I was sceptical about 'diversity training' preferring tailored conversations instead. Coaching hiring managers became a necessary part of this process if we were to properly serve the increased supply in talent with credible interviewers who would not make mistakes. It was about building confidence, empowering hiring managers to deal with diverse needs presented in interview. Rather than 'training' we unleashed two of the Diversity and Inclusion team, Lauren (visually impaired, entrepreneurial, smart and funny) and Mark (mobility scooter user, very 'blokeish', smart and funny) to talk with all the hiring managers. Part of the follow up to the Leadership Pledge was that anyone hiring people should go through this process.

We also held events for trainers and interviewers at partner organisations, especially Job Centre plus. They were people who appreciated an external intervention and a link to the Olympics and Paralympics. They were often dealing with a challenging client base and so our job was to offer 'actionable inspiration', to offer them a solution for their clients, to help them do their job.

Leadership Pledge and group leadership

After talent had been sourced, identified and matched, it was all about the hire. Hiring talent was a generally pleasurable experience for our recruiters, inspired by the Tutu Leadership Pledge and supporting infrastructure. This leadership process was a collective experience. Whether it was the Chief Executive reminding everyone he wanted an organisation that 'looked like London' or whether it was simply recruiters feeling able to speak freely about their challenges and successes with colleagues who were going through the same thing. The pledges were on everyone's desks or pinned to walls, the Diversity Action Team was in business, and the other support infrastructure from Champions to internal communications was alive and kicking.

Information sharing, target zones and high-frequency benchmarking

Instead of imposing compliance quotas or even specific targets on colleagues, we created competition among departments for diverse talent by assertively and proactively sharing information every month. We laid out 'target zones' with a range of attainable demographics based on the London labour market.[8] We then benchmarked every department every month on their hiring record. We ranked functional areas accordingly, for example their record on hiring women or hiring disabled people.[9] The resulting dynamic was fascinating – in the absence of quotas or specific targets, people held each other accountable for delivery. For example, two male directors who had never previously engaged in 'diversity' in their corporate career to date suddenly became fiercely competitive over their respective rankings in the female recruitment 'league table'.

This high-frequency monitoring and tracking built and maintained momentum. We tracked applications per month broken down by seven strands of diversity; gender including gender identity, disability, ethnicity, sexual orientation, age, belief (if any) and socio-economic status via postcode and previous employment status. We then tracked acceptances in any one month and rolling acceptances year-to-date by the same criteria. By matrixing this information across different functional areas, we could pinpoint detailed patterns and intervene early if we found any irregularities or persistent trends.

The role of information was therefore crucial. We tried hard to use information to create the proverbial 'level playing field' that would otherwise not exist. In the beginning, we discouraged staff referrals, to avoid recruiting similar people. We instead encouraged outreach, such as that explained above via our recruitment partners, Elevation Networks and so on. That outreach was important in providing information to those who were comparatively information poor. By giving information to the minority group we empowered them.

Individual accountability

To identify talent we used tracking – we kept details on and followed up on every person that came to a recruitment evening, joined the talent pool, or worked with our delivery partners. We could then match talent to opportunities. We deployed Andrew and Jackie solely to that critical task, and they were free to target functional areas, such as technology and venues, two of the biggest recruiting areas. This individual accountability was not just a process within the tent. With our Volunteer programme, we used the recruitment partner unique ID number tracking to benchmark our different partners and assess them against their recruitment plans.

Role models and peer review

Upon hire, we encouraged people to 'report back'; we had to create a feedback loop, a virtuous circle where diversity attracts diversity, where the culture was increasingly embracing of difference. So when local Muslim people were hired, we encouraged them to talk about it in their communities and supported the building of a positive cycle of interest from a community that had previously been isolated from the Olympic recruiting machine. We developed the idea of recruitment ambassadors – role models were created and promoted.

As the monthly reports progressed people were subject to peer review. Peer review is the idea of creating a positive, circular dynamic that is self-sustaining among colleagues. All Directors and Heads of Departments received and had access to full information on the diversity hiring statistics broken down by department. All staff had a top line summary on the intranet. This allowed anyone, at any time, to see how another team/department was performing and everyone knew that. Therefore, rather than relying on a compliance-driven 'diversity team' to 'push' departments into diverse hiring practices, they simply self-regulated. More than this, they were 'pulled' towards higher performance through friendly competition, rather than pushed. This was ultimately a more effective and sustainable strategy as people were wary of their reputation and standing among people they considered friends and colleagues. That could affect the quality of their life on a daily basis, far more profoundly than any compliance mechanism.

Group interviews

To save money and time we adopted group selection processes, instead of interviewing and choosing recruits one at a time. Instigated due to force of circumstances, this became a key inclusion tool. The reason is simple: people choose variety in bundles.

If you allow yourself one chocolate bar a week (or even each day!) you will probably choose the same one each time. It becomes a habit that you look forward to and since you only have one you have allowed yourself to eat, you are going to choose your absolute favourite one. If, however you allow yourself to buy five chocolate bars all in one go at the start of the week, you are more likely to choose variety, because it would seem less appealing to buy five of the same all in one go. In the UK, at Christmas time, we call these 'selection boxes'.

Evaluating in groups therefore produces a more diverse output. With this realisation we insisted on more than one candidate at a time rather than traditional 1–1 interviews wherever possible – groups of candidates in assessment centre type scenarios, where they can be observed as a group. Additionally, we encouraged more than one interviewer, but still an advantageous ratio for the organisation in terms of labour time and cost. This combined effect decreased subconscious bias and implicit association on the part of the interviewer, and increased peer-to-peer connections, via 'cluster hires' rather than recruiting isolated individuals. This gave inclusion a better chance. If we had realised this earlier on, or been cognisant of the literature, we would have established it as a process from the start.

Consultancy support and teamwork

We offered consultancy support throughout. It was teamwork in a real sense. Besides the relationships inside LOCOG between the Diversity and Inclusion team and HR recruitment managers and line managers in the various functional areas, there was also an important external relationship. The Diversity and Inclusion team brokered an effective relationship with Adecco, the official recruitment partner. Specifically we were able to make sense of the varied measurement systems we had inherited from the bid stage, starting with Excel spreadsheets. We built consensus on using the back office 'BOSS' system to track current 'as is' diversity and develop the recruitment pipeline measurement tool 'skillstream' to track it going forward.

Awards and recognition

Finally, awards and recognition were an important factor. To recognise individual achievement (and individual responsibility) we held regular features on particular hires, awards for the most improved functional area and any other way we could envisage saying thank you and rewarding leadership.

It's about inclusion

The supply and demand interventions worked well. The goal, however, was not the free market in and of itself. The goal was real inclusion and we had to measure it. Remember that it is possible to have diversity without inclusion? We implemented a way to measure inclusion to ensure we were achieving real inclusion, rather than superficial inclusion. We adopted a survey that asked 20 diagnostic questions every six months. By breaking it down by diversity category we could measure inclusion. And we could witness how minorities started to score above average. For example, 'The people I work with are committed to delivering a memorable Games', 'Working at London 2012 will enhance my future', and 'I am proud to say I work for London 2012' all registered very positive scores across the board. In 2008/09 minorities scored below or about average. This trend increased over time as the organisation became more diverse and by 2010/11 minorities were scoring above average in statistically significant numbers.

The constant drumbeat of days ticking away acted as a real focal point for all staff, regardless of identity. It also provided a rallying cry to deliver results and to have that conversation that you kept putting off. Deadlines were indeed a friend of inclusion.

Late in 2010, there was an all-staff meeting featuring two of my favourite LOCOG people – our Paralympics Director Chris Holmes and our Campaign Manager Gillian Millner. Chris is a superb presenter, completely blind and has an appalling sense of humour. Gillian is also a superb presenter, female with full vision and used to suffer from *Guardian*-reader syndrome. Standing next to each other in front of 500 people, Gillian's PowerPoint presentation failed. She cursed and exclaimed how she 'couldn't see a damn thing and was now presenting blind'. Then she stopped, went white as a sheet and held her head in shame. There was an intake of air and the room fell silent for about two seconds. Then everyone burst into communal laughter, Chris laughing loudest of all. The elephant had been slaughtered, a communal experience had taken place and we were en route to achieving real inclusion.

Takeaways – workforce

1 Achieving real workforce inclusion requires simultaneous and coordinated supply-side and demand-side interventions. This bifurcated and systemic approach differentiates Inclusion 3.0 from 101 or 2.0 approaches.

2 Supply-side interventions were designed to remove barriers to diverse talent applying, making the organisation an employer of choice.

3 Demand-side interventions were designed to create the 'new norm' where hiring homogeneously in a diverse world would seem odd. We decreased barriers, practised regular benchmarking and information sharing, and emphasised individual accountability, training, supports and recognition.

4 Other interventions that helped create 'the new norm' included a grounding in Inclusion 3.0 thinking, freedom from Diversity 101 compliance training, group leadership, teamwork, target zones, high-frequency monitoring and tracking. Above all, the deadline acted as a focus, and a driver for change.

Notes

1 See Chapter 3 for explanation of relational demography.

2 LOCOG document.

3 LOCOG document.

4 See Appendix, p 316.

5 Easy read is text that uses simpler words and sentence constructions in order to convey ideas to people with intellectual disabilities. It is an example of real inclusion because it also helps people who do not have intellectual disabilities grasp new ideas more quickly and fully than they may otherwise. For more information, see Chapter 19.

6 Andy from the volunteering team told me that the mother of a man with a learning disability had complained to them following his interview. The complaint was essentially that not enough fuss had been made of him at interview and he was treated like everyone else. She was so used to having 'special' treatment and being more centre of attention than was the case with us, that she didn't like it. When you actually spoke to the son, however, it was clear that he loved the fact that for the first time in his professional life, our staff had spoken to him directly and ignored his mother/carer. She had become unnecessary for the two-and-a-half hours he spent with London 2012. I told Andy that was the biggest compliment he could ever be given in terms of accessibility. It was a paradigm-shifting game changer.

7 Stephen Wright and Daniel Bates, 'Diversity targets drive up bill for Olympics', *Daily Mail*, Monday 2 April 2012, p 11.

8 See Appendix 2

9 See Appendix 3

Procurement

11

I never liked shopping. My understanding is that most men don't either. It therefore always perplexed me why most procurement departments I knew were virtually all-male teams. I wonder if 'Heads of Procurement' were renamed 'Heads of Shopping' whether it would go some way to shifting the gender balance in this area?

In 2007 I knew very little about procurement and had already assumed the area was dull and boring. Not only was this a discourtesy to the men and women who had built their careers in this space, it was also sheer ignorance of the game-changing role the supply chain can play in bringing about real inclusion. This, therefore, details the strategy of how we defied convention and published the majority of our $1.7 billion contract opportunities online, encouraged open competition and reached out to small businesses everywhere. LOCOG procurement was pivotal in creating Everyone's 2012.

The majority of our budget (any contract over £20,000) passed through the procurement team. There was an opportunity here to influence hundreds of companies to change the way they did business. They could also be the real change agents in these Games. Furthermore, a major risk to our vision of Everyone's 2012 was not simply our own behaviour, but the behaviour of our suppliers over which we had less control. The tragic and horrific collapse of a garment factory building outside Dhaka in Bangladesh used by suppliers to many Western clothing retailers in May 2013 reminds us of the interconnectedness of global supply chains.[1]

How could real inclusion help make the boat go faster?[2] We could make the big guys do stuff they wouldn't otherwise do, like implement a guaranteed interview scheme for disabled job applicants. We could also help the little guys get a slice of the pie. Literally, enlarging the pie for everyone. The rationale and overall inclusion philosophy in our procurement programme was to add not one penny to the cost of doing business but to create shared value wherever possible.[3]

This commercial approach, plus several rounds of beers, won over the procurement team and in particular their Director Gerry Walsh, who enthusiastically embraced and led on inclusion as an inherent part of his programme and how he and his team would define 'value for money'. Opening up our contract opportunities to a diverse range of suppliers was good news for them, but also good news for us because it helped generate competition, which is the best way to deliver value. LOCOG's procurement programme was of extreme scale and complexity. It required procuring to a fixed deadline and challenging budget in a new organisation with no existing supply base, all conducted under scrutiny from the government, media and general public. Laurie Neville was the cool-as-cucumber programme manager who we worked with to make real inclusion happen.

Supply-side leadership: the Business Charter

Our key approach on the supply side was the development of a Business Charter. This set out our values of great business relationships, transparency and the active promotion of Diversity and Inclusion. This was designed to make our procurement process as transparent as possible to increase competition, reduce costs and source innovation from organisations we didn't even know existed and certainly wouldn't be on a 'roster' (a list of established and 'preferred' suppliers). Above all, this enabled us to communicate with talent and innovation we didn't know existed. The designer of the Olympic Torch, or Thomas Heatherwick, who designed the celebrated cauldron, were not on any roster to my knowledge. They were both small businesses and they both contributed innovation, creativity and diversity to London 2012.

Being open: making the supply chain transparent and accessible

The first objective of the Charter was to make our own business opportunities accessible to a diverse range of suppliers. In other words, to open up our supply chain. Any business, of any size or background, could register online to have the opportunity to become part of the London 2012 supply chain. An online marketplace, CompeteFor, was created in partnership with the London Development Agency where all businesses could register and LOCOG placed most of its contract opportunities. We would put our contracts online wherever feasible. The only exceptions were where confidentiality was paramount, for example what we were buying for the ceremonies, and where certain Sports Federations stipulated which suppliers we needed to use for certain equipment such as basketballs and shuttlecocks.[4] As part of the outreach, again, akin to the recruitment outreach plans, we targeted small and medium sized enterprises (SMEs) and minority-owned businesses with multiple events and presentations all around the country. All of these events were held at minimal cost to LOCOG through engaging our partners and arranging value in kind; provision of facilities and refreshments and so forth.

With no existing roster, LOCOG attracted interest from diverse suppliers, minority-owned businesses and other SMEs via the CompeteFor 'dating website'. We tried hard to reach out to SMEs and to offer advice, signposting and heads-up on contracts coming down the line. As with recruitment, we targeted certain sectors such as catering, cleaning, waste, Ceremonies (with the potential for many small and specialised contracts) and security. We shared and promoted case studies and placed key messages in Seb and Paul's speeches to encourage more small businesses to apply.

We worked with Minority Supplier Development UK, East London Business Association, East London Business Partnership, the Federation of Small Businesses and Business Link to give advance notice of contracts with the evaluation criteria stated upfront. We also placed advance notice in the 'Nations and Regions' bulletins that went to small businesses all around the UK. We used the Community Relations team networks. This continued our policy of reinforcing existing infrastructure rather than creating new initiatives. The only new infrastructure we created was a quarterly meeting with those partners that requested it, such as those detailed above, followed by monthly email updates.

Most companies and organisations draw their suppliers from a limited pool. This is analogous to recruitment, which often views diversity as the antithesis of talent. This is again because the supply of skills required is perceived as limited and the demand for capacities is generally risk averse and biased, based on established networks and previous experience. We monitored the number of opportunities we were placing online and the diversity of organisations registered, to form our benchmark. Over 350 opportunities were placed which received more than 16,000 responses from prospective suppliers interested in bidding for a LOCOG contract.

We wanted to improve business relations with our stakeholders by minimising the amount of paperwork required, which was actually a barrier to small businesses in particular. I will never forget the front page of the *Hackney Gazette*, hardly a hard-nosed capitalist read, which lambasted well-intentioned 101 'equality policies' for creating onerous burdens on the very people they were supposed to be helping. Small businesses did not have a diversity team or even person who could take the time to jump through all the hoops and tick all the boxes. Perversely, large organisations did. We produced an easy-to-understand summary of our Terms and Conditions and only asked bidders a question once. By being light touch, less bureaucratic and more entrepreneurial, we saved time and costs – and were helping small and minority-owned businesses.

Ever more transparency and opportunity

The second objective was to push the policy down the supply chain, to act as a catalyst for greater change. We wanted to encourage organisations to whom we had awarded contracts to promote their subcontracts to an equally diverse range of suppliers by placing them back on the CompeteFor website. This was particularly valuable for smaller bidders who may not have the capacity to gain a Tier 1 contract but may be well suited to a sub-contract at Tier 2 or even Tier 3 Level from an already registered official supplier to the Games. Again, we tracked the uptake and usage of Compete-For by our suppliers and chased those who did not play by the rules.

Raise your game

Our third objective was to improve the performance of our contractors with regard to Diversity and Inclusion. There were two items here. One was the letter of the contract, for example requiring a dedicated point of contact accountable for inclusion within their organisation whom we could follow up with. More significant was the spirit of the relationship, above and beyond contract, that came not from compliance but from positioning this as free consultancy. Every single bidder, let alone successful contractor, who responded to a LOCOG opportunity, was challenged to think about their own performance in terms of Diversity and Inclusion. A number of suppliers chose to complete the online assessment anyway (see below), regardless of whether they won the contract or not. This demonstrated to us the potential of our stance and the validity of our mission, to use the power of the Games to inspire lasting change.

In many cases, this was about inspiring them to do more. To get them to go 'beyond the contract' we used our vision to motivate them to change; actionable inspiration. This was reinforced at the LOCOG Supplier Conference, see below. We also made materials available in a variety of alternative formats or languages as required. Basically, we agreed to remove any barrier we could and to try any sensible suggestion put forward for streamlining the process. The Commission for a Sustainable London 2012 remarked, 'The Diversity and Inclusion Business Charter represents a bold and potentially groundbreaking attempt to tackle the issue of diversity in the supply chain'.[5]

Demand-side leadership: Diversity Works

Our key approach on the demand side was the Diversity Works programme. This was about improving standards of Diversity and Inclusion practice within ourselves, our Tier One suppliers and then throughout their own supply chains. This was about improving reputation, increasing customer and stakeholder relations and minimising risk.

Diversity Works for London (DWFL) was a programme established under Mayor Ken Livingstone and continued (although less enthusiastically at first) under Mayor Boris Johnson. The aim was to promote the benefits of diversity within business. As with the Equality Standard for Sport, this scheme has been in existence for some time but was languishing. No company had yet completed all the assessments and achieved the Gold standard. That was a reflection both on the scheme and on business. In 2009, LOCOG became the first organisation to achieve the Gold Standard. The rationale was again similar to the Equality Standard for Sport. If we wanted to effect change in a sector (in this case business, rather than sports governing bodies) we had to lead from the front. Any request or mandate from us to complete this assessment would be more credible if we had already achieved it ourselves.

We therefore used the Gold standard to influence the supply chain as much as we could in the time we had available. It was a good fit with our approach of simple, free of charge and measurable interventions. We required all organisations awarded a contract to complete the free online assessment and supply results within 30 days of contract signature. This was mandatory. What was optional, but encouraged, was then to progress to Gold level by Games time. We relied on the London Development Agency (LDA) to be the lead on this. In effect, we acted as the front-end marketing agent, they were the ongoing accreditation organisation. It fitted with our approach to non-profit organisations, which was to say 'what can we do in the time we have to help you when we are gone?'

We developed a joint monitoring system with LDA such that we could track which of our suppliers had and had not completed the assessment. Laggards could be chased with a series of escalating letters from the friendly, to the final ones from our Chief Executive threatening legal action on the basis of breach of contract.

360 degree inclusion

We incorporated Diversity and Inclusion at all stages of the tender process. At the CompeteFor stage every organisation was checked for a basic equal opportunities policy before it could proceed any further. At pre-qualification stage there were a set of seven mandatory questions. At tender stage there were an additional set of seven questions where it was relevant (waived for small businesses where it would be a barrier to entry). Finally, at contract stage every contract issued included a stipulation about completing the DWFL assessment within 30 days and reporting results, with encouragement to go for Gold by 2012.

What was the overall objective here? Value for money. How did we define value for money? Via our Procurement Governance Model – see Figure 11.1. To govern all the above we developed an integrated programme management model and redefined value for money in procurement. In so doing we created a new norm in procurement. In summer 2010, the Chartered Institute of Purchasing and Supply (CIPS) came in to provide a rigorous, independent assessment of our Procurement function and how it operated within LOCOG as a whole. Not only did LOCOG reach the 'standard of excellence' by achieving CIPS Certification, but our policies, procedures and approach around Diversity and Inclusion were commended as best-in-class. So much so that CIPS has taken on our Business Charter as an example of best practice that its other corporate members should strive to achieve. Again, this was not an end in itself, but all about building momentum and credibility in our processes, leading by example, and encouraging others to follow suit.

It was important that we adopted a clear and concise framework, easily understood by all involved. We wanted procurement practices that were robust while also fair, transparent and encouraging of open competition, rather than backroom deals. To that end, we agreed on the Procurement Governance Model (PGM).[6] This was a process followed for all deals led by the procurement team, typically those above £20k. Diversity and Inclusion was embedded in the definition of value for money. In practice, this meant that Tom from the Diversity and Inclusion team was involved from the start feeding in requirements and flagging any risks or opportunities related to Diversity and Inclusion. To reduce work for the procurement team we partnered with Sustainability, Financial due diligence, Legal and Health and Safety to form one evaluation group, the LOCOG Evaluation Group, or LEG. This avoided one-to-one decision-making and dubious

FIGURE 11.1 Procurement governance model

LOCOG Procurement Governance Model

How LOCOG defines value for money	Kick-Off Project	Gather Info	Develop Strategy	Source Supplier	Mobilise Contract
Quality/Delivery/Disposal					
Commercial					
Sustainability					
Diversity and Inclusion					
Legal/Financial/Health and Safety					

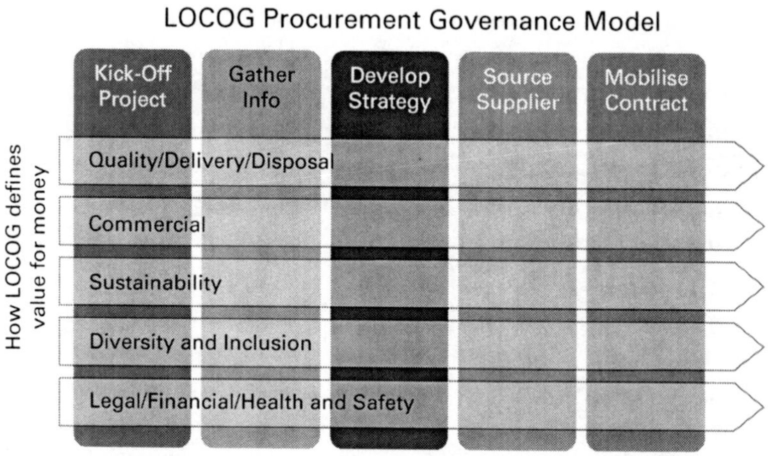

Developed by Laurie Neville and the Procurement team, including Richard Mould and Gerry Walsh

deals. Tom was part of the LEG and the PGM ensured that suppliers who offered LOCOG best value for money (based on all of the above criteria) won the contract.

Treating Diversity and Inclusion as a core part of the definition of value for money meant it was an assessment criteria at every step of the procurement journey, from kick-off project, through information gathering, strategy development to supplier sourcing and final contract mobilisation. These five stages comprised the full life cycle of procurement from identifying the need through to advertising the opportunity, tender process and eventual award. By Diversity and Inclusion being in there from the start it was an integral part of the process and we could avoid being 'the auditor' at the back end of the process and creating additional work for a procurement manager (if they would then even consider it) when they had already completed the majority of the process.

How the process worked

At kick-off project stage Tom would offer an early input of risks, issues and opportunities and identify relevant stakeholders that could help. One example would be interpretation services where we linked-in several deaf organisations to create innovative economies of scale in sign language provision.

At gather information stage, Diversity and Inclusion would support in drafting the specification so that all LEG requirements were satisfied in one document. Again, this was Diversity and Inclusion inputting into the existing system rather than creating an additional sign-off sheet. We ensured that specifications of the tender were inclusive to all. For example, we wanted to ensure the volunteer recruitment centre was accessible to facilitate easy logistics with regard to interviewing thousands of disabled people. This is the example I used in a speech in Toronto to demonstrate what we mean by value for money that caused the *Daily Mail* to claim we were wasting money (see note 7, page 162).

We would suggest additional questions that might be necessary at the next stage and then participate in evaluation at source supplier stage. One major bus and coach supplier, with the best financials of all the bids, initially point blank refused to complete the diversity questions. When they realised they were going to miss out on a major contract we finally had a meeting with their Country Chief Executive. Following civil dialogue they then understood our argument and changed their policies, which cost them nothing. Finally, the monitoring and benchmarking would come into play at the final mobilise contract stage, such as the Diversity Works (DWFL) self-assessment.[7]

Every tender was assessed in terms of Red, Amber, Green and no tender could be successful without achieving green status in Diversity and Inclusion. This simple RAG system allowed us all to talk the same language, and offered the right of veto in extreme cases.[8] Many contractors were initially red or amber and had to change their policies and improve in order to achieve green status and win a LOCOG contract. This was absolutely in line with our vision of using the power of the Games to inspire change. The colour was not necessarily an inhibitor – the real inhibitor to a contract was unwillingness to improve.

We maintained momentum through increasing engagement with contractors and profiling case studies constantly in a 'contractors corner' of our website and CompeteFor. We maintained an open door policy between Diversity and Inclusion and procurement to discuss anything at any time. We discussed measurement on a regular basis – as part of the procurement process, Diversity and Inclusion data across the seven strands was provided by contractors via an extranet at various phases prior to and after Games time. The PGM applied a rigorous project management approach to sourcing goods and services and it was important that the standards were seen as higher/more rigorous than standard procurement and that Diversity and Inclusion was an integral part of it. We were associating Diversity and

Inclusion with an improved system, not a worse one. A guiding principle for us was to reconcile commercial and Diversity and Inclusion objectives – all our policies imposed not one penny of additional cost on the contractor but did achieve significant added social value.

In January 2012 we brought our suppliers together and challenged them to articulate how they would achieve a legacy. The LOCOG Supplier Conference took place on 12 January 2012 at the Grosvenor House Hotel, London. It was attended by over 400 top executives, from sponsors and Games-time suppliers and from family-run SMEs through to large multinationals.

The 'ask' was for the big guys to do stuff they wouldn't otherwise do – to go for Gold on DWFL, to copy our monitoring system for their own internal processes, to adopt the business charter for themselves and to promote Diversity and Inclusion to their own contractors. Several of them voluntarily began the journey to Gold level and several achieved it by Games time, such as BT, Sodexo and Aramark.

The 'ask' for the little guys was to promote their slice of the pie and act as role models for other SMEs. They too could adopt the business charter. They too could improve their own Diversity and Inclusion performance. They too could take on board our work in the area of transparency to create untold new and innovative opportunities.

Takeaways – procurement

1 Understanding was developed and shared through our Business Charter. Supply-side outreach was critical in sourcing diverse suppliers who could compete and help lower costs, bring new innovative ideas and gain a slice of the Olympic pie in the process. Transparency and supplier diversity were positively correlated.

2 Leadership was promulgated through the Diversity Works (DWFL) Gold Standard programme. Demand-side education and consciousness was half the battle. By understanding that we were not seeking to lower standards, impose costs or otherwise harm the procurement function, procurement managers were encouraged to seek out new diverse suppliers to enhance the Games.

3 Delivery and monitoring was achieved through the Procurement Governance Model (PGM). The PGM focused on generating value for money, which we redefined to include diversity and inclusion.

Notes

1 BBC News Bangladesh garment factory [online] http://bbc.co.uk/news/world-asia-22476774.

2 This is a phrase frequently attributed to the British rower Ben Hunt-Davies.

3 See Figure 4.1 in Chapter 4.

4 In some cases, a sponsor had exclusive supply rights as part of a larger sponsorship deal.

5 Commission for a Sustainable London 2012 Annual Report, 2010.

6 Developed largely by Laurie Neville and LOCOG colleagues.

7 We failed here in not having more enforcement mechanisms because it did rely on good faith, which was sometimes lacking in the real hardcore anti-diversity suppliers who were the ones we really wanted to affect change in. See also Failures section in Chapter 25, p 292–93.

8 See Appendix, p 318.

Service delivery

12

The most complex intervention was service delivery; influencing upwards of 57 different departments (it varied over time) from catering to transport to the Torch Relay team. The challenge was to deliver inclusive Games services, accounting for all strands of diversity. There was little precedent I was aware of. There were also multiple portfolios, agendas and operating styles. There were at most two available Diversity and Inclusion staff to support these teams. How to inculcate Diversity and Inclusion within and across all functional areas to deliver inclusive service to our nine client groups? And how to do this at no additional cost, or even cost reduction?

The Diversity and Inclusion team was unorthodox and occasionally eccentric. They acted as internal consultants rather than auditors, with the offer of 'how can I help?' rather than issuing compliance edicts along the lines of 'you need to…'. We laid down the challenge to each department to submit a proposed project, attain some budget protection, deliver a groundbreaking legacy and make history. We proceeded in three stages.

In the beginning

To begin, every functional area was interviewed and consulted in order to determine their basic compliance requirements. We had to start from the basics, to ensure that everyone in venues was aware of the accessibility guidelines, building codes and so forth. We had to check that everyone in Catering was aware we were holding the Games during Ramadan and therefore needed to account not simply for different food types but also time of service to allow for post-fast late-night eating. This was the least palatable part of the conversation because it was toward the auditing end of the spectrum and against our overall philosophy. It was, however, essential, and in a few cases we did avert some potential embarrassments at an early stage.

Structuring the conversation

The more interesting second stage was to challenge functional areas as to how their service delivery could be strengthened through Diversity and Inclusion. This was more akin to our overall approach, positioning Diversity and Inclusion as a positive, value-adding programme, rather than a burden. We worked at successive meetings when asked to do so by the functional area in order to come up with some exciting ideas. The most compelling was the Volunteer programme, where a diverse workforce would undoubtedly strengthen the operational impact of the team, such as having a wider set of language skills and more confidence in dealing with the diversity of the London and global customer base. Or, perhaps more surprisingly, in venues, where several venue managers saw early accessibility provision as being in the interests of last-minute operational flexibility. Often the people lobbying for wider entrances, shallower ramps and the like were not the Diversity and Inclusion team and our access manager but the operational venues guys.

Show me the money

The most tangible third stage, however, was our request of functional areas to propose 'inclusive projects', those where they could excel and tangibly demonstrate what could be achieved with forethought, imagination and commitment. This was important, not only because they knew their business better than we ever would do, but also to get the functional areas to do the work, so that they owned the solution, rather than it being imposed on them. This was appealing to the good wolf, the 'what can you do to better the human condition' calling that is asked so rarely in professional life, but when it is it can evoke a amazing response. We also appealed to ego, the idea that this was a once in a lifetime opportunity and what did they want their legacy to be? Did they want to stage a ceremony, or did they want to stage a ceremony that would lift people and stand out with real meaning? Did they want to procure uniforms, or did they want to procure uniforms that would work for every shape, size, religion and person imaginable? Did they want to make their mark on Everyone's 2012. Could they make this work for everyone?

There was undoubtedly a lot of goodwill and leadership brought to the fore in these processes. It would be disingenuous, however, to suggest they were the only forces at play. It was well understood that this Diversity and Inclusion programme was now going places, with a real momentum and buy-in from all levels of the organisation. It was likeable, rather than threatening, and people wanted to be associated with it. All the more so if it didn't threaten their budget – and even more so still if it could actually help safeguard their budget.

People were conscious of the seemingly never-ending rounds of cost reductions. The regular budgeting cycle was feared by many and anything they could do to safeguard their own budget and protect their patch was welcome. By coming up with an 'Everyone's 2012' project which brought us onside and attracted allies outside their own functional area, including the Chief Executive who had oversight of these projects thanks to the Diversity Board, they stood a better chance of having their budget maintained in order to fulfil their project promise. This should not be overstated, but I know from several conversations that it was true for several of the projects;

TABLE 12.1 Everyone's 2012 inclusive work streams

Paid workforce	Ticketing
Volunteer workforce	Arrivals and departures
Contractor workforce	Security and screening
Uniforms	Catering
Procurement programme	Games Mobility and transport
LOCOG Overlay Access File	Event Services
Ceremonies, Torch Relay	OGKM (Olympic Games Knowledge Management)
Education Programme	Sports presentation
Cultural Olympiad	Southbank/PIE (Paralympic Inclusive Environment)
Website	Athlete guide
Equality Standard for sport	Live Sites

Each project had a point of accountability in the D&I team, in the Functional Area and they jointly reported every month again, it reinforced our approach that we were commercially savvy and operationally respectful.

In the end there were 97 projects submitted, far more than we had ever imagined. Using two bright interns, Ben and Garima, we applied basic cost benefit analysis in terms of cost, impact, legacy potential and likelihood of success. We compiled a shortlist of 22 projects, which we determined, given the limited resources of the Diversity and Inclusion team, we could just about support (See Table 12.1). We were mindful to cover all aspects of the project, from people to procurement to high-profile events such as the ceremonies and sports presentation, to logistical but essential projects such as arrivals and departures and uniforms. The most effective Everyone's 2012 projects, such as the Torch Relay, are detailed in Part Three.

How we tracked and managed the projects

Each project had a point of accountability in the functional area concerned as well as in the Diversity and Inclusion team. Both were accountable for the progression of that project. The two colleagues formed a close working relationship, evidenced through the regular meetings, pizza takeaway late-night working sessions, exchanging of mobile phone numbers, and simply the understanding that they could ask anything anytime. Getting the functional area to lead and take pride in the project was reciprocated by us showing empathy for their operational constraints. As ever, the question was *how can we help?*

The project team would produce regular updates using an analytical communication tool we jointly created. It was a simple monthly one-pager with basic information from current status (red/amber/green), current challenges, next steps to media headlines that could be shared with the communications team. These one-pagers (22 in total) formed part of the monthly Diversity and Inclusion report that went to the Chief Executive, Directors and Diversity Board, as well as the fact sheets that went to the Press Office. This was our principal information-sharing method and it helped maintain oversight and momentum.[1]

Momentum was maintained by the deadline, the drumbeat, and the days to go. It was maintained by the idea of legacy now – ask what you can do. It was also encouraged by the recognition efforts of our Diversity Board with regular awards and commendations communicated out to the wider team.

We therefore ended up with 22 Everyone's 2012 projects, designed to break new ground in terms of the way they include people, from the Torch Relay to the food we serve at Games time accounting for Ramadan through opening hours, food type and even 'Ramadan packs' for our fasting workforce.

With understanding of the issues, empowered leadership at all levels and a culture of delivery people had the conceptual framework for what we wanted to do. With clarity over the interventions that would make the most impact in the most efficient and effective way (workforce, procurement and service delivery) they knew where we wanted to do it. With all of these processes reinforcing each other and being iterative, constantly monitored and constantly improved, we were ready to do the best work of our lives. Let the Games begin.

Takeaways – service delivery

1 The method was business led, rather than departmental led by the Diversity and Inclusion team, activating people's own natural, human and personal desire for legacy. The question constantly addressed across all individuals and departments was 'does it make the Games better?'

2 The Diversity and Inclusion team acted as internal consultants, connecting different departments and ideas and creating resources and real value for colleagues. The question posed was always 'How can I help?', the goal to find resources for teams under pressure and become the 'go-to' people who could help get things done.

3 The resulting 'Everyone's 2012 projects' were monitored monthly. These high-frequency Red/Amber/Green reports were pithy, succinct but subject to peer review and maintained the momentum of inclusive delivery.

Note

1 Example in Appendix, p 315.

PART THREE
Talent

Introduction to Part Three

What real inclusion looks like

From courage, originating in Ancient Greece, to creativity, originating in the Age of Enlightenment, the third key ingredient in creating real inclusion, is talent. Talent, the most modern of concepts, is herein redefined as 'skill' combined with positive attitude and aspiration, rather than merely 'educational attainment' or other traditional definitions of merit. This is not simply to reflect the thousands of people without traditional qualifications who delivered brilliant work at London 2012, it is also a nod to the future. Talent comes in many guises and capturing that diversity is not simply an ethical concern, it is a very practical requirement in connecting the organisation to the world outside.

We are educating our children for jobs that do not yet exist. By the time a student undertaking a four-year technical degree now reaches graduation, the material they learnt in their first two years will be obsolete.[1] How can we sustain a traditional definition of talent when the world requires us to be far more discerning? This chapter showcases what modern diverse talent looks like and demonstrates how this cohort created the game-changing 'Everyone's 2012' projects that follow.

Don't get me wrong; I am as guilty of cynicism as the next person. When we witness bad behaviour, or see downright malice, it can be hard to see the 'talent' in an individual. I never forget one of my early school friends sharing his school report with me. He was naughtier than I was and the teacher had written in his report 'the wheel is turning, but the hamster is dead'. Many HR directors still believe talent and diversity are diametrically opposed, that in order to achieve 'diversity' one has to compromise on talent. To be clear, talent is not separate from diversity, but the product of diversity.[2]

Our 'results' were published on an ongoing basis, every month, and distributed to all directors and heads of department as well as the Diversity

Board and others. The purpose of this information sharing was to inspire further success, encourage people to overcome challenges and to maintain the constant drumbeat of progress and momentum. Paul Deighton was fond of saying that it was impossible to over-communicate. Our reporting covered all 22 Everyone's 2012 projects and focused on the three main interventions: workforce; procurement; and service delivery.

Every month, the workforce report would include a breakdown of numbers relating to the diversity of the current paid workforce but also numbers relating to each stage of the recruitment cycle; applications, interviews, job offers and offers accepted. These were further broken down by strand and by department. This allowed the benchmarking so crucial to encouraging competition between departments and among the Champions. As well as diversity measures it also included the latest inclusion measures, as determined by our YourSay survey. We also included the data for volunteering as the programme ramped up.

The procurement report would assess the diversity status of each supplier. We would know whether they had completed the Diversity Works (DWFL) assessment and implemented a Guaranteed Interview Scheme for disabled people. This information came from our partners at the Greater London Authority and in government. We had undertaken the front-end marketing for them, they supplied the data to track progress. It was resource light for LOCOG, as we were providing a mutually beneficial service to the public sector. The report also measured the distribution of contracts by sector (small businesses) and minority ownership (supplier diversity).

The service delivery report identified the successes and challenges for each of the 22 projects using a simple red, amber, green system, to evaluate the risks and issues. It allowed any of the directors to see at a glance whether we were on track not just to stage a brilliant Games from a technical point of view, but whether it was going to be 'Everyone's 2012' too. We later included National Governing Body progress in the Equality Standard for Sport.

It should be stressed that these reports were light. They were as succinct as possible, not only to help people with limited time to digest complex information, but also to reinforce the point that Diversity and Inclusion at LOCOG were commercial, smart and value adding, rather than bureaucratic, burdensome and costly. The Executive summary could be read in less than two minutes, and most people therefore read it.

In some ways, the results that now follow have been achieved against the odds. Jean Tomlin, a minority herself, had worked over 30 years in FTSE 100 companies and stated 'it has been truly heart-warming to be part of an organisation that despite each and every one of us having our own personal views has embraced Diversity and Inclusion in the receptive and open way that it has'.

Talent really does come in a variety of guises. It was a privilege to work with an array of superstars of all levels, shapes and sizes. The following pages show the results of that diverse talent, and speak to the potential of people set free to achieve in an inclusive environment.

Notes

1 Did you know? Video [online] http://www.youtube.com/watch?v=YmwwrGv_aiE
2 Scott Page, *The Difference* (Princeton University Press, 2007).

200,000 people: the workforce story

13

There were two headline-grabbing people stories from the Games. One was negative, concerning the people that never showed, after security firm G4S failed to deliver on its contractual commitments and we drafted in the military to man security checkpoints. The other was profoundly positive, about the diversity and welcome offered to people by the 200,000 Games Makers. This was a bigger story in the end.

This is the story of how we influenced the recruitment of 200,000 people, lowered recruitment costs, saved time and ended up with the most diverse workforce ever assembled for any Olympic or Paralympic Games. Above all, it demonstrates how we did not face a trade-off between 'diversity' and 'talent'.

We achieved or surpassed all our target zones across inclusion in the paid workforce – race (40 per cent black, asian or minority ethnic), gender (46 per cent female) and gender identity (trans staff included), disability (9 per cent deaf, disabled or having a long-term health condition), sexual orientation (5 per cent declared lesbian, gay or bisexual), age (36 per cent under 30 and 15 per cent over 50 with ranges from 16–79) and belief (all major faiths represented). Of the people we hired 36 per cent were previously unemployed and 23 per cent came from the poorest boroughs in East London.

Previous Games, and most companies and organisations, draw their talent from a limited talent pool. This is because the supply of skills required is perceived as limited and the demand for talent is biased based on networks and previous experience. The recruitment achievements of LOCOG therefore need to be viewed in that context. For LOCOG to match, and then exceed, the diversity of the generic labour market is game-changing when our recruitment is in many ways more specialised.

It was not only about diversity. It was about how we included that diversity. Whether it be adapted vehicles for disabled drivers, late hours food options for Muslims observing Ramadan or inclusive and flexible uniforms, people felt included. Above and beyond the numbers, we created a truly inclusive working environment. There will always be naysayers and individuals who are more comfortable with a less diverse environment but on the whole our approach generated widespread support that enabled us to deliver some groundbreaking results against our stated target zones.

Stories are the best results we can offer. One that stays with me still is that told to me by a straight, white male venue manager who had loved his team and frankly acknowledged that he 'would never have met people like that' in his previous or next intended professional setting. He wouldn't have talked to them in the street or a bar, let alone work with them. They weren't 'his kind of people' but they became his beloved team.

Female leadership

Our overall target zone (not quota) for women, as established by the then Mayor Ken Livingstone in 2007, was 46–54 per cent female across the board. We achieved 46 per cent female representation including some high-profile female leadership within the organisation, such as Debbie Jevans, the first female sports director of any Summer Olympic Games.

Of the 12 original directors, five were female (42 per cent). The Directors of Human Resources, Communications and Public Affairs, Sport, Strategic Programmes and the General Counsel were all women. These were five of the most high-profile positions in the organisation.

When Tutu delivered his speech in February 2010, there was a photograph taken with the heads of department showing 12 female heads of department out of 46 in the picture (26 per cent). This figure almost doubled across the organisation in the subsequent two-year period.

Craig Beaumont, a highly competent Government Relations Manager, worked for a female Head of Government Relations, who in turn worked for the female Communications Director. He commented 'it's important to me that LOCOG embraces diversity in all its forms, and it's great to work in an organisation where women hold most of the senior posts'.[1] Given the personalities he was working for, it was entirely understandable that the perception around the organisation was that this was in some ways a female-dominated environment. The high-profile jobs did seem to be controlled by women and they set the tone. The massive recruitment programme, the legal department, the sport itself, the strategy of the organisation, and our communications-led behaviour, were all controlled by women.

We produced a gender pin badge that also included transgender people (See Appendix fig A.4). There was some confusion when Jean Tomlin, LOCOG HR Director and Hugh Robertson, the Conservative Party Sports Minister, launched the pin at the European Women in Sport event in Olympic Park. I wasn't there at the time but I think they understood the arrow sign being for the man, the cross sign representing the women, but were unsure as to what the mixed one was.

Not all results were great, however, and indeed there were some lost opportunities. I will never forget the elderly male International Olympic Committee Member who patted a female LOCOG director on the bottom at the penultimate Coordination Commission. Rather than react professionally and promptly, she accepted it, much to my disapproval. Anyone who has worked with the Federation Internationale de Volleyball (FIVB) could be forgiven for thinking they had entered the 1980s. The board (94 per cent male, 29 out of 31 members) reluctantly allowed more modest 'uniform' sizes for the female players in March 2012 in the run up to London when it was clear that there would be a more diverse set of countries taking part.[2] Until this time the board had overseen the previous policy that was for women to wear either a one-piece bathing suit or a bikini with a maximum side width of 7cm.

Most of these antiquated gender failures were outside the remit of the Organising Committee. So too, arguably, was its own board, being a series of political appointees. Murziline Parchment was one of two female board members who lost her seat when Ken Livingstone was replaced as mayor by Boris Johnson, the new mayor appointing a man. It was noteworthy from this point on that at every meeting the only female in the room, besides Terry Miller, General Counsel and Secretary to the Board, was Princess Anne. We resigned ourselves to fighting other battles. As Paul Deighton had said to me 'judge me on what's within my control'. And to be fair to him, his Director team was and there were five forceful women on it.

The board aside, LOCOG's performance in gender equality was exemplary. We conducted gender pay audits, had flexible working policies, women gave equal or above equal inclusion feedback scores from the internal survey, and we hosted several events, such as the European Women in Sport conference. In short, we acted as a role model for how others might wish to behave. We were not, however, in existence long enough for us to change the predominantly chauvinistic culture evident in many of the International Sport Federations and offshoots of the Olympic Family.

Real ethnic minority inclusion

Our overall target zone for ethnic minority inclusion was 18–29 per cent and we smashed it, achieving 40 per cent ethnic minority representation among our paid staff[3]. High-profile hires included Charlie Wijeratna, our Commercial Negotiations Director and Jean Tomlin, our HR Director.

The Black, Asian and Minority Ethnic (BAME) group had played a key role in this, acting as internal champions of BAME inclusion and mentoring many prospective candidates. The BAME pin badge was produced and the group supported LOCOG hosting the Professional Footballers Association Black List Awards in 2011, the year before the Games. The >action on inclusion programme had worked, and it came into its own in the final few months of operations. We were trailing at just behind the lower limit of our target zone until the last few months when a full talent pool was reapplying for many new jobs being advertised and the success rate of these pre-screened people with experience increased significantly.

This level of inclusion was particularly gratifying because sports management in many places is such a white world. The stars of basketball, football and track and field are often black but the management remains white. When I took on our first interns from the Local Borough of Tower Hamlets, Abdul and Kohinur, it took a long time for them to open up and tell me their thoughts. They considered LOCOG to be a white place, full of West London folks who never left the spaceship that was Canary Wharf (our offices). To some extent that was true. There was a main route, the A1261 running just north of the offices and it acted as a Berlin Wall between the local population and us. People didn't know where our front door was, let alone how to get a job here. That wall took a few years to knock down, and we completely toppled it in 2012.

Early on, some directors, including the ones who had asked me to 'keep them honest', tried to persuade me that we could 'make our numbers' when we hired security contractors, that when the large, comparatively low-paid contracts came on stream we would hit our targets. I explained that we were in the business of using the power of the Games to create change, not reinforcing existing paradigms and stereotypes. We had BAME people at all levels of the organisation.

Unprecedented inclusion of disabled people

Our overall target zone for disabled people was 3–6 per cent and we achieved 9 per cent. The YourSay scores, initially below average ended up bang-on. In contrast, the Vancouver Organising Committee (VANOC) had the intention of '10 per cent by 2010' and employing 1 in 10 disabled people to stage the 2010 Winter Olympic Games. However they ended up with less than 1 per cent.

This happened to VANOC because there was no real Diversity and Inclusion programme with accountabilities. There was some understanding of what disability was and how to confidently interact with disabled people. There was some leadership on the issue with VANOC colleagues I met and knew being very supportive of disability inclusion. But there was no delivery mechanism, no process and no accountabilities. What gets measured gets done, and conversely the lack of delivery mechanisms for disability inclusion in Vancouver resulted in very few disabled people being employed there.

We were determined to be different, and an early start was imperative. Only two months into the Diversity and Inclusion programme, we launched our first recruitment outreach programme, >access now. The method is discussed above in Chapter 10 but the important thing is that it worked. Thousands of talented disabled people, understandably sceptical about employer platitudes, applied to work for LOCOG. The key element of the >access now programme, which convinced the sceptics more than anything else, was the guaranteed interview if they met the minimum criteria. This promise was enough to convince talented disabled people to spend the time and effort applying to us as they could guarantee that all-important first foot in the door. The guaranteed interview scheme had never been undertaken in a Games before. We followed it up with the talent pool, again discussed above.

The key element to successful disabled inclusion in the Games Maker volunteer programme was the early start. Disabled people could apply from 27 July 2011, in advance of 15 September, the date for everyone else. Like with the guaranteed interview scheme (GIS) in paid recruitment, it sent that all-important signal of seriousness of intent to our target group. Beyond marketing or literature or platitudes, it said quite clearly that we were serious about hiring disabled people. I worked with Stephen Duckworth, a board member at the Olympic Delivery Authority, and we pooled thinking to further the work. One thing was attraction, and that was working, but the other was retention. What would happen if all these disabled people were successful in gaining positions and then had their expectations let down by a terrible inaccessible work experience? We had to not only prepare LOCOG to be accommodating but moreover prepare the candidates for their own need to adapt.

We launched the disability pin badge in March 2011. This had been designed by our deaf and disabled network and so was authentic. It was very tactile with raised surfaces and lots of people seemed to like it. Beyond the stories and pin badges, we were thrilled to be included as the only positive disability story in the US State Department's Human Rights report 2012.

LGBT people

Against a target zone of 5–7 per cent, 5 per cent of colleagues identified as lesbian, gay or bisexual. Given the still homophobic nature of much of the sports management world, we were especially pleased to create a culture where staff could be open about their sexuality if they so wished. It is clear from research that people perform better when they can be themselves and there is a clear correlation in the staff survey between people feeling able to be out and their overall happiness and productivity in the LOCOG workplace. LGBT people were above average in their engagement scores consistently from 2009 onwards.

The launch of the 'pride pin' caused disquiet in some parts of the Communications team (Appendix fig A.1). Our LGBT group had come up with a simple, beautiful design of the 2012 logo and a Pride rainbow flag representing LGBT inclusion. There was concern we would be seen as 'activist'. There was concern in the International Olympic Committee that we were allying the brand with a political movement, prohibited under the International Olympic Committee Charter. But what was really going on was a general unease about associating with 'gay rights' or something seen as too radical for the conservative world of sport. Plus, it coincided with our Mascot Launch film *Over a Rainbow*. They would understandably be nervous about any potential confusion between rainbow-originating Mascots and gay pride pin badges. The mascots were diverse enough without being gay pride dolls to boot.[4]

Our Communications team initially vetoed the LOCOG pride pin but the internal lobbying of our LGBT staff group, plus partnering with the Deputy Mayor and other stakeholders, made it happen. Ditto with participation in London World Pride. A middle-ranking programme manager Craig Jones, in particular, acted way above his pay grade and inspired others through his determination to see this delivered.

The production of the pin badge was therefore a great result for all those who saw countering homophobia in sport not as a radical agenda, but as a long-overdue requirement. It was also one of the best-selling badges. The badge was well received in almost all media quarters and we received some amazing letters from LGBT people (and straight people) all around the world thanking London 2012 for taking a stand for gay inclusion. This was particularly amazing to see from Russia, Nigeria and even the Middle East. This was a first for the Olympics and Paralympics and it worked. It grew the customer market for the Olympic Games and as such was bang-on the mission of saving the Olympic movement by connecting it with otherwise disengaged audiences. The International Paralympic Committee much more readily embraced the pride pin, perhaps because they were hungrier for new fans and audiences.

We worked with the Education team to support their inclusion of anti gay bullying messages being sent out via the Get Set programme network to three-quarters of the schools in the country. We were a founder signatory to the Charter against homophobia and transphobia. I include trans specifically. Jackie Parkin on my team deserves the credit for recruiting the extraordinary woman Delia Johnston. Delia was a brave and inspiring member of the team who taught many others as well as me a great deal about trans issues. Delia 'kept us honest' about trans inclusion, such as with the World Pride preparations. She went through her transition during her time at LOCOG and in her own words 'couldn't have been in a better environment in which to become me'.[5]

Every generation and faith was on the team

LOCOG was a diverse organisation in terms of age: 36 per cent identified as under 30, above our target of 20–30 per cent; 15 per cent of staff identified as over 50. Our oldest employee was 79 and in the Torch Relay our oldest torchbearer was 101 and we had to take out extra insurance.

We launched the age pin in June 2011 (Appendix fig A.3). This celebrated the success of our >attitude over age programme, which had worked. We banned the retirement age (another barrier in need of removal) before it became law to do so. Seb trumpeted our lack of retirement age in several interviews and the Employers Forum on Age awarded us best private sector innovation award in recognition of our results. The Zimmers' experience lives with many of us still.

Every major faith as well as atheism and humanism was represented among LOCOG's people. The Inter Faith group produced a faith pin badge

(Appendix fig A.5). There was a multi-faith centre in operation in the Olympic Village for the five main faiths plus others, which went above and beyond requirements. We had quiet rooms at all venues back of house and quiet spaces front of house and even rooms on park for spectators. Ramadan went well and was celebrated. Duncan Green, a Church of England Minister on the LOCOG books, led on many faith issues for LOCOG and was adept at bringing the different groups together.

The most marginalised and externalised were now on the inside

There were 8,500 residents of the host boroughs working on the Olympic Park and the Village through the Olympic Delivery Authority. Thirty-six per cent of LOCOG's final workforce were previously unemployed (against a target of 7–12 per cent). Our host borough target was 15–20 per cent and after 50 recruitment events across the host boroughs 23.5 per cent of our paid staff came from the six host boroughs.

There were two principal factors at work here besides geographical proximity to the park. On the demand side we had been successful at creating a new norm internally that local people should be part of our organisation.

On the supply side, we had successfully positioned LOCOG as an employer of choice in almost every community in London. Given where we started, that was a fantastic team turnaround. On the supply side, the strength of relationship with the local job brokerage, and their level of competence, is evident. Greenwich had a great brokerage, was very engaged, and contributed 5 per cent of our people. Waltham Forest, for example, was less so, and contributed only half that number. We can only conclude that benchmarking works.

More important than the numbers, however, were the stories.

Alice was a female employee who came through our outreach event for local residents and gained a job as Security Team Administrator. In her own words:

> Before I started at LOCOG I asked myself if I would be capable of being part of such a big event and undertaking such a huge task. I remember standing in the interview assessments room and looking down from the window of the 22nd floor, thinking that I might have the opportunity to be part of the greatest show on earth. I realised how much I wanted to be part of London 2012 and that opportunity that Britain had been given the chance to deliver. After watching

the LOCOG presentation and video clips I saw and understood what made the organisation. It is LOCOG's passion to include and celebrate difference and to engage and embrace individuals from so many different cultures and walks of life. For that one moment I believed I could be part of this equation as one of many of the other candidates in the room. I am so glad I took the plunge and came to one of LOCOG's assessment days.

The Games Makers

Beyond the paid staff, there was the Volunteer programme. There were 240,000 Games Maker applications and we interviewed 86,000 people from February to April 2012. There were nine centres around the UK. Forty per cent said the Games inspired them to volunteer for the first time. In the end 70,000 Games Makers delivered 8 million volunteer hours after 1 million hours of training. The roles varied from welcome desk staff and ticket checkers to costume assistants, drivers and event stewards. We kept the barrier to entry as low as possible; requiring a minimum age of 18 on 1 January 2012, being available to work 10 days and attend 3 days' training. All 70,000 went through Orientation, then venue-specific and then role-specific training that featured inclusion throughout. For example, all 70,000 volunteers were taught the importance of addressing the disabled person and not their 'carer'.

Young Games Makers numbered 2,000 16–18 year olds who worked in 250 teams. LOCOG worked with BP, one of our sponsors, and national youth service 'V' to deliver a Young Leaders Programme for disadvantaged young people. We worked with Sheffield Hallam University to create a Press Operations module for 600 students to be Main Press Centre volunteers. The numbers for the Games Makers in terms of diversity are detailed in Appendix p 315.

The contractor workforce

LOCOG received diversity and inclusion data for all contractors that were major workforce providers. That, in itself, is a result – it allowed each contractor organisation to recognise and own the importance of diversity and inclusion as part of their current and future resourcing strategy. Registration and completion of Diversity Works (DWFL) progressed month on month from 66 per cent in September 2011 to 90 per cent in May 2012. As a direct result of our contractual relationship, over 75 organisations, employing millions of people, have now established a guaranteed interview scheme, creating a paradigm shift in the employment prospects for disabled people.

The workforce inclusion story of the Games is the creation of a team that represented London and welcomed the world, speaking the customers' language and understanding their culture. There was universal praise for our people as the face of the Games. We placed over 2,000 disabled people into roles at Games time, which is a paradigm shift in the inclusion of disabled people. To put that in perspective, the previous Games, Beijing 2008, managed 67 disabled people out of 1 million volunteers and that set a record then.

The numbers overall met or exceeded all our target zones. What they demonstrate is not only that real inclusion is possible but that the environment you create is the critical enabler. There is a pattern and a lesson. Where we had direct control, within LOCOG, the numbers were the most diverse. Where we had less control, in the Games Maker programme, the numbers were less diverse. In the areas of disability and LGBT, perhaps two of the more challenging aspects of diversity to communicate to third parties, we had the lowest incidences among the contractors, over whom we had least control. I cannot prove this but my deep hunch is that this wasn't just about fewer disabled people and fewer lesbian and gay people in third party contractors. It was more that those who were hired didn't feel as comfortable to be themselves because they hadn't lived our internal climate until the last minute. This demonstrates that it doesn't just happen. You have to create the climate for people to be themselves.

Overall, it was still an unprecedented result and the workforce was more than reflective of the customer base that experienced the Games than in any other comparable organisation I know.

Takeaways – the workforce story

1 The numbers speak for themselves. This workforce could have been a skewed representation of London due to the specialised recruitment and multiple other challenges presented. The fact that it looked like London, and in many cases was even more diverse, is testament to people working together to achieve real inclusion.

2 Beyond the numbers, real inclusion is evident in the stories of the men and women who worked on the Games. They demonstrate not

only the infinite diversity of 200,000 people, but also how they all had the same sense of what we were trying to achieve.

3 If the LOCOG team demonstrated anything, it was that talent and diversity are a virtuous circle, not diametrically opposed. This was far beyond Diversity 101 and 2.0; this was real inclusion, which unquestionably made London 2012 Everyone's Games.

Notes

1 Conversation with Craig Beaumont, July 2012.

2 http://www.fivb.org/EN/FIVB/Board_of_Administration.asp.

3 This compares with a UK statistic of about 10 per cent ethnic minority or in London of about 30 per cent. In either case, especially in the context of the zero-sum game issue, it raises a valid question of did we go too far? As we did not use quotas and all selection was merit-based it is hard to say that we proactively did. However, it does beg the question why most companies cannot even manage to attain results at least half-way to the demographic reality in which they operate.

4 See Chapter 15.

5 Conversation with author.

2,700 footballs and 22 tape measures: the procurement story

14

This is the procurement story of the Games. We found some brilliant 'off the wall' talent, saved $150 million and ended up with two-thirds of our contracts going to micro, small and medium businesses providing innovative products many of which we would never otherwise have known about, the Torch and the widely-acclaimed cauldron being two.

LOCOG procured over 1 million pieces of sporting equipment in the end, from 600 basketballs (each one needing to be tested and worn in) to 2,700 footballs, 22 tape measures for Boccia, 356 pairs of boxing gloves – and 150,000 condoms for the athlete's village. LOCOG ended up buying over £1 billion in goods and services in over 650 contracts over eight areas: artists, performance and events, security, services, soft facilities management and catering, sports, technology, transport and logistics and venues and hard facilities management.

The real inclusion results have been twofold. We created significant supplier diversity – there is a set of smaller companies who have gained contracts with London 2012, from Brickwall Films in Hackney and Clarity that employs visually impaired people, to Saffords, a women-owned and managed coach company based in Bedfordshire. We also changed the policies of the larger organisations – there is a set of larger companies who now have more inclusive policies and procedures as a result of working with us. That affects the wider economy.

Giving the innovative little guys a slice of the pie

Our business charter set out three clear principles that created shared value but added not a single penny to the cost of doing business. Transparency resulted in some fantastic innovation. Successful bidders placing subcontracts back into the system opened up smaller contracts for smaller companies with less capacity. And all suppliers of whatever size improved their diversity performance.

The majority of LOCOG's supply chain went online in a publicly available competitive bidding process. Most companies don't even place 1 per cent out to public tender. This allowed maximum competition, drove down costs, drove up quality and innovation – and crucially allowed new entrants, especially small businesses and minority-owned businesses, into the market. Our final procurement costs were $150 million under budget.

As Table 14.1 demonstrates, over two-thirds of LOCOG contracts were awarded to small businesses from every region of the UK. About 20 per cent of our suppliers employed less than 10 people. Ninety per cent of contracts (94 per cent by value) were awarded to UK-based businesses. The Business Network promoted opportunities at events all over the UK. They helped gear up business in legacy, even for those who were ultimately unsuccessful in winning contracts, by improving their Diversity and Inclusion performance. This is evidence that our opportunities were accessible, and that our procurement process enabled all types of organisation to win work with us.

Small businesses that won LOCOG contracts included Brickwall Films, a small East End business formed in 2005, the year LOCOG won the bid. It employed less than 10 people. Based in Hackney one of the six host boroughs, they were awarded a framework contract to produce short thematic films for LOCOG marking special occasions such as the fabulous *Two Years to Go* film (which was produced in Audio Description and subtitled versions too) as well as the excellent ticket films.

Clarity employs 47 registered blind and disabled people, making it a supported business. They supplied LOCOG offices with anti-bacterial hand wash and washing-up liquids after being introduced to a range of opportunities. 'Social Enterprise London were extremely helpful in pointing us in the right direction to these opportunities. The CompeteFor process was simple to use,' said John Stutchfield, Business Development Manager for Clarity. In return, LOCOG supported Clarity in raising their profile in the business community and offering mentoring for further contracts post Games.

TABLE 14.1 Suppliers awarded contracts directly by LOCOG Procurement (as of Aug 2012)

Size of organisation	No. of suppliers	%
Micro (1–9 FTEs)	109	20.6
Small (10–49 FTEs)	143	27.0
Medium (50–249 FTEs)	120	22.6
Large (250+FTEs)	158	29.8
Total:	530	100

Careline delivered the contact centre for disabled or socially excluded people to apply for the Games Maker programme. They adopted LOCOG's monitoring mechanism across all seven strands and continued after the Games every three months. LOCOG introduced Careline to the London employer Accord, tackling joblessness. Charles Cooper-Driver, Chief Executive, said, 'LOCOG has really helped us focus on employing people with disabilities, we have actively reviewed and updated our employment policies accordingly.'

Other small businesses that supplied the Games included Safford's, a small coach business based in Bedfordshire. Established in 1935, it is now wholly owned and run by the wife and daughter of the founder. Aquaclear is a micro business specialising in conservation, environment and habitat management. They delivered the weed removal services in Eton Dorney lake (rowing) and Serpentine in Hyde Park (triathlon swim). Redline buses is an Asian-owned, family-run business in Aylesbury. They supplied buses between the venues.

Within the small business sector, Table 14.2 shows the real supplier diversity achieved. The response rate suggests LOCOG was effective in its outreach with 24 per cent of responses being from women-owned business and there being a significant proportion of responses from BAME-, disabled- and LGBT-owned business too.[1] The capacity constraints of some minority-owned businesses are clear in the fall off from response to short-listing, meaning that they didn't satisfy our core requirements and standards. However the 'awarded' results are groundbreaking. For 15 per cent of our online contracts to go to women-owned businesses is a terrific supplier diversity result.

LOCOG used its massive list of requirements to create supplier diversity. But this was the by-product, not the intention per se. By advertising

TABLE 14.2 Supplier diversity of online contracts

Organisation type[1]	Responded[2]		Shortlisted[2]		Awarded[2]	
	#	%	#	%	#	%
BAME-owned	1,864	12%	885	11%	10	4%
Woman-owned	3,741	24%	1,821	22%	40	15%
Disabled-owned	316	2%	161	2%	8	3%
LGBT-owned	272	2%	145	2%	5	2%

[1] The above data for 'Ownership type' is based upon CompeteFor business profiles
[2] Data is for all LOCOG opportunities published on CompeteFor (up to Feb 2012)

widely, we made use of companies of all sizes, from all backgrounds, and across all parts of the UK in order to stage not only a great Games, but an inclusive Games. Take bus and coach requirements as a case in point. Here, we had a large, complex and high-profile requirement – transport was towards the top of our risk register. We met this challenge by engaging and then contracting with companies from all over the UK, including an Asian-run business from Aylesbury, a female-owned family business and disabled-owned businesses. By reaching out to every nation and region, a diverse range of operators from all over the UK and Ireland have benefited from London 2012 including many small businesses and women, ethnic-minority and disabled-owned organisations. There are many other examples of small businesses who won contracts with LOCOG, who provided innovation and value to the Games, that without our Diversity and Inclusion programme we would not have known about and certainly would not have contracted with.

Raising the bar for the big guys

The second result, in addition to supplier diversity and innovation, is the changed policies and procedures of the larger organisations. I have discussed how becoming the first organisation in the country to achieve the Diversity Works (DWFL) Gold Assessment was part of the method, not a result. Here, we can see the organisations that were contractually obliged to undertake the assessment subsequently. Our use of the DWFL measurement system improved the diversity performance of all suppliers.

In total, 250 suppliers and 71 per cent of UK-based suppliers, completed the online self-assessment toolkit. Many more bidders will have completed the toolkit without us knowing as it was referenced during the LOCOG Procurement process. Examples of large companies who employ many staff who have completed the online self-assessment tool include Agrekko UK Ltd, BBC, Google, Manchester United Football Club, Aramark, Sodexo Ltd, Transport for London and Xerox Business Services. Aramark and Sodexo pledged to go for the Gold Standard during the LOCOG Supplier Conference.

Half-way through our purchasing journey, an Italian gymnastics provider was refusing to provide us some basic information on their gender statistics. Finally, they called the press office to suggest our whole policy was a joke. The press officer who took the call later told me that in response to the gender question, the Italian male on the phone became very animated and told him that they 'had lots of beautiful women on the team', and with that slammed the phone down. In the end they did come on board with our reasonable requests, but this was the first time they had ever been challenged to talk about their diversity as a company.

LOCOG's policies and procedures for Diversity and Inclusion were viewed as above and beyond what was required by the Chartered Institute of Purchasing and Supply (CIPS) in their normal assessments of organisations. The procurement achievements of LOCOG therefore need to be viewed in that context. The Chartered Institute of Purchasing and Supply, as well as the Commission for a Sustainable London 2012, called the process 'groundbreaking'.

The CIPS agreed to consequently update the assessment questions in the CIPS standard to reflect some of the new work LOCOG had initiated. This means that every single organisation from now on that wishes to achieve CIPS Certification will be challenged to demonstrate excellent policies and procedures with regards to Diversity and Inclusion. This is a genuine legacy benefit and an example of using the Games to change things for the better.

Takeaways – the procurement story

1 We achieved unprecedented supplier diversity, with significant numbers of minority suppliers gaining a slice of the pie. Women-owned businesses accounted for 15 per cent of online contracts, for

example, as well as significant contracts being awarded to other minority-owned businesses that would have otherwise been left off the roster.

2 We made the big guys change their policies, from encouraging over 75 organisations to establish the guaranteed interview scheme for disabled people to encouraging improved diversity performance through the Diversity Works programme.

3 Transparency and supplier diversity led to competition, cost savings of $150 million and greater innovation, initiating a virtuous circle of shared value creation.

Notes

1 Ownership is defined as 51 per cent or more of the owners being from the minority group stated.

Logo and mascots

15

In addition to my boss's plane being struck by lightning and diverted en route to an International Olympic Committee meeting in Mexico, my first week in the job contained a Logo launch film that gave some people epileptic seizures and a mascot design process that took Diversity 101 to new extremes. These were two of the most high-profile 'Everyone's 2012' projects of the Games and a sobering story of how to get it right, and wrong, when diversity takes centre stage.

Every Olympic Games and Paralympic Games to date has created some form of logo or emblem, a visual identity that represents the Games and their host city. The usual format is to have the Olympic rings, alongside the host city name, underneath some simple representation of what the city and their Games stand for. Some have become design classics, such as the artistic paintbrush strokes of the Barcelona athlete for the 1992 Games, or the stars of the 1984 Los Angeles Games. The Barcelona paint strokes embodied artists such as Picasso. The LA stars embodied US identity as well as Hollywood glitz. The Athens 2004 logo embodied the laurel wreath bestowed on athletes in ancient times echoing the birth of the Olympic Games, and Sydney 2000's logo included a boomerang representing Aboriginal culture.

London's 'Logo-gate' began on Monday 4 June 2007. Not only had London created a logo that was unfathomable to many, the launch film also contained a sequence with the potential to trigger epileptic seizures. This did not appear to be a good day for Diversity and Inclusion.

The groundbreaking, diverse and innovative logo

There were actually two issues here, but as usual they were blurred in the media frenzy that ensued. Issue one was the logo itself, which a lot of people did not like, plain and simple. An online petition calling for it to be scrapped completely gained over 25,000 signatures. Over 3,000 messages were posted on the BBC Sport website. Perhaps people were expecting something linked to the Queen's Jubilee, something traditional, or something with the Union Jack flag. It would have been so easy to put Big Ben and a dove on top of some rings and tick the box. Perhaps they had become accustomed to the existing successful Bid campaign logo that comprised the River Thames in the form of a winner's ribbon over the words 'London 2012'. The new logo replaced this old logo, which everyone had loved.

Replacing something loved with something new is risky. Replacing something loved with something unfathomable is dangerous. But London 2012 was doing things differently, and I admired that. That different approach helped foster a great team atmosphere that carried us through our darkest days. However, on this occasion, that approach had also created one of our darkest days.

The new logo was based on the date 2012. I thought it was based on a cute little athlete with their arms raised, ready for the starting gun. Witty commentators likened it to a range of objects, from Lisa Simpson performing sexual acts, to an Iranian alleged Zionist conspiracy. I actually rather liked it. I liked it because it was different, it was brave and it was the antithesis of kitsch. Moreover, it was historic as it was the same shape for both Olympic and Paralympic Games. As discussed earlier, this gave the Paralympics an unprecedented platform for recognition and inclusion. It was the first time both Games had ever been united in their visual identity and the way they would be marketed to the world. To put this in context one only has to look at the Olympic logos of the Games over time. London clearly stands out as different. The colours are a rejection of the conservative logos that preceded it and embrace and reflect London's diversity. It put London 2012 on the global map and represented a step change in Olympic and Paralympic history.

For every day of the week of its launch, it was the most talked about global story online. The International Olympic Committee had to go on record in defending it, declaring, 'We love the logo.' At the time, Seb Coe responded by saying 'We don't do bland. This is not a bland city.' 'We weren't going to come to you with a dull or dry corporate logo that will appear on a polo shirt and we're all gardening in it, in a year's time. This is something that has got to live for the next five years.'[1] Seb was right, and it did survive. The design world, however, was deeply divided with a majority against, people tending to suggest a jagged logo was a patronising way to reach out to young people. At a Fulbright Committee drinks reception in central

London, a usually highly civilised affair, an irate member of the London design-world elite physically accosted me. He cornered me, publicly barracked me and spilt his wine all over the front of my suit.

The distraction

The second issue was the launch film for the new logo, which had the potential to cause epileptic seizures. Everything was produced on incredibly short deadlines, but there was no excuse for this important launch film not having been checked via a Harding test. A Harding test is a now standard procedure in the UK to check a piece of visual film for 'flashing patterns' with the potential to cause harm to people with epilepsy. Photosensitive epilepsy, in particular, affects approximately one in 4,000 people and 'is a form of epilepsy in which seizures are triggered by visual stimuli that form patterns in time or space, such as flashing lights, bold regular patterns, or regular moving patterns'.[2]

A part of the launch film showed a diver diving into a pool, which then produced a multi-colour ripple effect, as the 'shards' burst out to convey energy and excitement. We had to remove this segment of animated footage and apologise profusely, nay grovel. By failing the Harding machine test, the standard industry test, the film did not comply with the UK Communications Regulator guidelines, which was embarrassing. According to Epilepsy Action, who was enjoying their newfound authority, the film had even triggered 'breakthrough seizures',[3] where people have a relapse after being seizure-free for a long time. With 18 viewers reporting 'ill effects', London 2012 was following a tradition established in 1993, when an advert for Pot Noodles allegedly caused seizures in three people. It joined the esteemed company of Pokémon whose 1997 game edition allegedly resulted in 650 hospital admissions in Japan alone.[4]

Prof Graham Harding, after whom the test to measure photo-sensitivity levels was named, said, 'it should not be broadcast again'. Epilepsy Action was the first of a series of lobby groups to understandably try to use the platform the Games offered for their own agenda. Following the swift correction of this mistake LOCOG became best in class in terms of the accessibility of its communications, better than any other organisation I had ever worked for. Granted it needed to be 'up there', given its remit, but that took a lot of work and commitment, never acknowledged properly by many of the lobby groups whose own behaviour was sometimes questionable.

Approximately 23,000 people in the UK have photosensitive epilepsy, according to Epilepsy Action. This was their best chance, possibly ever, to gain a platform and to secure visibility and funding for their cause. That is not to deny it is a great cause, but it is to suggest that in the quest for visibility and funding a range of lobby groups used the Games and were sometimes loose with the facts in order to secure the outcome they wanted.

Our Communications team internally vilified our Brand and Marketing team. It was the beginning of their ascendancy. We tried to partner with them, to attend their team meetings, to offer one-page briefing documents and 'fact sheets', to build alliances with relevant stakeholders for rebuttal and to be on call 24/7. After the logo was launched, I was fully aware, if I wasn't before, that every move we made would be scrutinised in the press like never before. Every potentially embarrassing failure that could be seen as contradicting our 'Everyone's 2012' message would be blown up to a new proportion.

That was not just a challenge in terms of personal strength and dealing with 'friends down the pub' situations, it was genuinely troubling in terms of building an alliance for inclusion. All the sceptics, lobby groups, opinion formers and activists had to be brought onside and to believe that we were serious about inclusion. The level of media scrutiny and often factually incorrect or downright improper reporting would have to be challenged constantly if we were to win the trust of those we needed onside.

Part of the problem, as we learned over the years, was the complexity of the operation. While it was being played out in real time seconds, we had to coordinate internally in human, bureaucratic time. It was often very possible that the press department was taking calls without knowing anything about the Diversity and Inclusion issue at hand. Either because they had not talked with the right department, or because they were lacking in knowledge about epilepsy, or disability and so on, or usually both. Rather like the budget issue, the public did not care where the mistake was made, only that it was made.

However, in retrospect, Logo-gate, gave the Diversity and Inclusion programme an early boost. When other diversity practitioners are desperately trying to gain the attention of the Chief Executive and other senior members, here was the world pointing the finger for us. It was the media and thousands of people online, not the internal Diversity and Inclusion team, pointing out the fact that our launch film had caused ill effects and was the opposite of inclusive. The internal team, on the other hand, stood ready to help and advise. We were helped even more three months later, when we held a launch for our new commercial partner Adidas. As if to say, 'I told you so', world-beating Paralympian Tanni Grey-Thompson was forced to make a keynote from the floor, as she couldn't manage the steps up to the stage. The event organisers had presumably never considered the possibility that the keynote speaker could be a wheelchair user. We were able to revisit the 'it doesn't just happen' conversation and the Diversity and Inclusion team was on speed dial as standard practice henceforth.

It started with a sausage dog

Three years later, in May 2010 it was time to launch the mascots. As with the logo, there is a tradition of mascots in the Olympic Games, although only stretching back to Munich in 1972. It was in Germany that the first mascot emerged, a psychedelically coloured dachshund sausage dog named Waldi. The colours were supposed to represent the 'happiness and joy' of the world, but only two years after the swinging sixties, it reminded me more of a (allegedly) drug-induced episode of the French/British children's television series *The Magic Roundabout*. Waldi would have been right at home with Dougal, Zebedee and Brian the Snail.

Montreal followed up in 1976 with a forgettable beaver called Amik, and in 1980 Moscow introduced the world to Misha the bear, designed by the famous Russian children's illustrator Victor Chizhikov. In true Cold War style, the United States responded four years later with Sam the Eagle. As the United States had boycotted Moscow 1980, Russia boycotted Los Angeles 1984. We met another dog at Barcelona in 1992, Spanish 'Cobi', who even featured on his own television series. Perhaps most forgettable of all was Izzy the lobster, from Atlanta 1996. 'Izzy', the first computer-generated mascot, can perhaps best be (generously) described as a 'prototype', otherwise regarded as a 'drug ravaged bottom feeder'.[5]

Given this bizarre history, the logo launch three years previously, and the British press baying for blood now that things were going quite well, there was understandable nervousness in the team about the mascot launch.[6] This time we had insisted on Harding tests, and the communications team had also insisted on every other type of test imaginable. Here again, though, was a genuine, decent and brave attempt to do things differently and to demonstrate inclusion in everything we delivered.

Again, the Paralympics benefited from association with the Olympics and both mascots were launched together. They were called Wenlock and

Mandeville. Wenlock was named after the town where the modern Olympics were born in rural Shropshire, in the Midlands of England. Mandeville hailed from Stoke Mandeville, the site of the first Paralympic Games after World War Two. Not only did they combine credible British history, they embraced modern inclusion. They had a lot more credibility in terms of story, purpose and design than Waldi the dachshund and some of the other aforementioned previous creatures. We were self-aware enough not to take them too seriously, although they did have their own website, computer games and Facebook pages.

They were launched at a multicultural school in East London. LOCOG could not have tried harder to make these as diverse and as inclusive as possible. One of the key people behind the mascots, Maria Ramos, conferred with me and the Diversity and Inclusion team at every step. They had one eye, were 'gender neutral' and couldn't have been more diverse and inclusive if they tried. Having seen some of the earlier candidates for London mascots, one of which (adopting the sustainability ticket) involved a natterjack toad[7] (think modern-day Izzy), these were definitely the best result. A leading critic said, 'Both are clearly of the digital age. And we have to say, we think they look rather good...'.[8]

However, my friend Andrea, a human rights lawyer and diversity supporter, refused to buy one for her son on the pretext that 'they scare children'.[9] The design community agreed with her. Stephen Bayley, founder of the Design Museum, called them 'atrocious' and 'hideous creatures'. He said that his daughter could have done better. Apparently she called them 'rubbish earrings'. Bayley said: 'the logo was hideous enough but now we have these ridiculous, infantile mascots. Who is to blame for this I ask you?'[10] A Canadian newspaper suggested that the pair were the product of a 'drunken one-night stand between a Teletubby and a Dalek'.[11]

In the story of the logo and the mascots we witness the search for the guilty and the persecution of the innocent (Stages 4 and 5 from Chapter 1) play out in real time on the world stage. The logo and mascots are two projects that are not only a protocol requirement of staging the Games, they are projects and requirements common to most organisations with a public profile in one form or another. The fact remains that while both projects were somewhat of a rollercoaster ride, ricocheting between the dangerous and the absurd, both projects were brave, creative and created a step change in inclusion for the Olympic and Paralympic movements. Even if you hated them, they certainly started a conversation and raised consciousness, which is, after all, half the battle.

Takeaways – logo and mascots

1 The London 2012 logo and mascots embodied Diversity and Inclusion. Diversity – they were nothing if not different. Inclusion – they both embraced a joining together, of people and in an historic sense, representing a step change in the history of the Olympics and Paralympics

2 These projects demonstrate the need for courage and creativity – the risk of negative reaction was outweighed by the contribution they made to a step change in inclusion. But that was not, and could not have been, known at the time.

Notes

1 http://news.bbc.co.uk/z/mobile/uk-news/magazine/6719805.stm

2 http://en.wikipedia.org/wiki/Photosensitive_epilepsy

3 See note 2.

4 http://www.csicop.org/si/show/pokemon_panic_of_1997

5 Conversation with Izzet Agoren, Internet entrepreneur, NYC, June 2013.

6 This is now 2010.

7 http://www.bbc.co.uk/nature/life/Natterjack_Toad. These creatures are Europe's loudest amphibians and are poor swimmers, having a tendency to drown in deep water and an inability to jump far. They may therefore be suitable logos for some organisations, but perhaps not for the world's pre-eminent sporting event.

8 'Wenlock & Mandeville: London's Olympic mascots'. *Creative Review*. Retrieved 16 May 2012.

9 Conversation with Andrea Coomber, July 2011.

10 http://dailymail.co.uk/news/article-1279736/London-2012-Olympic-mascots-meet-wenlock-mandeville.html.

11 http://theglobeandmail.com/news/world/behold-the-one-eyed-compromise-monster/article-1367664/

Who got tickets?

16

If the London 2012 ticketing experience taught us anything, it was how commercial necessity and Diversity and Inclusion can happily coexist. Yet, as with the logo and mascots, a healthy dose of courage was required. The ticketing programme was critical, not just because it raised a third of LOCOG's operating budget, but because it demonstrated beyond doubt how catering to different needs (niche marketing), not treating people the same under the illusion of 'fairness', and getting seats filled were inclusion goals, as well as commercial goals.

We had to sell over 11 million tickets in order to raise about a third of our operating budget (£700 million), and as a consequence stressed from the outset that there were no free tickets. That potential floodgate had to stay firmly closed. There were 8.8 million tickets made available for the Olympic Games and 2.2 million for the Paralympic Games. We called the campaign 'the greatest tickets on earth'.[1] Commercially, the need to raise £700 million, a third of our operating budget, placed huge pressure upon the Ticketing Director, Paul Williamson. Aside from being a Manchester United supporter, Paul was a fantastic guy and we worked together from the outset with him and his brilliant team. Louise Jolly in particular was relentless in coming up with new inclusive ideas to make the ticketing programme work for everyone. We appreciated the commercial imperative from the start, and they appreciated the need to thread inclusion throughout this most high profile of commercial activities.

An impossible game

While overall demand was high, and all the modelling confirmed this, it was highly variable, as well as volatile. There was an opportunity to target niche markets to tap under-demand for certain events as well as ensure the political objective of 'bums on seats' was met. However, in return for the potential use of diversity to help fulfil commercial gaps, we needed to also ensure that everyone would get a fair shot at the inevitably popular events, especially athletics, cycling, swimming and the Ceremonies. We had worked so hard to create accessible venues and an inclusive events policy that it would be rather ironic if the crowd were not a diverse crowd and a representative slice of society that would benefit from all the planning. So we agreed: diversity to the rescue in those areas where it could help fill under-demand, but an allowance for diversity where it was, quite frankly, not needed from a commercial perspective, at the oversubscribed events.

In addition to diversity weaved into the overall ticket campaign messaging, we launched targeted campaigns in East London, as well as in niche LGBT, minority and disability press. We used the full database we had amassed over the diversity recruitment cycle and leveraged relationships with all our delivery partners. Pakistani and Indian Brits were particularly interested in the hockey. Jamaicans were especially interested in the athletics, with Usain Bolt expected to beat the world record in the 100 m. Sometimes the stereotype could go too far – not all gay men were interested in the diving, and besides, we had no trouble selling that to straight women.

The Diversity and Inclusion team was therefore a marketing tool to diverse communities, based on the relationships we had established and cultivated to date. It was imperative that local people got tickets. However the propensity to be a) informed and b) ready to buy was disproportionately higher among the 'non target' groups predominantly in West London and among existing Olympic observers online worldwide. I was annoyed when I discovered we were targeting tube travellers with advertisements rather than bus travellers. Tube travellers are more likely to be the audiences who were already well-engaged with the ticket marketing programme and had pre-registered in their millions. Bus users, especially in the East End where the tube network is less developed, were in far more need of engagement. This oversight was partially corrected with ultimately more up-weighting of advertising in the East End.

We included Diversity and Inclusion analysis on ticketing sales for the first time ever to my knowledge, which allowed us to determine who had bought them. It was in many ways a typically commercial result, with higher income, better-postcode individuals leading the charge. However, there were a significant number of people who were not in this category and that undoubtedly would not have occurred to the extent it did without our targeted efforts. And, back to the earlier agreement, diverse crowds did not occur only in the modern pentathlon and archery that had less demand. I was in the Stadium on 'Super Saturday' with my godchildren on my one day off, watching Usain Bolt, Jess Ennis and Oscar Pistorious. The crowd was diverse. There were clearly people there, including families with young children, who had never been to such an event before and who were from East End postcodes.

We wanted to achieve affordable tickets and managed to achieve £20 entry-level prices for some of the top events, including Super Saturday. The more expensive tickets subsidised the £20 and £20.12 tickets (the affordable tickets marketed for the Opening Ceremony to reflect the year). Thirty per cent of Olympic tickets were £20 or less, 40 per cent £30 or less, two-thirds £50 or less and 90 per cent were £100 or less. The consequence of this 'win' for Diversity and Inclusion however was an astronomical rise in demand due to the extremely high price elasticity of demand in respect to price. So although we had achieved £20 tickets for the top events in the Olympic Games, terrific from an inclusion perspective, we had at the same time disproportionately increased the demand for these tickets.

Real inclusion is hard

There was a parallel with the mascots and logo. In a genuine groundbreaking attempt to be more diverse and inclusive, in this case by offering extremely low-cost entry points for tickets, it had resulted in phenomenal demand that ultimately could not be met. In a genuine attempt to be more inclusive, it had resulted in some ways in many people feeling excluded because the supply could not meet the demand. Demand was greatest for the Opening Ceremony where we had lead £20.12 tickets available (over 2 million requests) and athletics (over 1 million requests for the men's 100 m final) as well as the popular sports of track, cycling, swimming and artistic gymnastics. The stadium had 80,000 seats and after adjustments for cameras and commentary boxes it was more like 60,000. As we finalised seating bowls (including wheelchair spaces) then we released contingency tickets but it was still not enough to meet the demand.

In true British fairness tradition, the people who were unsuccessful in earlier rounds were prioritised, however this had the negative effect of excluding anyone who was late to the party in the initial round, which was disproportionately those target groups. A helpful innovation was selling park tickets for £10 and £5 for young people and seniors so many more people could simply experience the park at Games time, which was alive and vibrant and an unforgettable experience.

Over 50 per cent of Paralympic tickets were £10 or less and 75 per cent were £20 or less; 95 per cent of all Paralympic Games tickets were £50 or less and entry prices for Paralympic park tickets were again £10 or £5 reduced. Given that all tickets (even the £5 ones) included a travel card for all London transport (worth more than £5) it represented an extremely good deal and we were satisfied it could not have realistically been made any more affordable. There were free events too, such as the road cycling, race walking, triathlon and marathon.

One of the main challenges with the ticketing campaign was that many of the London media elite, who are accustomed to buying opera tickets on the door any night of the week, found it harder than usual to go. Indeed on some occasions they couldn't get tickets. These people, like everyone else, were prisoners of supply and demand dynamics. However, they were disproportionately more vocal about any rejection they may have experienced. The Olympics is bigger than opera and no matter what your experience to date with other events, there will always be someone else with a valid claim to what you perceive to be your entitlement. The London 2012 tickets did categorically not all go to VIPs and sponsors, it was an open ballot, and it was another win for inclusion.

Seventy-five per cent of all 11 million tickets were available to the UK public through the domestic application process. This was higher than previous Games, higher than the FA Cup Final or Champions League Finals (football/soccer). In Beijing, the Organising Committee made 50 per cent of just over 7 million tickets publicly available. Twelve per cent were purchased by National Olympic Committees and this caused us some problems as some (for example Germany) placed their allocations online and British fans then went online to buy them abroad creating confusion and allegations of unfairness. Only 13 per cent were for purchase by 'Olympic family' and sponsors, stakeholders, broadcast rights holders, international federations, prestige ticketing partners and Thomas Cook the official travel agency sponsor. This is a small percentage compared with any equivalent event.

Inclusion issues and triumphs

We worked with the sponsors to create a 'Ticketshare' scheme. Through a levy on hospitality, 10,000 serving troops went to the Games for free and 200,000 ticketshare tickets were donated to schools and colleges via the Get Set Education network. We introduced a 'pay your age' scheme with special prices for young people (under 16 at start of Games on 27 July 2012) who were eligible to pay a corresponding sum in pounds to their actual age across one-third of sport sessions. Seniors, aged over 60, had a special price too with a flat fee of £16 so they could 'feel young again' and join the teenagers. The pay your age scheme was in operation at over 200 Olympic sessions allowing families to take their kids along for between £1 and £16 per child and grandparents for £16. No other Games had instituted anything of this nature. A key test for us was whether a family on welfare support, without any current job, could afford to go to the London Olympic and Paralympic Games. They could, and they did.

We were perceived as having an issue with babies. We were attacked for our 'babes in arms' policy as we originally held the position that every human being needed a ticket for licensing reasons. However, under pressure from family groups and women's organisations in particular we relented on part of the policy and admitted babies under 12 months attached to a parent for free. We couldn't do this for the existing venues of Wembley, St James' Park, Old Trafford and North Greenwich Arena owing to the specific restrictions on their existing licensing agreements already in effect. The issue was mainly that people had bought tickets before the child was born and then wanted to bring it along with them. Explaining to senior commercial guys in LOCOG about expressed milk and mother/father roles became rather complicated. So we ended up with a fudged policy, not ideal but determined by the variations in different venue licensing agreements rather than any strategic diversity guidelines.

We had developed four different ticket types, in addition to the above tickets, for disabled people. Wheelchair users could buy tickets in all price categories in every event of both Games. Tickets included a companion seat and the option was available for families to sit together. Because of demand, these sold out and the media portrayed it as us not letting people sit together. Not true. It was actually a sign of success, rather than failure that wheelchair seating sold out. Disabled people attended both Games in unprecedented numbers. We had innovated with tickets allowing deaf people to specify they needed a seat with a direct view of the big screens to read the subtitles or see the screens for general comprehension. Visually impaired people could specify that they needed a seat closer to the action so that they could feel the action and activate their senses more than if they were further away from the sport. Any customer with access requirements or limited mobility could request step-free access or seats closest to the entrance/exit with fewest steps. Audio augmentation and audio description were available to those who needed it free of charge, subsidised by a nominal charge for people who did not need it but wanted to pay for an enhanced experience.

In all these ticketing cases, we did not ask people if they were disabled. We did not seek to ask their identity or be seen to be invading their privacy. We asked about requirements, not about them. This allowed people who did not identify in the way others may perceive them to get the help they needed in the most dignified, and for us efficient, manner possible.

We also established accessible transport shuttle services, free disabled parking and assistant-dog spending areas (doggie toilets) at every venue. Changing places toilets were at all major Games venues. These were large toilets and changing rooms with a bench and a hoist for disabled people with high care needs. Accessible seating was spread throughout venues to avoid perceived segregation of those with access requirements and to offer choice for everyone.

There was also the issue of how to accommodate assistants or 'carers' to disabled ticket holders. To charge such assistants for a ticket could have been legitimately challenged on grounds of equal access and a reasonable adjustment. If a disabled person could not attend without an assistant then charging the assistant was in effect charging the disabled person double that of an able-bodied person with no need for assistance. We had originally aimed to include these situations within the ticketshare programme. However, under increasing pressure, the communications team changed it to 'ticketcare'. Of the 1,315 people who applied for complimentary second tickets under the scheme, 100 per cent were successful. Phew. This was available for every session at every venue in every price category. It meant that in addition to additional spaces for wheelchair users, any disabled person attending the Games, whether a wheelchair user or not, who needed an assistant brought them free of charge. Alongside all the other innovations to build an inclusive experience for disabled people, this represented a step change in accessible inclusion at public events.

Given the commercial imperatives, the high-profile nature of the programme, the intense scrutiny and multiple agendas, I think we pulled off a great inclusive result with London 2012 ticketing. Whereas 'babes in arms' and various ticket products for disabled people could be argued to be net costs, the net effect was overwhelmingly revenue adding, with the diversity of families, disabled people and age groups we were able to attract, all bringing their hard-earned wages to spend during their trip of a lifetime to the Games.

Takeaways – who got tickets?

1 The ticketing programme, inclusion included, was a fantastic commercial success.

2 Diversity and commercial imperatives can, and did, happily coexist.

3 Diversity and Inclusion made the games ticketing experience better – we enhanced our reputation, we increased our recruitment of new customers and customer penetration, we mitigated risk (that had resulted in lawsuits at other Games), we grew the market and we produced an ethically sound programme.

Note

1 For an example of the campaign see http://www.youtube.com/watch?v=
LMd3bDJW8iQ.

Education and the Cultural Olympiad

T here is an untold aspect of the Games beyond the sport. It is the story of how we encouraged new audiences for the Arts and influenced the curriculum of three-quarters of British schools. It is a compelling case of how issues of inclusion are brought to the fore and how children instinctively understand Diversity and Inclusion better than adults do. It's a humbling reminder of how we can learn from them. We just need to become more childlike sometimes, and strip away the inefficient baggage that we have picked up over the years that still keeps holding us back.

The original Olympic vision of founder Baron Pierre de Coubertin was Sport, Education and Culture, a general human improvement programme. However, in the modern commercial world, the latter two have somewhat lost out to Sport, which has reigned supreme in all recent Olympic Games. London, being London, and the UK remaining a creative, if no longer economic, superpower, Education and Culture were to receive their biggest boost in years with the London Games. As Seb said upfront 'We are serious when we say that London's Cultural Olympiad is an important part of the 2012 Games. These are not just warm words. Together with education and sport, culture sits at the core of the founding of the modern Games and retains that role in today's Movement.'

Creating a market for Diversity and Inclusion

Spread over four years, the Cultural Olympiad was designed to give everyone in the UK the chance to play a role in the Games, should they wish. It was designed to inspire creativity across all forms of culture, especially among young people, and bring in new audiences, taking 'culture' to groups who would never visit a museum or library. The culmination of the four-year programme was the London 2012 Festival, which brought together leading artists from all over the world from 21 June through the duration of the Olympic Games and Paralympic Games. The aim was to build on the UK's already strong cultural sector and be a step change to allow everyone to celebrate London 2012 through dance, music, theatre, the visual arts, film and digital innovation, leaving a strong arts legacy in place afterwards.

'Culture' can be notoriously elitist. I never cease to be amazed whenever I frequent a gallery opening or new show at the potential for arrogance and ignorance of some of the people present. In defiance of this, we were opening up culture to everyone. In the four-year run up there were 3,673 free London 2012 'Open Weekend' Community events, more than 1,000 cultural events in 150 locations across the UK and Diversity and Inclusion were integral principles in the planning and delivery of them all. The Cultural Olympiad aimed to offer something for everyone regardless of age, gender, location, background or previous exposure to the arts. An audience development programme ran throughout the Cultural Olympiad. Its aim was to attract new groups and to leave a legacy of inclusion within cultural institutions, them having now introduced and excited new audiences.

A highlight of the programme included the largest commissioning programme for deaf and disabled artists anywhere in the world, reflecting the values of the Paralympic movement. This was called 'Unlimited'. This programme of commission of new work from the UK's finest disabled and deaf artists encouraged collaborations and partnerships between disability arts organisations, artists, producers and mainstream organisations to celebrate the inspiration of the Games and create new original and exciting work. Brian Oakby from the Mayor's Office said, 'it's a celebration of diversity, it's a celebration of creativity'. Culture was free of charge to 10 million people.[1]

Jenny Sealey, of Graeae Theatre Company, invented a new sign (in British Sign Language) for Unlimited. It consisted of an outward and upward movement of both hands. This symbolised everything about what we were trying to do – a new sign, a new method, and new opportunities that represented a step change from the past. As Jenny said, 'for the first time ever, we will be viewed by millions and millions of people'.[2] Artist Deb Williams said it's about 'engaging with things you've never engaged with before – it's our big chance to say – globally – we're here'. And the late David Morris from my team said that Unlimited was a 'very important initiative because it will give credibility and support to artists that may not have had access to mainstream support before. I think the work we can do can inspire change everywhere'.

Unlimited challenged our understanding of inclusion. Superficial inclusion would see no need for a separate 'disability arts movement'. It would assume that we should just 'treat people the same'. This unfortunately results in people being either ignored or subverted to the dominant paradigm, should they fail to 'fit in'. It's analogous to how the French state seeks to treat diverse citizens 'the same' with minimal comprehension that different people respond to different stimuli. Russell Parton argues that:

> It's some leap, however, from greater visibility and opportunities for deaf and disabled artists to there being a level playing field with mainstream Arts. Five years ago, the London Disability Arts Forum hosted a debate at Tate Modern with the motion: 'Should disability and deaf arts be dead and buried in the 21st century?' It was defeated and found little support – to suggest we're all in the mainstream now is dangerously complacent.

Katie O'Reilly, one of the prominent artists involved in Unlimited, discussed the practice of theatres casting non-disabled actors as disabled characters, a tradition she labels 'cripping up'. This can be understood as an analogy or corollary of white actors 'blacking up' to play Othello. In Hollywood, it is still the case that straight actors play gay characters.[3] At some point, we will hopefully allow people to play themselves. 'I hope the impact of Unlimited and the work that's been happening is that in time we will be as embarrassed about non-disabled people cripping up as we are now when we look back and see people blacking up,' she says. 'I really do hope in time it will just be part of that great wonderful human variety; a celebration of all that's possible.'

A large-scale programme of artists and curators sharing the cultural diversity from every nation competing in the Games was another expression of Diversity and Inclusion within the programme. The River of Music saw musicians from 206 countries performing at River Thames stages free of charge to half-a-million people. Poets from every country in the world performed together at Poetry Parnassus, at the South Bank Centre. The Photographers gallery and Gulbenkian Foundation jointly commissioned and celebrated a photographer from every country competing in the Games in the series 'The World in London'. Throughout libraries all over the UK 1 million children created and enjoyed stories from around the world. Most celebrated was the World Shakespeare Festival, a celebration of the Bard as the world's playwright. The Royal Shakespeare Company (RSC) produced this in an unprecedented collaboration with leading UK and international arts organisations. Globe-to-Globe offered the complete 37 works of Shakespeare, but from 37 different countries in their language with subtitles.

A major barrier to participation has been socio-economic factors in terms of cost, role models and opportunity. Just as there were free sports events, from the marathon to the road cycling, there were now 10 million free opportunities to participate in London 2012 Festival events, removing cost as the main barrier to engaging in culture. Fourteen million people across the UK participated in a Cultural Olympiad event.

The Inspire Mark was an innovation that helped make this happen. As the Olympic and Paralympic properties are heavily protected in view of the exclusive marketing deals done with commercial sponsors who fund the Games, there was a need for a very creative solution to offer association with non-profits or arts-based charities. The Inspire Mark was a brilliant 'fix' between offering enough shape of the logo for it to be recognisable as 2012 (thank heavens for that awful logo, Mr Bayley) but it omitted the rings or agitos to keep the sponsors happy. Over 900 Inspire Mark projects were awarded in sport and 500 in culture, across all aspects of diversity.

A phrase I had used in speeches to lesbian and gay audiences in the past was 'if you want a world where you can walk down the street and hold your partner's hand, then maybe you need to walk down the street and hold your partners' hand, for then you will live in such a world'. It was a phrase not lost on David Watkins, the founder of A Day in Hand (the same-sex hand-holding relay) which became one of the Inspire Mark projects. He rebuffed the superficial inclusion mantra that there is no need for this. He said, 'I hope that, eventually, we'll all get used to it.' Only then would there be no need. He referenced Zack Rosen who, in his blog for *The New Gay*,[4] said, 'You see one person walking a unicorn in the park and it's headline news. Three months later you'll see 200 people walking unicorns in the park and call it a Thursday.'

Inspire a generation

The original bid promise was to inspire a generation to choose sport. The Education programme therefore took on new importance. We partnered with Nick Fuller, LOCOG Head of Education, and his team early on and they were enthusiastic and creative adopters of the Diversity and Inclusion ethos and helped inculcate it throughout the programme. In particular, Kathryn McColl was unyielding in her passion and ability to think about inclusion in every aspect of the Education programme. There were two main parts to the London 2012 Education programme, Get Set (domestic) and International Inspiration, at a global scale.

In total, over 2 million young people were involved in the London 2012 Education programme. Through Get Set, LOCOG encouraged over 25,000 of the 30,000 UK schools and colleges to use the Olympic and Paralympic values to explore and address the main strands of Diversity and Inclusion. For example, materials were provided that promoted the Paralympic values with athletes helping to engage young people in learning about and accepting disability. Children and young people are intrinsically much better at doing this than adults are and therefore the only regret about this programme is that it wasn't the other way round. In Chapter 3 we discussed the child who is the only person in the room that asks the wheelchair user an awkward question. My friend Brooke Ellison, the first quadriplegic person to graduate from Harvard, echoed the importance of this. 'If we adults could learn from our children, it would make my life, for one, more real and make me feel more included.'[5]

Films, assembly materials and activity ideas were distributed to schools to introduce the Olympic truce and to encourage young people to use sport to build bridges between communities and accept difference. There were activities focused on learning languages using healthy recipes from the different countries competing in the London Games. There was a 'shine a spotlight' competition where students were rewarded for living an Olympic or Paralympic value. For example, the London 2012 Mascot Mandeville visited Calum at Osbaldwick Primary School in my hometown of York to reward his display of 'determination'. Calum had represented York at boccia in the North Yorkshire Youth Games and he plays disability football and wheelchair basketball. It was 'very cool' for Calum to get a visit from the London 2012 mascot and impress all his friends.

Through Get Set Goes Global, promoting global learning and intercultural exchange, schools were encouraged to follow and support at least one Olympic and Paralympic Team (in addition to Team Great Britain and Paralympics Great Britain, of course). They then celebrated the team(s) they had been following at London 2012 World Sport Day on 25 June. Over 4 million young people took part in each of the National School Sports Weeks.

Curwen Primary School in Plaistow, East London, joined the Get Set network in April 2010. The school has since used a variety of different projects to learn about the history of the Paralympic Games and its athletes. This included the Paralympic values and the wider theme of disability and inclusion using dance, poetry, music and art. They went on to establish their own Paralympic sports club with boccia, goalball, sitting volleyball and wheelchair basketball offered to students. By focusing on the Paralympic Games, it has helped pupils and teachers learn about disability and change attitudes.

St Mary's Grammar School, a Catholic School in Northern Ireland worked with a local Protestant School, culminating in a trip together to London. For anyone who knows Northern Ireland, this is not an insignificant event. Liverpool Community College worked with local lesbian, gay, bisexual and trans (LGBT) groups to break down homophobic barriers in sport and education. Brightside, a student-led LGBT group, held a series of activities based around sport and the Olympic values to promote LGBT history month. They then developed a weekly drop-in session for students to support anyone coming out.

We worked with the *Schools Out* organisation to help them achieve breakthrough in their messaging around homophobic bullying. They had been working tirelessly for years but had not managed to reach the scale LOCOG had in a short timeframe. So, in the spirit of 'It Gets Better' we sent their bulletin to all of the schools in the Get Set Network and over 2 million children received a lesson plan that homophobic bullying had to stop. This was courage in action and it contributed to systemic change.

Hackney Community College supported their female students, and female students at nearby schools, with careers in construction, a traditionally male-dominated career where the opportunity is taken up mainly by men. The college ran a 'Women into construction event' and developed a role model project inspired by the Games. The college saw a marked increase in the number of women applying for construction courses. This was about providing information to people who had not had it before, and giving them options that previously did not exist.

At a global scale, International Inspiration was designed to leave a sports legacy and enrich the lives of 12 million children in 20 countries worldwide, through high-quality and inclusive physical education, sport and play. The programme was supported by UK Sport, UNICEF and the British Council and delivered with the Youth Sport Trust. The objective was to change lives, encourage self-empowerment, health, inclusion, excellence and simply the joy of taking part.

As a direct result of International Inspiration 12.9 million children and young people actively participated in sport, physical education and play, many for the first time in their lives. This included children in Azerbaijan, Brazil, Bangladesh, South Africa and Tanzania. Around 119,000 teachers, coaches and young leaders have been trained to lead sport, physical education and play in their schools and communities, learning new skills. Thirty-five policies, strategies or legislative changes have been influenced by or implemented in response to International Inspiration. There are 244 International Inspiration Schools worldwide linked to 244 schools in the UK.

The debate around legacy started before the Games began. Was the Cultural Olympiad 15 minutes of fame for disabled artists and the Education programme a one-class experience for kids at a key stage in the curriculum? Or were they an intervention that will make a difference in the long term? Perhaps we will never know.

We do know that Heart n Soul and Graeae, disabled theatre companies, have received new commissions as a result of the Cultural Olympiad and are now darlings of the UK and international arts scene, challenging stereotypes every day and growing the disability arts market. We also know that the same-sex hand-holding relay continues and that the International Inspiration projects continue in multiple countries worldwide. What we will never know, and in some ways can never find out, are the totality of the individual stories, whether some child somewhere was saved that day in class, whether that disabled person's career trajectory was dramatically altered or whether somewhere, someone found actionable inspiration that they would never have otherwise come across.

Takeaways – education and the Cultural Olympiad

1 The Cultural Olympiad reached out to new audiences and grew the market for culture – and the economy in the UK. Inclusion provided new business opportunities.

2 The Education programme connected young people domestically and globally to the Olympic and Paralympic movement. In that sense it 'educated' a generation, but moreover it saved the Olympic and Paralympic movements from ageing decline by recruiting an enthusiastic new audience for them.

3 The Education programme showed at scale how young people often understand, lead and deliver better than adults. At minimum, it is a two-way learning process.

Notes

1 Russell Parton, *The Guardian*, 'London 2012 and disability arts: 'we'll be famous for 15 minutes', Russell Parton Tuesday 28 August 2012.

2 Conversation with Jenny Sealey, June 2011.

3 For example, the Michael Douglas and Matt Damon film *Behind the Candelabra* (2013).

4 *The New Gay*: http://thenewgay.net/2008/08/homos-hold-hands-some-words-in-defense.html

5 Conversation with the author, July 2013.

The Torch Relay

18

The modern Torch Relay was an invention of Nazi Germany. Carl Diem invented the protocol of transporting the Olympic flame via a relay system from Greece to the Olympic venue for the 1936 Olympic Games in Berlin. The Krupp armaments company produced the torches in wood and metal.

Thankfully, there are different authorities in charge of it today, and the London torches were produced by a small business in East London with 8,000 holes to represent the 8,000 diverse torchbearers. Before we arrive in 2012, however, let's revisit 2008, our 'test event' for the London Games.

A counterfactual

The Olympic flame is a symbol representing the universal values of peace, unity and friendship. Unfortunately, to many, the Beijing 2008 Torch Relay represented nothing more than China's debatable human rights record. This was our opportunity to observe how not to do a Torch Relay.

When the Beijing 2008 International Olympic Torch Relay came to the UK, I was stationed in the central London section between Park Lane and Bloomsbury and had the responsibility of marshalling four disabled children and the Sugababes. The Sugababes were promising pop stars in 2008. Although not a music industry expert by any means, I believe they are not so promising in 2014.

The day began with me failing to persuade the Sugababes to leave their Park Lane hotel suite. They had been watching the BBC and could see the demonstrations that planned to meet the Olympic Torch Relay as it progressed through central London. The Chinese human rights record was under attack by various UK and international lobby groups and we were about to run the gauntlet of public opinion.

Seb Coe arrived at the hotel and managed to persuade the Sugababes to come downstairs, I suspect by saying that there were four disabled children who had travelled far and wanted to meet them. The four children each had a parent or guardian and were the winners of a *Blue Peter* competition[1] to take part in the Olympic Torch Relay. Today was supposed to be a memorable day for them, meeting their pop idols and carrying the Olympic flame.

As we boarded the bus I made eye contact with a police officer on board. There was a knowing exchange of looks, in a very British understated way, which said, 'I completely understand that we are both aware of the situation and both share the same doubts'.

We departed on a double decker bus, somewhat behind schedule, with the Sugababes, Seb, the Olympic flame and the four disabled children upstairs on the top deck. It had been slightly awkward getting them up there – and the children! I had watched nervously as one of the children, who used crutches, was placed on top of an upturned milk crate in order to have a view over the side of the bus. 'Crikey', I thought, 'Everyone's 2012'. Downstairs, besides the driver, was a mixture of police, security service agents and Chinese special agents in blue tracksuits. The 'Chinese blue tracksuits' had gained notoriety as the strict guard of the Beijing 2008 Olympic flame, striking fear into all who came too close.

As we turned into Oxford Street the shouting started, 'Shame! Shame! Shame!' The crowds were angry, and much bigger than I had expected. The 'shame' was directed primarily at the Chinese, but also, I suspect, partially at us for being collaborators in what the crowd perceived as a sanctioning of China's human rights record.

This was an intimidating spectacle for me, let alone for the children. It was definitely an intimidating spectacle for the Sugababes and I made a compensatory fuss, running up and down the stairs fetching Cokes and chocolate brownies.

As we continued down Oxford Street I became progressively more worried and had conversations with the police officers on board. The crowds were now starting to surge around the bus still shouting 'Shame! Shame! Shame!' When we stopped for a moment, they began throwing eggs. This was not good.

We escorted the children downstairs as one fell from the milk crate. Her crutches went flying. I remember descending the stairs with screaming Sugababes (I think one got egg yolk in her hair) and crying children. Downstairs, it was a case of more Cokes (sugar-free Diet Cokes for the Sugababes) and chocolate brownies all round. And more chats with the officers.

I was at the front of the bus and so had a clear view out of the windscreen for what happened next. Since my Stonewall days, I have known Peter Tatchell. He is an insatiable human rights campaigner and the bane of many corporations for his incessant lobbying. You can't help but respect the guy. I was there when he was awarded a medal by the Gay Police Association for having been arrested over 300 times, but charged only once. He disliked Stonewall, the gay rights charity, perceiving it as 'fruits in suits' and at the beck and call of corporate interests, but he had time for me and I had coffee with him shortly after taking up the Olympics post.

It was as I stood at the front of the bus next to a police officer that I saw Peter Tatchell run out into the road with a placard and then disappear under the front left wheel. Just before he went down, he stared right at me and we had one of those moments of eye contact, not unlike with the police earlier, except this one was Peter shooting me a look of pure disappointment as I was clearly sleeping with the perceived enemy.

That was my first thought, quickly followed by my second which was 'Oh my God, we've just killed Peter Tatchell'.

Not only was this a potentially horrific situation in itself, it was also horrifically ironic if the Head of Diversity and Inclusion had been present on the vehicle that killed one of Britain's most famous human rights campaigners. 'Unfortunate' would have been a typically British understatement.

The bus shuddered to a halt and I only hoped the noises we heard over the Sugababes' protests were traffic cones popping, and not human limbs. Out of the side door I could see Peter Tatchell being dragged away by police waving his fist at me and the co-conspirators on board. The driver stepped on it and we moved quickly into Bloomsbury Square.

Things deteriorated, however. While we now had the children and Sugababes downstairs and everyone in an egg-free environment, the crowd started to rock the bus. It rocked from side to side at increasingly alarming angles and we radioed for help. If the bus had gone over it would not only have been dangerous for the occupants within the bus – but potentially deadly for those on the wrong side outside.

We managed to force our way forward and the driver stepped on the gas again and we hightailed it into a side street north of the square. It was at that point that we took the children and the Sugababes off the bus and into waiting cars where they sped away quickly in opposite directions back to the hotel. It had been an eventful morning, not proceeding totally to plan.

Everyone's 2012

That experience, as you can tell, lives with me still. Pragmatism should trump idealism on occasion. And so when I had the opportunity to work with the wonderful Deborah Hale and her team on the 2012 Torch Relay, there were a few lessons we could apply with authority.

The London 2012 Olympic flame was lit in Olympia, Greece on 10 May 2012. It journeyed around Greece, as is tradition, before departing for the host country. It arrived in the UK on the evening of 18 May at the RAF base Culdrose onboard a British Airways plane.

It had already been decided to make the 2012 Torch Relay a UK domestic affair, which was a sensible and safe option given people's differing views on UK Foreign Policy past and present. It also allowed us to do something more concentrated and really well, rather than something spread too wide at higher cost and less impact.

So we managed to design a route that was within 10 miles (by public transport) of 95 per cent of the population. That meant that 57 million people were within a cheap commute of seeing the Olympic flame pass through their own community. It travelled 8,000 miles over 70 days visiting every part of the UK. There was an advisory group in each region that helped us select 66 evening celebrations, 6 island visits and the 1,000 communities, towns and villages along the route. It visited landmarks such as Snowdon in Wales, Loch Ness in Scotland, Stormont in Northern Ireland and Stonehenge in England. But it also visited poignant, lesser known places and people.

Defying the sceptics, we went to Shetland in the far north, Lands End in the far south, remote Scottish islands and inner city mosques, churches, community centres and gay monuments. A theme was emerging about 'de-dramatising' potentially controversial topics by just doing them in a very calm, effective, competent way.

For example, Alan Turing was a surprisingly little-known national hero who had been a key 'code breaker' in World War Two and whose work had probably led to the saving of thousands of lives as German U boat attacks were flawed. A gay man, Turing was prosecuted in 1952, when homosexual acts were still illegal in Britain. He was subjected to a UK government-sponsored treatment programme of injections of stilboestrol, a synthetic oestrogen. After one year, the treatment rendered Turing impotent and caused gynaecomastia, or swelling of the breasts. He took his own life by eating a poisoned apple in 1952, aged just 41 years old. After Prime Minister Gordon Brown had apologised on behalf of the nation following a campaign led by the computer programmer and author John Graham Cumming,[2] we decided it was appropriate for the Olympic Torch to visit the Turing statue and pause for a minute, in Canal Street, heart of Manchester's modern-day thriving gay community.

It was acts like this, which needed forethought, a little planning and teamwork, but which cost nothing, that made inclusion come alive in the

Torch Relay. The Diversity and Inclusion team were in touch with many John Graham Cummings and we fed into a sympathetic Torch team on a regular basis, both parties in aggressive agreement that diversity made the Torch Relay even better.

The other key variable, besides the route, was the 8,000 Torchbearers themselves. We applied our learning from the volunteer programme to rapidly educate the Torch team on how to recruit a diverse team of volunteers to carry the flame. Selection was based on 150-word 'nominations' about how an individual had 'pushed past their personal best' and there were regional selection panels that were given a copy of our guidance. The result was the most diverse Torchbearer cohort to date. We published the names of the Torchbearers online, again to aid transparency. Each Torchbearer carried the flame for about 300 metres with about 110 people taking part each day.

We asked all Torchbearers to complete Diversity and Inclusion monitoring forms and the return rate was about 75 per cent (it varied by question). Of the responses, 42 per cent of Torchbearers were women and 23 per cent had a disability or long-term health condition (3 per cent of Torchbearers were wheelchair users and 4 per cent required some form of assistance to carry the Torch).

This was quietly radical, because this was the Olympic Torch Relay, not the Paralympic Torch Relay. Not even the International Olympic Committee, who had to approve almost everything, found the courage to reject our proposed diverse mix of Torchbearers. It would be hard to say, 'remove the disabled ones'. Once we had undertaken our supply-side recruitment outreach and our due diligence in selection, there was very little any opponent or sceptic could do. Again, this is an example of courage. This was not blind courage exercised recklessly, but courage exercised in the context of a clear 'understand, lead and deliver' framework and played out in a democratic organisation.

Of our Torchbearers 17 per cent were under 18 years old, the youngest being just 12. The oldest Torchbearer was 101 years old and counting. 67.3 per cent of our Torchbearers, more than two-thirds of the British public, told us their sexual orientation and of those 2.5 per cent identified as lesbian, gay or bisexual. The same number told us their religion, if any, and every major religion was represented in the Torch Relay, the largest groups being Christian and no religion, followed by 'other' then Muslim, Hindu, Jewish, Buddhist and Sikh. Of the 71.9 per cent who told us their ethnicity, 80 per cent were white British (against a population of 89 per cent) and the remaining 20 per cent included all major minorities as defined in the recent UK census.

The important fact about this is that people in Britain could see themselves in the Torch Relay as it passed through their local community. What critics would call 'social engineering' we demonstrated was merit-based selection with a view to diversity, executed in a devolved regional decision-making panel system. No one-to-one interviews, but group discussion, and diverse, brilliant outcomes. A Torch Relay that represented the best diversity of modern Britain, and provided everyone with a role model.

Again, confounding the cynics, relatively few sons of Chief Executives or sponsors made it on to the list, and even the allocated sponsor places were heavily influenced by our Diversity and Inclusion strategy. For example, Lloyds used theirs for staff recognition with due regard for diversity. Places were donated to wounded ex-service men and women. Coca Cola gave places to a vast array of the population, including the brilliant Casper ter Kuile, a gay social and environmental activist who is the least 'corporate' person I know.

We used alternative formats, such as easy read, and made adjustments to support virtually any accessibility requirement requested. Everyone was able to carry the flame, in a dignified manner with pride. This applied to both the Olympic and Paralympic relays.

The Paralympic Torch Relay was LOCOG's design completely, being without the traditions and protocol of the Olympic flame. We lit four separate flames in the four country capitals and united them at Stoke Mandeville for a 24-hour relay to London. As with our approach across the board, we integrated the planning and policies for both Olympic and Paralympic activities into one organisation. The Olympics therefore had a heavy dose of disability inclusion and enhanced accessibility that it had never experienced to date. It simply made operational sense for us. Why have two separate policies for two events when we could save time, money and 'training' by having one?

The Torch Relay, and moreover the men and women who carried the flame, demonstrated how merit-based selection, subsequent to strong targeted marketing and empowered, devolved group decision-making can produce great outcomes. What began as a tool of Nazi propaganda in 1936 became a beacon of inclusion in 2012. It was the modern-day equivalent of the black athlete Jesse Owens winning three gold medals in the Berlin Olympic Games, and would probably have annoyed Hitler just as much. The population, wherever they were on the diversity spectrum, loved it.

Takeaways – the Torch Relay

1 Courage and creativity, from including disabled people in the Olympic Torch Relay as well as the Paralympic Torch Relay to visiting the Alan Turing Statue in Manchester's Gay Village, infinitely improved the project.

2 Measurement was critical, both in the recruitment of Torchbearers as well as in presenting the results. The Torch Relay is what real inclusion looks like.

3 Achieving diversity was less an exercise in social engineering and more a case of representing a diverse reality to everyone. By holding up a mirror to society, everyone could discover a role model, have their stereotypes challenged and discover how talent comes in many forms.

Notes

1 *Blue Peter* is a legendary and popular British TV show for children.

2 blog.jgc.org/.

Use your LOAF: accessibility inside the tent

19

Accessibility is about people being able to interact with their environment. Things that many non-disabled people take for granted, from shopping to going to the toilet, from working in a job to having sex, can all be less accessible affairs for disabled people. In an attempt to empower disabled people and those with less mobility, accessibility has arisen as a field of work preoccupied with improving access. However, as with Diversity 101, it has in many cases achieved limited success because it is still viewed as a separate work stream, and by necessity an additional net cost in any project.

The potential for additional cost for London 2012 was extremely significant. In order to stage the Games LOCOG needed 3,500 cabins, 200,000 temporary seats and 10,000 temporary toilets – enough to service the entire population of Malta (assuming no disabled people). Further requirements included 16,500 telephones to be installed across venues, 76 miles of temporary fencing and 350 miles of cabling (which usually had very inaccessible 'hump' covers over them as they were fed over walkways). In addition, LOCOG needed 2,500 tent units totalling 2.5 million square feet, enough to cover Hong Kong completely, and 350,000 fixtures and fittings just in the Athletes Village alone (hence the importance of procurement). We also required 9,000 wardrobes, 11,000 sofas and 22,000 pillows in 2,818 apartments. There would also be a 5,000-seat dining facility in the Athletes Village and 500 cash registers installed in the megastore.

Given the above, the idea of another work stream, with additional costs, to ensure all of the above were accessible to disabled people was unappealing, to say the least. Anticipating the position of the Diversity and Inclusion team, the Venues and Operational teams, under enormous cost pressure, were preparing their argument. They would argue for 'reason' and a 'realistic and pragmatic approach', in other words to accept that much of the Games would be inaccessible. On the other hand, the lobby groups, and their expectations, coupled with global media scrutiny present in London constituted the most forceful accessibility advocates anywhere in the world. There were a range of powerful and vocal groups that would argue the exact opposite of the architects and the engineers, that this was a key human rights issue, that we were currently ratifying the UN Convention of the Rights of persons with Disabilities and the eyes of the world would be upon us. The Diversity and Inclusion team sat right at the nexus of these two opposing forces. How to square the circle?

Universal and inclusive design

There is extensive literature on 'universal design', which is a term coined by the architect Ronald L Mace to describe the concept of designing environments to be 'usable to the greatest extent possible by everyone, regardless of their age, ability, or status in life'.[1] In 1963, Selwyn Goldsmith authored a classic book *Designing for the Disabled*, which established a milestone in the creation of barrier-free access for disabled people.[2] He is most famous for the creation of the dropped curb. In 2008, the Chinese government bulldozed 28,000 pavement curbs in central Beijing to make the centre of the city accessible to disabled people in the run up to the 2008 Paralympic games. It was a significant achievement.

However, in most cases other than China hosting the Paralympic Games with an unlimited budget, *universal* design remains a separate work stream. The British government, along with most organisations, has to be more plural in its thinking and encourage others to see how inclusion is in their interests too. LOCOG moved to *inclusive* design to make the design process not just something for disabled people, but for everyone, and not something with fixed immovable standards, but something that could be adapted to better serve individual and cultural needs. A design and management process that works for mums and dads with screaming kids in buggies, last-minute operational flexibility with regard to dramatic Ceremony decisions and venue managers who had broken their leg 'skiing'. This is inclusion, when everyone benefits, when the pie is enlarged and when people understand it is not always a zero-sum game. Indeed, as life expectancy rises and modern medicine increases our survival rate, including those with significant injuries and conditions, we with all be a lot more in demand of inclusive design.

We did it our way

So we created the LOCOG Overlay Access File, or LOAF. 'Overlay' is the infrastructure placed on top of an existing venue in order to 'dress' it and make it ready for Games time. The Olympic and Paralympic movements love acronyms. The irony, as you may have experienced in this book, is that acronyms are not in themselves that accessible. The Olympics has almost invented another language, which is in many ways another barrier to accessibility – and we jumped on the bandwagon by establishing yet another acronym. It was in no small part the creation of Diversity team member Mark Todd, a mobility scooter user with a wild sense of humour and an entrepreneurial flair. Mark had worked in television and was nothing if not a showman. The phrase *du jour* of the Diversity and Inclusion team in conversation with colleagues throughout the organisation (in addition to 'how can I help?') became 'use your LOAF', referring to a common British saying encouraging people to engage their brain on issues of importance.

One of the most tangible aspects of service delivery was the accessible and inclusive venues. All 134 competition and non-competition venues had to comply with the LOAF. It gave practical, clear direction enabling us to deliver high-quality accessible venues for all client groups in all front as well as back of house areas. It was developed from a combination of existing standards, the emerging International Paralympic Committee Technical Manual on Accessibility, previous Games experience and innovative thinking. It was very much a living document that could be continually added to and updated as the Games progressed, and indeed in legacy. There were succinct one-page 'files' on all key issues including wheelchair spaces, accessible toilets, athlete changing facilities, pedestrian screening areas, refreshment counters, queuing systems and cable covers for those not already undergrounded.

It also included files on issues traditionally thought of as outside the scope of accessibility or universal design. For example, we included several entries ('slices') on faith provision including washing facilities, prayer facilities and quiet rooms. This was, after all, about inclusion, not just disability. It was a work stream affecting all of us, rather than being a niche interest. It helped us deliver venues that worked for everyone.

The LOAF was therefore our attempt to make architects design accessible venues and to encourage managers to run them in an accessible manner. It was a common set of accessibility and inclusion standards, which were applied to temporary overlay across all our venues to ensure LOCOG delivered a high and consistent level of accessibility. We aimed for a consistent level of look throughout every Olympic and Paralympic venue. There were a wide variety of venues, each presenting different, sometimes unprecedented, challenges. The aim was to create a consistent client experience across nine client groups and across all 134 venues. Among other things, it allowed us to save on operational costs while allowing full flexibility among allocating our disabled and non-disabled workforce.

We broke the venues down into four types and designed accordingly. With permanent, purpose-built venues, such as the Aquatics Centre in Olympic Park, the Olympic Delivery Authority built them to meet their Inclusive Design standards. With temporary venues such as Hadleigh Farm (mountain biking), or the Equestrian events at Greenwich, LOCOG was able to design the venue and the associated overlay. The goal was to match the purpose-built venues in terms of overlay accessibility standards. Established venues, such as Wimbledon (tennis) and the football stadia, provided the most challenging environments. They already had their own infrastructure, systems and policies in place and these were often inadequate for our standards and the increased expectations of our nine client groups.

Wembley arena, for example, had a limit on the number of assistance dogs that could be admitted for 'health and safety' reasons. This had never been challenged. Yet we knew from our recruitment progress that we were going to have more than six visually impaired people per training session and so we had to escalate this to the Chief Executive in order to have their policy changed. There are countless examples of this nature. In my view, this is precisely what 'using the power of the Games to inspire change' is all about. The fourth and final set of venues were those that were already established but would have a changed use for the Games, such as Lords Cricket ground that hosted the archery.

As with all Everyone's 2012 projects, the LOAF was interdependent with other projects. For example, in order to support the new ticketing product types we sold, we needed to design accordingly. We created a new design of seat layouts in venues that allowed visually impaired people to be seated nearer the front in order to 'feel' the live sporting action. Deaf people could request designated seats with a direct view of the big screens for subtitles and sign language interpretation. People with mobility impairments had a choice when buying tickets of being near fewest steps and/or on the end of a row. Companion seating was designed to offer a mix of options, so disabled and non-disabled people could sit together. Too often, in the past, disabled people were segregated and 'placed' somewhere. 'Able bodied' folks were separated from them. This new arrangement allowed mixed groups of various sizes to be seated together.

Zero-sum game

One of the major challenges to our work, and overall approach, was what Games junkies lovingly call 'Seat kill'. At the Games Operations Planning Steering Group there was a recommendation put forward on 16 June 2008 to reduce the Olympic and Paralympic accessible (wheelchair) seating numbers. The proposing department was Venues and they were recommending the use of local design codes (accessible stadia) to calculate the number of wheelchair positions for Olympic events and the use of the 2007 Paralympic technical manual to calculate the number of wheelchair positions for Paralympic events. This was a material change to the bid commitments, and the recommendation was to ignore the Bid Book.

Initially Ticketing and Sport backed this position. None of these departments were being spiteful, they all had an incredibly complex project to deliver and they couldn't see how they could make the numbers when the opportunity cost of a wheelchair space would be several regular seats. Practically, design-wise and financially it was a tough sell. We had long conversations about this seemingly zero-sum game and worked towards a practical solution that resulted in more wheelchair spaces in the stadia than any previous Games.

LOCOG's work was not undertaken in isolation. The wider circumstances outside the tent are discussed in the next chapter, but in terms of pre-work, the Olympic Delivery Authority and Margaret Hickish deserve credit. We built on the inclusive design process started by Margaret at the Olympic Delivery Authority that ensured, for example, that the wheelchair seating areas were located surrounded by other seating rather than being positioned in segregated areas removed from friends and family. We brought Margaret onto the team to replace the irreplaceable Dave Morris when he passed away in 2010. Prior to this, at the Olympic Delivery Authority, she had established the Built Environment Access Panel (BEAP) a consultative forum of disabled and non-disabled people that reviewed its work. Among other achievements, Margaret had led the undergrounding of much of the cables necessary in the delivery of the event, saving all people from much inconvenience and creating access and flow for all. When we held accessibility 'walk-throughs' post Test Events and pre Games time, we included non-LOCOG colleagues in order to challenge our thinking and to help us with last-minute changes.

Breaking new ground

One of the step-change outputs of our work in this area concerned Games Family transport. The Olympic and Paralympic family are accustomed to a fleet of vehicles and drivers to whizz them around at Games time. Here was our chance to influence a key client group. We worked with our automotive provider BMW to provide adapted vehicles to allow disabled people to drive, as well as be driven, challenging in the most direct way we knew how the concept of disabled people and what they can and can't do. We worked with the disability organisation Mobilise during the Volunteer outreach campaign. We identified and selected fully qualified drivers at our general selection events, using the access requirements we included in the recruitment questionnaire. Disabled people became a core part of the almost 10,000 volunteers aged from 18–79 that were part of Games Family transport operations. We included women drivers, disabled drivers and one 75-year-old driver for whom we had to get extra insurance.

A key inclusive design output was the first ever Games Mobility Service. For the first time at an Olympic and Paralympic Games a dedicated mobility service was designed and offered to provide assistance free of charge with spectator movement from entrances through public circulation areas to individual seats. It was a key concept tested in our client journey planning. It included the free loan of mobility scooters, wheelchairs and power chairs. After the Games, the plan was to pass vehicles on at subsidised rates to local shop mobility schemes and the National Health Service to upgrade their current fleets, splitting the cost of the equipment over its life cycle to save costs to each stakeholder. We created accessible viewing areas, and areas for wheelchair and pushchair and buggy storage. There was a golf buggy shuttle service at large venues, a wheelchair pushing service to help spectators to their seats and a guiding service for visually impaired spectators.

The Games Mobility Service was managed centrally from hubs. These hubs also distributed audio description and commentary devices for visually impaired spectators. They enabled blind people to have the action described to them, or to tune in to live commentary. Anyone could pay to rent one, in order to receive an enhanced spectator experience, but they were free of charge to any visually impaired person that requested one, no questions asked and no proof required. This saved on administration costs and training. Games Makers assisted spectators with accessibility needs by directing them to these hubs, especially when they did not know the answer to a particular question. The hubs could contact central control at any time, who in turn could access the Diversity and Inclusion team at any time and get the customer an answer in real time. The hubs also distributed spectator maps and guides in a range of formats such as large print, Braille, sign language and audio version. For learning-disabled folks and people whose native language is not English, we distributed Easy Read format fact sheets. These were documents that contained a lot of pictures and are made easier to understand by using plain language, simple phrases and ideas, short sentences and minimal abbreviations.

We had problems with over-demand for hub services and people not having ordered items in advance that were hard for us to produce in real time. I can only conclude that inclusion is a two-way street and while I remain of the belief that LOCOG created a step change in accessibility, we of course fell short some of the time. Some people were unreasonable some of the time.

Total customer service

We trained all 200,000 Games Makers to *ask*, rather than assume. This sounds simple but was in fact a step change in how customer service is delivered to disabled people, and anyone who might otherwise be ignored. Above all, we taught all 200,000 staff to talk to the person, not their 'carer', parent, personal assistant, boyfriend, dog, pet or inanimate object. In other words, we trained people to see the person, rather than make an assumption about their disability. This was the simplest of acts but it meant the world to disabled people who had become accustomed to being talked 'at' or 'about' rather than 'to' or 'with'. This is something I was particularly passionate about, having worked on the 'see the person' disability campaign back in my advertising days. This did not just apply to the Games Mobility Service team, all Games Makers were trained as part of their core training on disability confidence. We trained all 70,000 Games Makers to ask, 'How can I help you?' (rather than assume anything) and then to offer an elbow to any visually impaired person that wanted a guide.

Part of the understanding we had inculcated among LOCOG staff was the philosophy that we wanted to remove attitudinal as well as physical barriers that stop disabled people from being included. This was about removing barriers to anyone taking part. We incorporated inclusive design into the success criteria of the nine client groups. What would improve the experience of a member of the Olympic or Paralympic family or a member of the

press? How could it work for them but also their colleague/mum/dad/child/
personal assistant? The aim of the LOAF was to offer practical, clear direction enabling LOCOG to deliver high-quality accessible venues for all client
groups in all areas. For example, not assuming that we could use steps 'back
of house' because disabled people wouldn't work there. With LOCOG, they
did work there.

Online accessibility

In Sydney 2000, the Organising Committee ran into trouble when their
online results were inaccessible to some people. Mindful of this, we worked
to be inclusive online in terms of both accessibility and usability as well as
content and profiling our inclusion work and values. We engaged a range of
users to feed back on the website, as well as work with specialist providers
on accessibility. The end result was an exceeding of accessibility standards
not only in commissioning but also in editorial, design and coding. We went
beyond the Web Accessibility Initiative, Equality Act 2010 and the Disability Discrimination Act. We used plain English throughout the site (as well as
French, officially used by the Olympic Movement). The font size and style
was changeable on demand allowing visually impaired or dyslexic people to
access all information.[3] There were alternative formats. We worked with the
Royal Association of Deaf People so that users could find key info in sign
language and key videos with subtitles. Blind and visually impaired people
could find key videos and audio description and download free software
allowing them to have the content of the site read aloud to them.

The hope is that the LOAF, Games Mobility Service and other inclusive design outputs set the standard for future Games. As London proved it
could be done without significant extra cost, suppliers of component structures and supplies will update and modernise their stock to meet LOAF
standards and be ready for future Games. By starting early, significant
economies of scale were achieved and in many cases costs were reduced,
such as by designing for both Olympic and Paralympic Games at once and
minimising the need for transition between Games. By making the Olympic Games accessible, the Paralympic Games simply benefited from another
(albeit major) test event. We constantly reminded people of the slides shown
in the 'understand' conversation concerning the two separate views Dave
and I had of the same sport at the Beijing Paralympic Games. We constantly
reminded people that it doesn't just happen. And through maintaining the

conversation we were able to unlock innovation among engineers and architects who had previously been oblivious or even hostile.

Looking back now I appreciate more than ever the environment we created, especially in the Park. We created something special. An accessible environment that worked for everyone. Step free, highly tactile, with easy navigation and accessible transport on call. But it was not just in a physical sense. The staff and volunteers were trained to be inclusive.

Boarding a recent flight, I was pushing my mum in a wheelchair. The attendant asked me 'Does she know what flight she's on?' The way my Mum was disempowered in an instant defies words. Here was the first woman in her family ever to go to university, a naturally kind and clever woman and a teacher of 30 years being talked about as though she were a vegetable. In stark comparison, the Olympic Park in the summer of 2012 was a glimpse of how life could be.

Takeaways – use your LOAF: accessibility inside the tent

1 LOCOG moved on from 'accessibility' and even 'universal design' to inclusive design. The importance of an early start and systematising the operation was seen in the outputs, an environment that worked for all people.

2 Inclusive design allowed economies of scale and efficiencies not realised under conventional segregated accessibility policy.

3 The Park and the Games Mobility Service and transport outputs demonstrated what inclusion can look like, for everyone.

Notes

1 Universal design: http://www.ncsu.edu.ncsu/design/cud/aboutus/usronmace/htm.

2 See the 1997 edition (Architectural Press) of Goldsmith's famous book.

3 Visually impaired people generally need as much contrast as possible between text and background to make the letters stand out. Dyslexic people generally prefer the opposite with more subtle shades to aid reading and comprehension.

Transport, screening and a walk along the South Bank: accessibility outside the tent

20

Transport, along with security, the weather and the possibility of a death in the upper echelons of the Royal Family, was top of our risk register. In the end, the logistics worked brilliantly, with queue times under five minutes, the most diverse customer base imaginable and a utopian atmosphere created in the Olympic Park, if only for six weeks. Furthering our inclusive design work, creating environments that work for everyone, this is also the story of how we made a large part of central London accessible for disabled people.

Inclusion remains a theoretical concept for many. A fantastic way for us to make it tangible, and to demonstrably use the power of the Games to inspire change, was to improve the physical condition and accessibility of a large part of central London.

The Paralympic inclusive environment

On the South Bank of the River Thames in central London, the riverside walk was improved in terms of access along a mile-long stretch from Westminster Bridge to Tower Bridge, and slightly beyond. This provided an accessible and inclusive zone of significant size that could not only be enjoyed by disabled people, but anyone who had access requirements; mums and dads with buggies, older people, roller-bladers, inline skaters and cyclists. It opened up a large part of central London to groups who had difficulty accessing it in the past. The £4 million budget came from central government and was awarded to the Greater London Authority and the boroughs of Southwark and Lambeth. They spent it on improving pavement layouts, better lighting and signage, more seating and access ramps and handrails.

English Heritage were allegedly against the improvements we wanted to make in one section of the river walk.[1] It was a cobbled section by the 'Clink' prison not far from London Bridge. We of course want to be respectful of tradition and heritage but trying to cross these cobbles in a wheelchair was like being a ball bearing in a slot machine. And don't even mention heels. I suspect that both wheelchairs and heels were not common in medieval England when the original streetscape took shape. As with our approach to sewage and public sanitation, we have improved and moved on. So we should with cobbles. All tradition is invented and we can invent a new one. We retained the beloved cobbles, only this time there was a mere few millimetres depth between each one rather than inches, resulting in a smoother ride for wheelchair users, high-heel wearers and all concerned.

Following on from the LOCOG Overlay Access File (LOAF), we decided to call this the PIE, or Paralympic Inclusive Environment. In times of high stress and high workload the baking analogy could become wearing, but nobody seemed to mind. The PIE was a continuous safe and accessible route for everyone along the South Bank that passed major world cultural institutions, from the National Theatre to the Southbank Centre, from the Hayward Gallery to the British Film Institute, and from City Hall to a series of Live Sites during Games time.[2] By linking to the bridges it provided accessible routes to points north of the river. Easy way-finding was aided by photo routes developed by www.enabledcity.com and there were downloadable routes and information sheets for people with learning disabilities, non-English speakers (tourists), and sign language users. This was the brainchild of David Morris, who sadly did not live to see its completion.

Empowering people through information provision

One of the main barriers to disabled people accessing and enjoying London, especially at Games time but also in legacy, was lack of information and also the lack of credible and consistent information. To help, we joined forces with the mayor and a company called Direct Enquiries, to provide a one-stop website, www.inclusivelondon.com, with information on bars, restaurants, accommodation, shopping, entertainment and convenience stores including banks. The main innovation, besides its breadth and impartiality was user feedback, so it was not just owner promotion. The website achieved over a million hits before the Games even started, demonstrating its worth – and the potential new market.

Accessible transport

Transport was a major inclusion issue. Our work determined that if we did not intervene as early as possible in the client journey then a paying customer could be a frazzled mess by the time they reached the venue. We would then be playing catch-up rather than building a net positive client experience. When David Morris worked for the Mayor of London, before I stole him to work for the Games, one of his biggest legacies had been working on creating the world's biggest accessible bus fleet. For the Games, we went further and made the London bus fleet even more accessible, revamping 300 buses to create five to six wheelchair or buggy spaces per bus instead of the standard one space. This allowed wheelchair teams to travel together, plus additional seating for up to 21 non-disabled team members.

There is potentially a zero-sum game here, what venue planners call 'seat kill'. For one wheelchair space to be created, more than one regular seat is removed. From a commercial perspective, therefore, there is a potential revenue loss. I do not yet have a commercial answer to this conundrum, other than to offer the general growth and ethical argument of the benefits that accrue through different people being able to come together.

All London buses were therefore low floor, wheelchair accessible and delivered audio/visual announcements of stops. All London piers were wheelchair accessible and we worked with the ferry companies to develop an underused accessible transport mode for anyone with access requirements. London's famous black cabs were all wheelchair accessible with a ramp and space to manoeuvre. The only constraint with the cabs was some of the cabbies and their attitude. Many were brilliant, but even the Olympics had a hard time changing some remaining attitudes there.

Transport for London developed 'humps' on many major underground train platforms to permit level access on and off trains. Overnight, this increased the concept of London for millions of people. Now they could access previously inaccessible stations and new parts of the city. Part of the argument we used in lobbying for these 'humps' was the classic temporary argument. If you argue something is temporary, it is often easier to successfully navigate planning control. Gustav Eiffel knew this when he successfully completed his tower in Paris in 1889 for the World Fair. He only had a permit for the tower to stand for 20 years, after which time it had to be dismantled. As the tower was an instant tourist success and valuable communication platform, it remains to this day. Without that original framing of the project as 'temporary' we would be denied its current existence. Let us hope the same occurs with those humps. Call it an experiment and let it be a legacy.

Twenty million spectator journeys were made in London during the Games, 3 million on the busiest day. Public transport was used by 800,000 ticketed spectators on the busiest day and 600,000 pieces of luggage were handled during the Games at Heathrow airport, 203,000 on 13 August, the busiest day of all, or 35 per cent more than normal. The end-to-end client journey planning therefore aimed to ensure accessible and inclusive facilities at all points of entry and departure. LOCOG worked with British Airways, major airports, relevant companies and government at a 'Flying Round Table' to share best practice and improve the client journey. Tanni Grey-Thompson was incredibly helpful and vocal on these issues, for example testifying how her wheelchair would repeatedly be treated as luggage and subsequently damaged. We undertook our 'understand, lead and deliver' process with various stakeholders in order to smooth the client journey.

Security

LOCOG worked with a reference group to develop security policies and procedures that would be seamless for everyone, a step change from anything done before. We shared our training for all staff and specific disability confidence training with the largest security contractor, G4S. As it happened, G4S failed to deliver on their contractual commitments, could not deliver the staff and we were too late to train the military. Still, of those staff that were trained, they interacted with the military well and we received surprisingly few complaints from the thousands of disabled people who crossed the screening areas each day.

All pedestrian screening areas had at least one accessible entry point and all raised walk-through metal detectors were ramped at a gradient of 1 in 20 (easy). There were access lanes for those who could not stand for long periods of time. Accessible lanes were clearly signed with the international wheelchair symbol and had level access with a width of at least 1.2 m (wide enough for even large chairs to pass through and turn). Pat-down checks were mandatory for all wheelchair users (inclusion is a two-way street) and staff were trained to ask permission first and ask whether there were any sore or delicate areas on the person. Kirpans (a Sikh article of faith) were permitted as long as the blade was small enough. This sensitive, respectful approach was clearly beyond business as usual and overseen by a diverse team. People could ask for a more discreet search, or reasonable adjustments for spiritual and cultural value of religious items.

Athens had made the Acropolis accessible, Beijing the Great Wall. London made the less glamorous South Bank accessible, but it arguably made a bigger difference, opening up the centre of a global capital to all people. The deadline forced opposing factions to the negotiating table. The power of scrutiny also ensured no borough wanted to be seen as laggard in this area. When the central government was prepared to offer the money, the mayor was prepared to oversee it, and one borough came on board, it would be normal behaviour for another borough to oppose. That did not happen in this case because of the deadline, because of the scrutiny and also because of the framing of the subject matter.

Combined with the policy changes (such as screening) and process changes (such as the public transport underground 'humps') we were able to create lasting change. At the end of the day, this was simply about making environments work for all people.

Takeaways – transport, screening and a walk along the South Bank: accessibility outside the tent

1 Inclusive design outside the tent demonstrated the importance of partnership working. The Paralympic Inclusive Environment (PIE) shows what can be achieved when you don't care who takes the credit.

2 Because inclusive design is not generally understood or accepted, it requires leadership. The transport and security outcomes demonstrate how this is hard work, but ultimately successful.

3 The deadline was a focus for all parties to come together and to agree delivery of certain actions by a certain date. The client journey allowed us to analyse and determine how accessible environments could become, or would need to become, when 10,000 wheelchair users were arriving at the same time.

Notes

1 Conversation with Margaret Hickish, September 2012.

2 See Chapter 22.

Trapped in polyester

21

In Maslow's hierarchy of needs, two of the basic physiological necessities of life are food and clothing. Given that the Games impinged on one of my favourite Maslowian basics, sleep, it was imperative that we ensured the sanctity of the remaining ones. Furthermore, if the overall goal of real inclusion is to attain the top of the pyramid, to empower self-actualisation among our people, then it is imperative the basics are taken care of first.

Uniforms

However, and by way of confession, 'Uniforms' is one department I didn't take seriously at the outset. Maybe it's analogous to how many people still view Diversity and Inclusion. I just couldn't equate dressing up staff with the gravity of building and running 134 venues. I quickly learned, however, that uniforms are a serious business, both in terms of cost, but also in terms of logistics. If you get uniforms right, your staff will love you. Get them wrong, and you open a whole can of worms. How you dress people is indeed one of the fundamentals of professional life.

Uniforms were provided to over 8,000 paid staff and 70,000 volunteers; 766 miles of fabric was required. They also had to be easily mimicked by the remaining 130,000 contractors, in order to maintain an overall 'look and feel' of the Games. We were contractually bound to work with Adidas and Next, our two sportswear and home retail partners, respectively. So we undertook a series of structured conversations with them about our Diversity and Inclusion strategy, in a similar way to those we'd had inside LOCOG. We wanted to create a uniform that worked for everyone irrespective of size, shape or religious belief. During the development process, we reiterated the image used in our 'understanding' conversation, the image of the England football team with a supporter from every country in the world, wearing the same shirt; Diversity and Inclusion.

We worked closely with faith groups, especially the Inter Faith Forum, and disability groups to design a uniform that was distinctive and, if at all possible, *à la mode*. It would represent the face of the Games to the world, while allowing people with specific needs to make adaptations or adjustments within set guidelines. For example, people wanting to wear additional garments such as a Burqa, Hijab or Sikh turban were permitted to do so but ensuring they were plain in design, unbranded and black or white or of neutral colour. The same was true of people wishing to carry additional baggage due to their disability or long-term health condition.

We had a dedicated tailoring service and specific design adaptations for amputees, wheelchair users or anyone else if required and ensured sizing ranged from XS to XXXL. Simon Cartwright, the global VP of Olympic sports for Adidas said that the uniforms included 'perfect thermo regulation, light materials and the requirement that uniforms are practically adaptable for people with disabilities'.[1]

The uniform was universally praised for all its inclusion aspects. It could indeed be worn by people of various sizes, shapes and faiths. However, I personally wasn't enamoured with the design, being one of the few gay men in the world who is not remotely interested in fashion and avoids shopping wherever and whenever possible. In theory, here was another real inclusion example: fashion and real inclusion being happy bedfellows, just as with the commercial imperative of ticketing and inclusion, detailed in Chapter 16. However, my far more stylish and contemporary friend Madiha summed it up perfectly when she blamed me for recruiting her and 'trapping her in polyester'.

It is true that it wasn't the nicest feel next to the skin. It is also true that Madiha, more accustomed to a chic cocktail dress and a pair of Prada heels, was somewhat lost in the heat-trapping, skin-cladding polyester and flat trainers supplied with her job. Madiha, I can only apologise.

Others, however, went further. One Games Maker, Suzy Aldridge, made me laugh with the observation that she was contained in a 'Polyester prison'. She picked up her uniform before starting her role at the Millennium Stadium in Cardiff (football). She found the purple and red 'utterly garish' (I concur) but she 'couldn't help but enjoy the epaulettes'. It is true that epaulettes are a treat. However, her main issue, and indeed the main issue for many others, was that the job was often physically laborious and as a consequence she felt the Games Makers were 'cooking' in their 'polyester prisons'. Some people may have felt the uniforms were 'cool' in design terms, but it seems that they were unfortunately not in 'thermal' terms. This was an example of where, when you get the basics wrong, the inclusion triumph (or even debatable fashion triumph) is somewhat forgotten.

Food

Another of the fundamentals in Maslow's hierarchy of needs is food. Besides clothing our people, we had to feed them. And 11 million spectators and thousands of athletes. There are of course a huge variety of cuisines in London. The UK went from being the butt of international jokes on food to being one of the lead countries for food in the 1990s and 2000s and the country embraced its multiple food diversities. There exists a strong restaurant, market and shop culture, with a diverse range of food from all over the world. LOCOG published its food vision in December 2009 and the result was more diverse, more affordable and better food than any previous Games or equivalent sporting event.

When I was working at Beijing in 2008 I became accustomed to exploding takeaway rice dishes that miraculously 'self boiled' upon pulling a piece of string. They were just about edible. At baseball Games in the United States, we ate hot dogs of questionable meat served up with a stale roll and a variety of processed sauces. So in this context, the diversity and quality of British food served up at scale for the London 2012 Games was a triumph. Part of the credit goes to our catering and procurement teams who engaged with small suppliers, not just the big guys. That allowed quality specialist food to make its way to the public, as well as keep the big guys on their toes that they did not have a monopoly on all things edible.

We had children's portions and low counters for wheelchair users, with extensive use of iconography, to help all people order what they wanted, irrespective of intellectual disability or language – there were no barriers to having a good meal. This was not simply about inclusion, this saved time, reduced queue times and increased sales.

The Olympic Games took place during the final two weeks of Ramadan. We had adapted services during this period, such as late-night food options for the breaking of fast, and Ramadan packs for the workforce. We had worked with the Faith Reference Group to better understand specific needs and offered high-quality Halal and Kosher meals that surpassed levels such as the European Halal Development Agency's standard. Of course in any operation of such size and complexity there were hiccups. That is understandable, indeed expected, given that over the Games period, 14 million meals were served for all client groups.

On the first Wednesday of the Games I encountered an unhappy Muslim colleague in the Park. He had just returned from his meal break at the Common Domain main dining area. What was the matter? Was it the faith rooms not open? No, they were open 24/7 and used by people of all faiths and no faith as required. Was it a colleague that had been inappropriate or even discriminatory? No, the training seemed to have worked well and everyone was getting along just fine in their common uniform. The problem was the menu. After two consecutive days of pork being the meat option, he was understandably crying out for a change of tack. This particular Wednesday change happened. Unfortunately, the change manifested itself in the form of a beef and ale pie. I apologised, caught up with the relevant catering manager and it didn't happen again.

For some, therefore, a 'low light' of the best Games ever was the uniform and/or the food. However, this must be set in context. Compared to any other Games I have experienced, they were a triumph and credit should go to all concerned. However, after interviewing several 'Games Makers', I feel fully briefed to tell the story of a wonderfully inclusive, but in some ways unpopular, uniform, as well as well-intentioned meal options that sometimes fell at the final hurdle. This is the evidence to prove the point that basic considerations should sometimes come first, in order to achieve the best outcome for everyone. In order to achieve the top of Maslow's pyramid, we sometimes need to start at the bottom. Diversity advocates forget this at their peril.

Takeaways – trapped in polyester

1 Style and practicality are inclusion considerations. We understand now that asking people what is important to them (such as 'thermo-regulation' when carrying out laborious work) is better than assuming.

2 Client requirements can be incorporated into mass scale operations. Beef and ale pie aside, we were able to accommodate every global faith and every disability presented during the course of 14 million meals.

3 The uniform was the face of the Games. In our 'understanding' campaign, we had used an image of people from every country in the

world all wearing the England football team uniform. That had now been scaled up 1,000 times to represent the diversity of the world, working together as one team.

Note

1 Simon Cartwright interview, LOCOG policy document/report 2011.

The ceremonies 22

The Opening Ceremony of the London Olympic Games started at 20.12 (8.12 pm) on 27 July 2012. This is the moment my colleagues and I had been working constantly for, for over five years. David Luckes and Richard Sumray had been working on them since the late 1990s. Eighty Heads of State were in the stadium, 205 countries were represented, more than are members of the United Nations. We had done everything we could have done and now we waited to see how the world would react. It was quite a moment.

Isles of wonder

The Opening Ceremony, directed by Danny Boyle, began very humbly with a nod to low-key British idiosyncrasies; our love of the 'Green and Pleasant Land', a journey down the River Thames and the four national songs of the four constituent countries of the United Kingdom, including England, Scotland, Wales and Northern Ireland. The British Press had mocked the unveiling of the countryside model concept at a press briefing earlier in the year. But, as with Maslow's pyramid, it was important to start with the basics and this is what the world was expecting from Britain. It was the stereotype they wanted us to deliver on, and, in a fashion, we did.

Perhaps the most poignant 'traditional' sequence was honouring those who gave their lives in war for the freedoms we enjoy today. As one of the volunteer performers tweeted online after having watched the playback of the ceremony afterwards: 'I didn't realise everyone stood for the poppies section. I was holding back the tears while performing but when I just watched that I cried so hard.'

However, as the Opening Ceremony progressed, we began to challenge the Green and Pleasant Land stereotype. The Industrial Revolution was showcased in a brutal, honest and direct way with chimneys shooting up from the destroyed countryside ground. A Victorian paradigm shift was set to modern dance music from Underworld. Diversity sprang forth in the form of the Suffragettes, demanding women's rights, and in the form of the *Windrush* ship, that carried the first African and West Indian immigrants seeking jobs and prosperity in Britain. The Ceremony went on to showcase a wide variety of diverse backgrounds from the unrivalled Dame Evelyn Glennie, a deaf drummer and musician who teaches hearing people 'how to listen', to the first gay kiss broadcast on any global live feed, beamed around the world to all territories. Sir Tim Berners Lee, inventor of the World Wide Web, typed on his keyboard, as Emeli Sande sang *Heaven*, and the words 'This is for Everyone' were beamed around the stadium.

The four ceremonies (Opening and Closing for both Olympic and Paralympic Games) embodied the best of courage, creativity and talent.

Courage, because we defied protocol in including disabled people in such a visible way in the Olympic Opening Ceremony, rather than 'confining' them to the Paralympic Ceremony where it would have perhaps been 'understandable'. We were not only acting outside the norm; we created a new inclusive norm. 'Kaos', a mixed deaf and hearing children's choir sang the National Anthem. It was courage to include a gay kiss that was going to be seen in countries that still had the death penalty for gay people. It was courage, because we were defying the stereotype the world expected us to display, including the Queen 'jumping' from a helicopter with James Bond in tow. For the medal ceremonies, a little-known subversive process change we undertook was to swap the gender protocol of the medal presenters. At London 2012, boys offered flowers to winning athletes and girls offered the medals, and no one noticed, at least until it was too late.

The ceremonies were also supremely creative. The Paralympic Opening Ceremony was called 'Enlightenment', echoing the historical era that gave birth to the modern creative movement as detailed at the start of Part Two. It was in some ways even more important for inclusion than the Olympic opening. In it, Stephen Hawking, perhaps the most famous disabled role model in the world, encouraged us all to 'be curious' and to 'look up at the stars, not down at our feet'. Disabled and non-disabled people performed as protesters with placards calling for equal rights. There followed a rendition of the controversial song *Spasticus Autisticus* by Graeae Theatre Company.

In the same way that the LGBT movement has attempted to reclaim language used to oppress it, here too was the ultimate reclamation of language by the disabled movement, and on a global platform. The centrepiece of the sequence was a huge statue of the Marc Quinn sculpture 'Alison Lapper Pregnant'. Alison was born without arms and with truncated legs. Having attempted to use artificial limbs, she chose to discard them and simply be herself, as born. This was visually and morally challenging to many people, being a complete reversal of the disabled stereotype so frequently played out in everyday media. Did disabled people really have sex? And they could give birth?

The talent involved in the ceremonies was infinitely diverse and presented as such on a global stage. As with the athletes achieving their own potential so did many of the 10,000 Britons that were involved in the Opening and Closing Ceremonies in a volunteer capacity. They were actively encouraged to bring their whole selves to the stage and if you look closely at the films, you can see multiple individual personalities shine through.

Our Brazilian guests in the Olympic Closing Ceremony, Pele and colleagues, embraced our inclusive vision as they shared the event with British DJ Fat Boy Slim performing to an inflatable and expanding octopus. So too did the disabled pilot from Aerobility, when he flew over the stadium for the Paralympic Opening Ceremony. 'Look Up' said Stephen Hawking, and we did, to appreciate disabled talent presented like never before. In order to hire a diverse cast of performers and presenters, we applied all our learning from the recruitment process to help the ceremonies team. The end result was that everyone worldwide who watched the ceremonies saw someone like them in the cast.

Mike Brace, who is visually impaired and a former Chair of the British Paralympic Association, told me that having sat through nearly 20 Olympic and Paralympic Opening Ceremonies, this was the first time in his life he had any idea what was going on. London 2012 was the first Games ever to include audio description as standard in all of the ceremonies. Of course, this did not just happen. We worked with the Ceremonies Company for years to support them on their inclusion journey. They suffered from *Guardian*-reader syndrome to an even more severe degree than the main LOCOG organisation. Yet I can't help concluding that the presence of diversity forced creativity.

When Martin Green was appointed as LOCOG's Head of Ceremonies, he recruited a fantastic and diverse team, from Jenny Sealey as Creative Director for the Paralympics to Danny Boyle for the Olympics to Stephen Daldry and Catherine Ugwu as Executive Producers across all the shows. There was then a good chance the tipping point had been reached. We were consulting to the converted. Our questions of 'how can I help?' were enthusiastically embraced and we shared everything we had learned to date to help the Ceremonies team excel.

The ceremonies were especially poignant for me. I had managed to buy tickets to the Paralympic Games Closing Ceremony for my mum and dad as a thank you for everything they had done for me in my life up to this point.

My dad died unexpectedly in February 2012 while out on his bike, and so did not get to see the final result that he had been looking forward to. I took my mum and sister along and they enjoyed it. The Closing Ceremony is always a party, and this one was fantastic. It was also the final ceremony of the Games, and I felt able to relax a little, knowing that tomorrow we could lie in and if things didn't go totally to plan we could still take heart from the extraordinary spectacle that already lay behind us. As Coldplay blasted out the final song and the stadium sang along to *Paradise* I couldn't help reflecting on loss as I simultaneously looked around the stadium and saw 80,000 people having the time of their lives.

Including people outside the stadium

We applied a lot of the learning we developed in ceremonies' preparation to the presentation of the sport too. In the same way as we saw the Olympics and Paralympics as one overall show, we cross-fertilised the two events with regard to the sport too. Paralympic sports such as wheelchair basketball were exhibited and marketed at half-time entertainment at some of the Olympic Games competitions. We worked with the Royal National Institute of Blind people semi-successfully to provide enhanced audio description or commentary of the sport – and not just for the Paralympics. Commentary for all blind or visually impaired people who wanted it was provided at no charge, with a nominal charge for all others to cover our costs. This was a first for any multi-sport event. Information was also provided in sign language to allow deaf people to interact with the Games. This was inclusion – take gymnastics, for example. In this sport I watched and watched and still didn't have a clue what was going on, until I could access commentary, and alongside visually impaired people, begin to understand the sport for the first time.

In order to bring the action to people in towns and cities across the UK, LOCOG instigated a Live Sites programme. This involved a series of large screens in 22 public spaces where people could follow the Games for free. In addition to these permanent sites, there were a further 47 temporary sites. They were paired with news and community events and each site was designed to be as accessible as possible. We developed a 'Live Sites toolkit' that was distributed free to the relevant local authorities and is a legacy document for improved accessibility in their town. Working with the broadcasters and other providers, LOCOG ensured an accessible display of content using plain English and text content as part of the video presentation. Over 500,000 people celebrated at Live Sites every day during the Games.

Inclusion ran through the planning of the ceremonies as well as their execution. As Martin Green, Head of Ceremonies said, 'we want the country to be engaged with it we want them to come along on the journey... for the first time of any host country we are going to share (in advance) some of the content of the show... we want people to get involved'.[1] The ceremonies were in many ways the most memorable and impactful of the 'Everyone's 2012' projects. From suffragettes to dancing nuns on roller blades, immigrants and disabled choirs to the first gay kiss in any Olympics ceremony, this is a story of how we infused the ceremonies with inclusion in a non-worthy, stylish and popular way that worked.

Historically, I think they will be judged strongly – they walked the line between being so stereotypical that they changed very little thinking, and being so radical that they were ignored or dismissed. They managed to satisfy so many requirements without resorting to rule by committee output, and as beacons of inclusion, they will stand the test of time.

Takeaways – the ceremonies

1 The overwhelming benefit of the Opening and Closing Ceremonies, besides sheer joy, was that millions of people worldwide could see what real inclusion looked like. As with the Torch Relays, the ceremonies offered the opportunity to make the nebulous real, and to use emotion as a business imperative for change.

2 Rather than additional 'initiatives' inclusion was weaved systemically throughout the whole process and output, reflective of our approach to work through the line rather than as an external department.

3 In a very real sense, the ceremonies delivered on the overall mission, which was to use the power of the Games to inspire change.

Note

1 http://www.bbc.co.uk/news/uk-england-16758749.

PART FOUR
Legacy

Introduction to Part Four

The inclusion imperative

In the Opening Ceremony of the London Olympic Games, the actor Kenneth Branagh, playing the British engineer Isambard Kingdom Brunel, addresses the men and women of the Industrial Revolution. As he stands on the replica of Glastonbury Tor, and Elgar's Nimrod symphony stirs in the background, he quotes from Shakespeare's *The Tempest* and implores the citizens not to be afraid of change.

> Be not afeard; the isle is full of noises,
>
> Sounds, and sweet airs, that give delight and hurt not.
>
> Sometimes a thousand twangling instruments
>
> Will hum about mine ears; and sometime voices,
>
> That, if I then had waked after long sleep,
>
> Will make me sleep again: and then, in dreaming,
>
> The clouds methought would open, and show riches
>
> Ready to drop upon me; that, when I waked,
>
> I cried to dream again.
>
> —William Shakespeare, *The Tempest*

But change can be scary, unsettling and upsetting. By its very nature, it can create massive disequilibrium that, if poorly managed, can cause chaos. The *Pandemonium* sequence, which in my view is the most beautiful aspect of London's Opening Ceremony, was named after John Milton's definition of hell in his 1667 book *Paradise Lost*. It echoes the confusion, hurt and loss than can occur during the process of change. One thing I consistently fail to do is show sufficient compassion for the victims of change, as well as sufficient understanding of those who fail to embrace it. It is something I need to become better at. But we need not be 'afeard' of real inclusion. In the end, it has the potential to save us more than it ever does to harm us.

The legacy debate raged before the Games were even won, and it will rage for many more years yet. What is legacy and what is the inclusion legacy of the Games? Government, organisations and the media are constantly searching for evidence of 'legacy', some tangible proof that all the money spent was worthwhile.

To many, legacy means physical regeneration; that the local environment looks different. After years of inaction, dithering and infighting, the East End of London has finally been cleaned up after World War Two. Unexploded bombs have been removed, soil has been washed, and water has been cleaned. In and around the Park 8.35 km of waterways have been cleaned, with 30 new bridges crossing roads, rail lines and rivers, linking the city East–West and bringing the poorest part of the capital back into contact with the rest of the city. In two 6 km-long tunnels 200 km of electrical cables were laid, allowing 52 overhead pylons to be removed. Over 4,000 trees, 60,000 bulbs and 350,000 wetlands plants have been planted – the largest such project ever undertaken in the UK. Queen Elizabeth Olympic Park is set to be the major new Hyde Park of our times; and in East London, the part of London most in need of it.

To many others, legacy means sporting regeneration, the promise to inspire a generation to choose sport. Some claim that 500,000 people were inspired to choose sport with a £135 million investment in 1,500 facilities, clubs, playing fields and participation programmes. Every permanent new venue was only built where a business case supported it, legacy operators were in place before the Games even started and there will be a vibrant sports complex in the East End of London, including London's only velodrome, cycling tracks and community pools.

Few, however, have yet considered the Diversity and Inclusion legacy. A concerted, strategic four-year team effort has produced tangible results. LOCOG achieved the most diverse workforce of any Games to date with 40 per cent ethnic minority inclusion against a national figure of 10 per cent. Five Directors and 46 per cent of staff were women, 5 per cent of the staff were openly gay or lesbian and trans people were genuinely and naturally included as part of the team. Every faith, and no faith, was represented in multiple ways, volunteers ranged from 16 to 101 years old and over 2,000 disabled people were placed into genuine Games time roles on the basis of merit.

Groundbreaking supplier diversity led to two-thirds of contracts awarded to small businesses, 15 per cent of CompeteFor contracts awarded to women-owned businesses, the largest supplier diversity mobilisation of large UK corporations to date and changes in major global corporation diversity policy. LOCOG's work re-wrote the rules of the professional body's standards.

In service delivery, sports governing bodies were benchmarked on their diversity record for the first time and a National Charter against homophobia and transphobia was launched for the first time ever. A series of pin badges alongside the Olympic rings went global and symbolised minority inclusion at the heart of the world's greatest event, a Games first. The ceremonies were infused with diversity, from Evelyn Glennie's soaring drums to the first gay kiss ever in an Opening Ceremony, broadcast worldwide. The most accessible Games ever included a new accessible River Thames South Bank, adapted vehicles and 8,000 diverse, role model Torchbearers. The most successful Paralympic Games ever reflected the inclusion of both the Olympic and Paralympic Games in one single planning team. London 2012 was the first time a Saudi woman has competed in the Games and the first time all countries had women on their teams.

The hard truth, however, is that the work is never complete. There is always more to do. In a dynamic world the work can never be complete. The above list of achievements did not just happen. They happened because enough people intellectually, emotionally and practically bought into an idea and made it part of their day job. They understood inclusion, they led on inclusion, and they delivered inclusively. Thousands of people working hard, to shared values, in a limited timeframe created an unprecedented and key differentiator for the London Games.

Every Games has its passions and priorities. London chose a key differentiator which had never been achieved before, which cost comparatively little and achieved significant return on investment. We created an unprecedented culture of inclusion that infused the entire planning and staging of the world's greatest event. This also happened against the odds. Most change programmes take time but we had limited time and an immovable deadline. Most inclusion efforts require significant resources but we had an incredibly constrained budget with unprecedented scrutiny. Perhaps most significantly of all however, most 'diversity programmes' are party to vested interests and merely reiterate current thinking. We used the power of the Games to create lasting change, create paradigm shift and tackle significant vested interests in the wider social interest.

In many ways, Diversity and Inclusion work is pushing against human nature, like salmon swimming upstream. We like to associate with people like ourselves. We are suspicious of difference. And so without constantly swimming upstream, there is always the risk of being pulled down by the current, of the work sliding back, of retrenchment. Counter-stereotyping is an ongoing process, not a 'flick of the switch'.[1] We see it in sectarian conflict every day all over the world. We persist in our dislike of diversity and we persist in an embracing of superficial inclusion. We are living on a knife-edge and, even in the information age, we still draw comfort from ignorance.

In Part One of *The Inclusion Imperative* we discussed what real inclusion is, why you might want to achieve it, and introduced the principal case study of the book, both inside and outside the London 2012 tent. In Part Two, we discussed how to achieve real inclusion, the process, the interventions and the priorities. In Part Three, we discussed what real inclusion looks like and analysed some of the results, from a diverse workforce, to an innovative supply chain, to an inclusive customer experience that exceeded the expectations of our nine client groups. In the final part, I attempt to give due diligence to four important legacy questions.

These concern the theory developed, the tools created, the lessons learned and applicability to other organisations. First, what have we learned about the value of real inclusion? Second, what were the key game-changers, the tools that created the results we achieved? Third, where did we fail and what did this teach us? Finally, where do we go from here – what is the applicability to other organisations that want to achieve real inclusion?

Milton's book *Paradise Lost* was written in 1667, the Industrial Revolution happened in the 18th and 19th centuries, and with reference to both, Sir Hubert Parry wrote the well-known British anthem *Jerusalem* in 1916, seeking to build heaven on earth for all people. A century later, we find ourselves in the middle of the technological revolution, the information age, an era of unprecedented and exponential change. We may have lost Paradise a long time ago – but, for too many people, we have yet to replace it.

Note

1 Melissa Thomas-Hunt, 4 April 2013, 'Condoning Stereotyping: How Awareness of Stereotyping Prevalence Impact Stereotype Expression in Negotiations and Beyond'. (Seminar, Harvard Women and Public Policy Program, Cambridge, MA)

The theory: what have we learned?

23

An important point made to me by Iris Bohnet, Academic Dean at Harvard's Kennedy School, is that we cannot take learning for granted. People actually have to be taught how to learn. Many of us, disproportionately those who have most social reinforcement (usually white men) talk more than we listen, see the world from our point of view, rather than from others', and like wearing our own shoes, rather than wearing someone else's. If we learned how to listen more, if we were to build on someone else's argument, if we were to live someone else's life for a day, we could contribute to something bigger than our own agenda. This is not pure generosity of spirit, or philanthropy of thought. It is a very practical necessity in building an inclusive society that, in turn, benefits us all.

In learning to learn, I think the London 2012 experience has taught us six things.

To understand

First, we have learned the importance of understanding real inclusion. We are talking here about real, deep understanding rather than a nod and a smile to get the HR person to leave your office. We are talking about being positively conscious of difference, as opposed to Diversity 101 'top tips' for dealing with black and female customers. We are talking about the type of understanding that only occurs through the killing of any remaining elephants in the room, so that as few questions as possible remain unanswered.

We learned that people need space (and confidence) to ask the difficult questions. Without common understanding that disabled people really do have sex, Muslims can in fact go to the bar and women on otherwise all-male teams significantly aid better decision-making, we cannot achieve effective teamwork. We will continue to work based on assumption rather than fact, and we will fail to manage diversity.

In part, this necessary consciousness is achieved through a credible, real and fully understood business case based on customers, employees, growth, mathematics and ethics. I have seen different groups of colleagues respond to different parts of the business case in whatever area strikes the strongest chord for them. I have seen individuals make different personal connections to different arguments – the pie has been enlarged in their minds through actionable inspiration that resonated with them personally. I have seen thousands of colleagues respond to the removal of barriers to their own self-actualisation through the re-framing of the conversation as why wouldn't you? To respond better to being asked a question rather than told an answer.

In part this consciousness is brought about through reflection and gaining perspective. We learned that in the heat of battle, it was critical to 'get off the dance floor', take a step back and analyse what's really going on. Only then can we begin to understand the system as opposed to individual personal dynamics. If diversity remains in the realm of the personal then inclusion will remain a prisoner of office politics and interpersonal dynamics. Real inclusion will remain a pipedream.

When we get caught up in personal dynamics we become distracted from the real work. That's why it's important to distinguish between the role you play in the system and your own self-preservation. As a black woman, or a white man, people are going to judge you before you have even uttered a single word. We all play a role in the system, it's not personal. There are bigger forces at work here.

We have understood that diversity is a reality, whether we choose to acknowledge it or not. Perhaps most surprising of all, we have learned that diversity is the opposite of 'fluffy'. Far from the stereotype of a bunch of tree huggers holding hands by the campfire and singing *Kumbaya*, diversity has been laid bare as full of conflict, challenge and creativity. It is contested, raw and political. The skill of the inclusive leader is to make sense from the mess and work effectively with a diverse team. The reality of diversity couldn't be further from the truth of how many people (perhaps in less diverse environments) perceive it to be.

We have understood the limits of superficial inclusion and the value of real inclusion. We have learned to differentiate between systemic change/paradigm shift and what is simply window dressing – 'initiatives' always have a time and/or cost implication. Furthermore we have learned that diversity is not a panacea, there are negatives to it, from lower team cohesion to lower motivation to even lower economic growth. Inside the organisation I have witnessed and experienced poor team performance due to clashing world-views and wildly differing norms, as I suspect you have. Outside the organisation I see, and am affected by, the negatives of diversity in the media every day, as we all are.

We have learned that Diversity 101 can be perceived as self-interested, and therefore never achieve breakthrough with dominant groups that think they will consequently lose out. Still, many interest groups persist. Perhaps they will only ever understand diversity as self-interest. It is in this context that quotas and affirmative action fail, victims of a world perceived as zero-sum.

As I write this book I am incredibly conscious of the work that has gone before. Anyone today who enjoys any aspect of civil rights is standing on the shoulders of giants. Men and women have literally fought and died for the freedoms we now take for granted, for the rights we enjoy and for the lives we lead. It is unconscionable to forget that. But the best legacy we can create to honour that work is not to now be trapped by it. The best future we can build for our own careers, our organisations, our society, is to adapt to the realities we *now* face, not *did* face. And so it is important that for there to be a legacy we need to move on from Diversity 101 to the brave new world of inclusion, with all its imperfections and possibilities. There is limited legacy in Diversity 101 or 2.0.

To lead

Second, we have learned to lead. Critically, we have learned that anyone can lead, with or without authority, and this empowered almost everyone to maximise their contribution to the overall mission of the Games, whether it was working weekends, establishing a disability or LGBT group, providing superb customer service or some other form of captured discretionary effort. We witnessed how leadership is a group process, rather than a solitary pursuit. We learned that we can't do it all on our own, and the result would be worse if we did.

We learned the need to partner with others, and build relationships based on shared values. Often the most valuable partnerships were those formed with someone very different from you. Outside the tent, for example, we had no idea where or how to source disabled drivers, but Mobilise, a small charity did – it was their core purpose. We were wildly different organisations, with different infrastructure, cultures and backgrounds. But we needed each other. And because we were both committed to empowering disabled people, we were able to work together. Inside the tent, we scaled up through building allies – those in positions of authority – but also those 'culture-carriers' and opinion-formers who possess significant informal authority and generate followers. At LOCOG, we had to build alliances horizontally to thrive in an organisation with vertical silos.

How did that partnering come about? By sharing our inevitable ignorance, by failing publicly, we make ourselves vulnerable. But we learned that it is, after all, our failures that connect us more than our successes. By admitting when we are wrong, by avoiding talking nonsense,[1] by being humble. This realisation cuts across almost everything we are taught in professional life, from how to structure a CV to how to conduct an interview.

But to err is indeed human. Nobody is perfect. It is only through leadership being a group process that this has been possible. Had we promoted a classic view of the solitary male hero, people would have resisted sharing, especially men. We had to explicitly create this new norm and we had to reiterate publicly that failure was permitted, even encouraged. Knowing the group was going through what you were going through decreased the fear factor and encouraged people to offer more of themselves to the larger team.

We learned that partnering is not a passive activity where you cede all demands the other side put forward. The value of partnering comes from robust, not benign, conversation. Take the Equality and Human Rights Commission, for example. Despite one of their commissioners leaking a story that portrayed us inaccurately, the overall result was positive. We proved that a different approach to diversity (different to compliance) can result in better outcomes for everyone. Or consider the interactions with some disability charities. Had we given in to their quota demands we would never have persisted with a programme that placed over 2,000 disabled people into Games time roles.

New norms can be created. People do change attitudes. We don't have to rely solely on cohort replacement, literally waiting until 'the problem' dies! Change has happened (albeit slowly) in female career advancement. People who previously blocked female advancement onto corporate boards have changed tack.[2] The UK House of Lords, hardly the most progressive of institutions, overwhelmingly backed gay marriage in 2013. The average age of peers is 69 and therefore proof that you can teach an old dog new tricks. There is real progress toward integration, albeit in isolated examples.

We learned that leadership was about bringing your whole self to work. People perform better when they can be themselves. Real leadership was about being authentic and building your individual style, celebrating and leveraging your diverse talent. This is incredibly empowering for everyone, but especially for minorities who feel they have had to contain their potential to 'fit' in to company culture in the past. As Steve Girdler, the Chief Executive of HireRight, has brilliantly articulated, 'sod company culture. We want every individual to self-actualise and reap the collective benefit of that, rather than level down.'[3] Of course there is a balance, we cannot do work at the zoo, but there is a line to walk and most organisations I have worked with in the past are operating way below their people's collective potential.

Every day we had to make a choice whether to manage, or to lead. Management was hard, the technical challenge of the Games was formidable, but by managing we would only ever deliver the Games. To create Everyone's 2012, we had to exercise Leadership. Leading on inclusion was an art. We had to be sensitive to where people were coming from, but never apologise for what we were trying to do. We had to throw the work back and offer to help.

Leading people through change, and especially loss, is challenging. We had a very difficult relationship with one major disability charity in particular. At the time I could not understand why they would be opposed to our intention to recruit as many disabled people as possible. Only later did I appreciate that they were not fighting us because of the change we wanted to bring about per se. They were fighting us because they stood to lose. While I thought we were enlarging the pie, they thought we were going to beat them in a zero-sum game.

Most of our stakeholders were operating under a charity model of 'helping the disadvantaged'. We were operating under an inclusion model of enabling the 'disadvantaged' to help themselves. If we 'stole' the charity's limited talent pool, they would lose their raison d'être. Worse, if we demonstrated that our method worked, questions would be asked about their own approach. Often, the inhibitors of progress are the very organisations (people) who you would assume would be most supportive.

To deliver

Third, we have learned to deliver inclusion, which requires an ability to 'let go'. It requires an appetite for measured risk and for putting out fires when people, newly empowered, mess up. It is bound to happen from time to time. This requires having some tolerance for imperfection. I can best think of it as letting dad do the laundry. You know he won't do as good a job as mum would have done, but we need to empower him. Change won't happen without him.

We learned that delivery needed to be systemic. Interventions at the personal scale often fail. While they can be transformative for an individual, they are rarely transformative for the organisation. I know of a leading FTSE 100 company who has delivered an award-winning programme for its female executives. The feedback is excellent from all concerned; it has tangible outcomes and makes them an employer of choice for women. However, because they then 'send' these women back into unreconstructed workplaces, they ultimately fail. They have changed the women but not the environment within which the women operate. By focusing on workforce, procurement and service delivery we adopted a systemic approach that gave 'changed' or 'inspired' individuals a better chance of success because the organisation was swimming in the same direction they were. For example, by applying our workforce and procurement policies to our contractors, we ended up with excellent customer service delivery. Complex realities require intervention in complex feedback loops. Better procurement and better recruitment in unison led to better customer service.

We delivered relentlessly at LOCOG and on occasion it was exhausting. But nothing would be more demotivating than people not pulling their weight and hence the importance of delivery being an individual accountability. It was not just a question of working harder; it was most definitely a question of working smarter. In the past, minorities have been underleveraged and their expertise has been wasted in groups. Similarly, some minorities, 'empowered' by quotas, have coasted and failed to drive themselves. This time, these Games, every one was encouraged to self-actualise.[4] On the one hand is the carrot; an empowering, group leadership environment where you can be yourself. The quid pro quo is an environment of individual accountability where you contribute your marginal productivity, not enjoy a free ride.

One way of checking the free-rider problem is through promoting competition over compliance and capturing the power of peer review. Peer review is far more challenging to free riders than a compliance programme any day of the week. They stand to be assessed by their peers, whom they respect and whose friendship and loyalty they require to be human. This is far more core to human needs than satisfying an anonymous regulator. Compliance programmes are easily avoided by non-attendance. There is a whole industry helping individuals and organisations avoid compliance every day. Peer review applies to minorities as well as the dominant group. Everyone is in danger of free-riding at times. Everyone can maximise their potential with barrier removal on one side and individual effort on the other.

FIGURE 23.1 Walking the talk matrix

	Talk	Do
Give	Diversity 2.0	Real Inclusion
Take	Diversity 101	

Adapted from David Aikman World Economic Forum, Myanmar, 2013.

Measurement and benchmarking allows us to demystify inclusion. Applying the age-old KISS principle allows everyone to understand and take part. We convert the cynics through delivering results. It is better to demonstrate practical outcomes instead of engaging in theoretical conversations. That of course necessitates working very hard, and meeting all KPIs, before time and under budget. But this walking of the talk minimises reasons people can give for not coming on the journey too.

A very succinct (and endearing) way of explaining this was developed by David Aikman, a colleague at the World Economic Forum. He developed a simple matrix as per Figure 23.1. The world is full of givers and takers, as indeed the organisation is also populated by talkers and do-ers. Real inclusion is about the givers and the do-ers. Not out of naivety, but out of the fact that by doing so we enlarge the pie. It is a wonderful build on the diagram at the start of Chapter 3 (Table 3.1). The takers and the talkers will forever be stuck in a negative and depressing zero-sum game. Conversely, real inclusion gives us cause for optimism and offers us hope – actionable inspiration helps create better business and build better societies.

To be courageous

Fourth, we have learned to be brave. Courage is not recklessness, it is based on the confidence to follow your values and make a sensible calculated risk in the interests of the greater good. It is about standing in your purpose, not being confined by your role. Paul Deighton, the LOCOG Chief Executive, described his job as 'absorbing risk' so that the people that worked for him were freer to do their jobs. Andy Ellis, a male PA, defied the stereotype every day, and came out for the first time in his professional life, in a sports organisation to boot. Debbie Jevans, Sports Director, navigated a male world every day and didn't let it stop her championing what she believed was important such as the Equality Standard that many of the men were fiercely opposed to. I suffered two attacks by the *Daily Mail* and one by the *Observer*. We survived.

This is not heroic, this is simply brave. Sometimes there seem so many limits on us being brave even a little courage seems radical. If we upset the norm in a group will we be uninvited to team drinks? If I go over my boss's head or act as a whistleblower how safe is my job? If we upset the line manager in any other way, regardless of their behaviour or ethics, how safe is our job? So many leadership books talk about leadership in a vacuum of courage or personal resolve. The truth is that sometimes we are scared. Three to four per cent of CEOs and Senior Staff are on the spectrum of psychiatric disorder.[5] That statistic is four times the population at large. We need to be brave to blow the whistle on occasion.

But in all of these situations, we do not have to be alone. Through partnering, through building allies, through being authentic we can attract decency and even common sense. Try this; next time you have a disagreement with someone, rather than raising the stakes and instigating a zero-sum game, trying sharing a failure instead. Try expressing the issue from their point of view and demonstrating empathy. Consider it a professional challenge to try turning an opponent into an ally. This is pie enlargement – in their interest as well as yours.

When I was in the bus on the Beijing Torch Relay and the disabled kids and the Sugababes were panicking and I felt a complete failure it was a low moment. But when judged on what was within my control, I feel differently. When the *Daily Mail* attacked me personally,[6] instead of feeling like I had on the Beijing Torch Relay I felt almost validated, as I knew we had achieved success in order to provoke such a spiteful and nasty reaction. I received fantastic support from colleagues, which did nothing other than bring us closer together.

To be creative

Fifth, we have learned the value of creativity. And we have learned that, almost by definition, diversity is a key ingredient in creating creativity. The more diversity, the more availability to select from. Variation leads to amplification of the best talents, and the process of human evolution continues. More than anything, we have learned that new norms can be created. That is the most optimistic fact we can take away from this work. Diversity and Inclusion work need not be in vain, change really is possible.

We have learned the necessity of creativity in order to challenge people's preconceptions of diversity as demonstrated by earlier approaches.[7] Creativity has enabled us to move beyond Diversity 101 and 2.0 and demonstrate through evidence how new 3.0 techniques, methods and ideas worked. For example, the bifurcated approach of supply-side and demand-side interventions to build a diverse and inclusive workforce is much more effective than previous attempts, which tended to focus on only one side of the story, demand or supply, but rarely both in unison. Following a talk I gave to the UK's Office of Fair Trading in January 2010, their Chief Executive John Fingleton said, 'You obviously have a huge task on your hands, but showed how keeping focused on the issues within one's control can lead to a legacy of innovation around Diversity and Inclusion.'

Of course a downside to creativity is failure. But the best organisations, from Google to Novartis to Research and Development laboratories worldwide, allow, even encourage, failure. Review and adaptation are essential. As is an ability to be humble; we don't have all the answers, you can't do it all alone and the result would be worse if you did. Remember, failure is one of the best things that can happen to you – you just need some allies around to help pick you up and carry on with the experiential learning. The best organisations make it part of the overall programme.

Understanding, leadership and delivery are iterative processes and to keep them tip-top and fresh we need to subject them to regular challenge and review. In the same way people dislike change, people resist adaptation. But we have learned not to be afraid to adapt – the feedback loop is essential for walking the line and organisational survival. Some Chief Executives need to re-read their Darwin. By proactively seeking feedback from a range of anchors and people whom you respect (not people like you who will give you the answer you want) you can achieve a free early-warning system that will help you in the long run.

To set talent free

Finally, we have seen what talent looks like. We have learned that talent comes in an infinite variety of guises, from the athletes, to the Games Makers, from the Ceremony performers to the technical staff. From the international 'Games junkies' to the locals who live in the East End of London and played a key part in the word's biggest and most complex event.

But in order for that talent not to feel isolated and leave before it has fully contributed, we need to reach critical mass as soon as possible. Gay rights in the UK, and possibly the United States, have reached this tipping point now. In the space of only a few years, minority support for gay equality has become majority support for minority rights. Most people (who are not gay) now see gay rights as: a) non-threatening to their own rights; and b) good for collective social happiness and structure. London 2012 provided a significant boost to many minorities and their quest for greater advancement and rights. Through positioning inclusion as a time and cost saver for HR we were able to go fast on recruitment and ensure that the one black guy or solo senior women were soon joined by others, and they didn't reject real inclusion before they had given it a chance.

We have learned how to create new norms. It is hard to control individual subconscious bias and therefore group interviews helped – that's invoking the system rather than relying on the fallible individual. Putting the onus on the system allows the individual greater chance of success. We all stereotype – that is normal, as it is a necessary cognitive shortcut to cope with modern life. But people are less inclined to stereotype if they think it is a minority interest. We made Diversity and Inclusion a majority conversation, not a minority conversation.

In a hotel, if you tell guests that they have to re-use their towels they most likely won't. If you say that most people in *that* room re-use their towels, they most likely will too.[8] The power of collective norms should not be underestimated. Diversity and Inclusion moving from a minority issue to a majority conversation was perhaps the biggest legacy of the inclusion work we undertook at LOCOG.

We created a culture where the expectation and belief were that individuals were working against stereotyping. That's partly what 'Everyone's 2012' was about, the embrace of infinite difference, to seek it out. Bad behaviour decreases when it is thought to be a minority activity. When driving, people speed because they think everyone does it. If people thought everyone obeyed the limit, then fewer people would speed because speeding, not being 'boringly compliant', would be outside the norm.

So while there is much talk of physical and sporting legacies, I think there is a learning legacy. We have learned that Diversity and Inclusion can be undertaken very differently. We have learned how to understand, how to lead and how to deliver. We have learned the value of courage, creativity and talent. And we have witnessed it, bottled it and now need to share it. We have had a glimpse of Paradise found, just ask any minority who worked for

LOCOG vis-à-vis their work experience to date. We now need to ensure we move forward and we do not again encounter Paradise Lost.

Takeaways – the theory: what have we learned?

1 People still think diversity is 'soft' and a nice 'thing to have'. The reality at LOCOG showed that diversity is in fact messy, contested and creative – and yet it is because of this that it is impactful.

2 Achieving superficial inclusion is easy but of little value. Achieving real inclusion is hard but has both measurable and immeasurable potential and value.

Notes

1 Or bullshit – see http://en.wikipedia.org/wiki/Bullshit.

2 Matt Huffman, 25 April 2013, 'Female Managers and Gender Inequality: Evidence from Private Sector Firms'.

3 Conversation with Steve Girdler, May 2013.

4 Melissa Thomas Hunt, 4 April Seminar WAPPP, 'Condoning Stereotyping: How Awareness of Stereotyping Prevalence Impact Stereotype Expression in Negotiations and Beyond'. When people feel threatened, they often tend to close down the conversation, especially around a 'controversial' area like inclusion. This makes breaking down the barriers, and inclusion itself, even harder to achieve. To prevent this double whammy, we taught our team to avoid words that might shut people down. For example, if you replace 'you need to do this' with 'imagine why it might not be so' or 'how do we know that?', the conversation is less threatening and has a better chance of proceeding to a fruitful outcome.

5 Forbes article 'why (some) psychopaths make great CEOs' 6 April 2011.

6 See note 5.

7 *FT* article 'Creating creativity' [online] http://ft.com/cms/s/0/d433d3b0-8195-11ez-ae78-00144feabdc0.html.

8 Women and Public Policy program seminar, Cambridge MA, February 2013.

The tools: game-changers

24

When we launched the Workplace Equality Index at Stonewall in January 2005, showcasing the most gay-friendly employers in Britain, seven organisations out of the 'Top 100' did not want to be named. They were afraid of association with a gay Index or a gay charity. By the time I left Stonewall in May 2007, and we had published our third Index, they were fighting to get in and be publicly credited.

Systemic change happens. In this case, it happened very quickly, in a mere two years. Positive change is possible and can be created – if the conversation is framed effectively. It takes understanding and correct diagnosis, and it takes leadership and persistence. I would argue that one of the tools that helped bring about the rapid change highlighted above is benchmarking and competition. This is a tool we made a lot of use of at London 2012. Reflect, if you will, that white male Chief Executives ended up competing to be top diversity dog. This paradigm shift speaks to the importance of the tools, just as much as, if not more than, the nature of the subject.

There are several tools that became game-changers. Game-changers are those tools that created systemic change and helped achieve real inclusion, as opposed to decorating the tree and perpetuating the current paradigm. These are the paradigm-shifting methods that differentiate Inclusion 3.0 from Diversity 101 and 2.0 and offer the professional a new arsenal that can be employed to effect change. I have broken them down into our familiar workforce, procurement and service delivery intervention areas.

Workforce game-changers

Recruitment Action Plans

So many organisations have difficult relationships with diversity lobby groups or stakeholders. This is due in no small part to the fact that they can never fully satisfy their demands, according to the existing rules of the game. For example, organisations can never offer enough apprenticeship places, or environmental improvements. The lobby groups will always want more. This conundrum leads many organisations to avoid interaction with stakeholders altogether – that is a huge missed opportunity for benefiting from difference and enlarging the pie.

Recruitment Action Plans (RAPs) are a way not only of managing challenging stakeholder demands, but also getting them to do the work. Our partners (as they became) were much more expert in their own areas than we were. We did not want to be lobbied. We didn't have the time to manage a relationship for such little output. But by implementing the RAPs we not only strengthened their purpose and efficiently directed their effort, we helped them to help us. These can be a very cost effective, efficient way of accessing niche talent that would be harder and more expensive to access otherwise.

>access now/guaranteed interview scheme

We established the >access now programme to increase the employment of disabled people. In 2008 disability lobby groups had aggressively pushed us for a fixed quota of 10–20 jobs for their clients. We held steady, developed an alternative approach and in 2012 placed over 2,000 disabled people into Games time roles, in dignified uniforms, becoming the proud, inclusive face of London 2012. By rejecting orthodoxy, we achieved a result 100 times greater than expected.

They key part of >access now was a guaranteed interview scheme, which costs nothing. It does not employ sub-optimal hires because only an interview, not a job, is guaranteed. It is merit-based, legal and ethical. It requires pithy, accurate and specific job descriptions to be able to reject clearly unqualified candidates. However, I have yet to find a more effective intervention in terms of challenging the understandable cynicism and barriers that many disabled people face in the labour market, as well as capturing massively underutilised talent coupled with unlocked discretionary effort. This guaranteed interview scheme remains in legacy and I encourage you to set one up.[1]

>action on inclusion/talent pool

Many organisations may claim to operate talent pools. Many in fact do, but they are mostly confused with their personal and professional networks, as evidenced on Facebook and LinkedIn. This actually reduces diversity and can work against inclusion. It is the same for rewarding employees for referrals – they usually refer people like them.

In order to achieve real inclusion, talent pools of people different from you need to be created. This is harder to achieve, hence the importance of efficient use of the recruitment system and not wasting the time and effort already invested in second-choice candidates. By building talent pools of diverse skill sets and diverse communities it directly challenges the usual excuse for not hiring difference, 'we couldn't find any'. It also helps future proof the organisation – demand for labour tends to operate on shorter timelines than the cultivation and supply of it. Get it ready, now.

Leadership Pledge

The Leadership Pledge aroused some suspicion at first. The sceptics thought it was token and didn't have teeth. The believers wanted 100 per cent of people to complete it. What could have been naive ended up being a tremendously motivating communal leadership tool. If positioned effectively, as aspirational rather than compliance-based, most people wanted to opt in rather than opt out. Especially when they were joining the senior people and the opinion-formers in doing something they were partaking in too.

Had it been obligatory we would have had 100 per cent sign-up but mental ambivalence and perhaps only token commitment. As it was voluntary, it became a campaign, a goal, a desirable result. By making it voluntary it requires thought and consciousness, rather like signing a cheque or a contract. It provided everyone with a common reference point, a comparable set of actions and a personal stake in the inclusion success of the organisation. Their reputation was on the line too. Perhaps more than anything, the Leadership Pledge shows in black and white how we are removing barriers. It is an effective and resource-light way of empowering people.[2]

Group interviews

As we have seen, when people interview one-to-one, they think they are being objective but they are unfortunately biased. In isolation, this bias proceeds unchecked and is presented as an objective decision in the form of a successful candidate.

There are two interventions we can make to correct this. One is to have more than one person interview, so that different biases from different people can to some degree counteract each other. Better still, have more than one candidate, preferably a bundle, so that you can see skills (as opposed to experiences) play out in real time. We choose variety in bundles. When people are analysed in groups their individual characteristics (eg gender) are less salient and their skill sets and how they interact with the group are more so. Even the most ardent diversity sceptic is unlikely to select a bundle of sameness (eg all men). This is one of the most effective tools in your arsenal for reducing cost, saving time and increasing diversity.

Benchmarking

Instead of quotas or other fixed, inflexible measures, benchmarking allows a better interaction with current time-sensitive organisational realities. Inside the tent, teams can be benchmarked on their progress in terms of hiring to create a competitive dynamic and a market for diverse talent. Outside the tent, recruitment agencies should be benchmarked in order to calculate your return on investment. In all cases, peer review, instead of compliance quotas, is the driver. This is based on high-frequency, real-time information sharing (monitoring), which not only maintains momentum and democratises the workplace; it is by definition closer to the mission of the organisation than compliance measures ever would be.

Job brokerages receive public money to place unemployed and/or disadvantaged people into meaningful work. However, many job brokerages are broken. They are incentivised to place people off their books but not to place them into any kind of meaningful long-term employment. We also came across cases where certain job brokerages would claim credit for other job brokerage placements, a fight over humans, if you will. London 2012 benchmarked these agencies and held them to account for delivery. We benchmarked the supply of talent and the placing of that talent, in both paid and volunteer positions and can demonstrate that; Mobilise, for example, a small charity with limited resources was successful in placing most of its disabled drivers into Games time roles. A major charity, one of the largest national charities with huge resources refused to work with us, fearful that London 2012 would take away its best volunteers. The life chances of the said human beings in question were not considered.

The benchmarking concept can also be applied in procurement, using a Red/Amber/Green traffic light system on Diversity and Inclusion for all tenders over £20,000 and supplier ownership as a proxy for the candidate. It can also be applied in service delivery, through monthly reporting. In these areas where there is a lack of external benchmarks, and no precedent or equivalent, use your own timeline, benchmarking against yourselves at monthly intervals. Again, competition and benchmarking can be used outside the tent with providers and stakeholders, as we did with the Equality Standard and Sports Governing Bodies. Internally, we used partnering to achieve systemic change through the line. Externally, we used partnering to achieve systemic change between organisations.

Procurement game-changers

Online procurement (transparency)

Placing contracts online permits transparency, greater participation, competition, cost savings and increased innovation from previously 'unrostered' organisations. These are perhaps new, start-up companies with a new innovative product that you are not aware of. This is supplier diversity mobilisation by default, yet the reward for small businesses is greater than 'initiatives' that only ever offer token pieces of the supply chain.

Our use of CompeteFor has very much been a demonstration of what can be achieved with the system – we helped convince other bodies to embed it into their own process and so far the Metropolitan Police, Westminster Council, some government departments and major programmes such as Crossrail are all now using a system that was originally designed and built for London 2012. When this transparency increases competition, reduces costs and sources innovation you may not otherwise know about, the question for other organisations is not 'Why would you?', but 'Why wouldn't you?' The system remains in legacy, and I encourage you to use it.[3]

Legacy Evaluation Group (LEG)

This cross-functional team oversaw all procurements over 20K and at first sounds like an additional bureaucratic burden. In fact it was an economy of scale, bringing together multiple functional areas that would otherwise have each required separate management by the procurement function. By regulating and suggesting improvements that did not impose costs but did create shared value, it encouraged improvements across the board in suppliers. For example, organisations were encouraged to complete free online

Diversity and Inclusion advice through the DWFL programme. This online assessment produced a step change in our suppliers' attitude to Diversity and Inclusion, as they had to analyse themselves in this respect, often for the first time. Natasha Landers, who ran the DWFL programme, said there was, 'real understanding and acceptance that diversity is fully integrated in all that is done'. That not only added value – in an age of global supply chains and social media, it also mitigated risk. The system remains in legacy and I encourage you to use it.[4]

Service delivery game-changers

Immovable deadline

In one sense, none of the people at London 2012 can be credited with the business and social change achieved. Not all of the changes were premeditated, designed or even intended. In these cases, the credit is not ours; it is due to the laboratory experiment taking place in the LOCOG crucible. The immovable deadline of 27 July 2012 forced a certain intensity of purpose that was outside the control of any one individual, whether they were pro or anti social change. The wonderful opportunity of London 2012, however, was the possibility to demonstrate change that would normally take decades, in a considerably shorter space of time.

Why the London 2012 experience is so valuable is because it forced adaptive change over technical change. In the absence of an immovable deadline, intense media and political scrutiny and forced stakeholder engagement it would be far easier to pursue a quiet path of technical work and system tweaking. In this very real sense, therefore, the deadline was issue-resolving more than fear-inducing. Deadlines are your friend, they force conversations. If you don't have a deadline, create one. If you can't do that, call a friend and have them partner with you to monitor your progress.

Sponsors Forum and Diversity Board

While Inclusion 3.0 was in many ways a democratic affair, driven bottom-up and with a circular conversation, the use of authority was at times helpful. Specifically, the creation of the Diversity Board and the commercial driver of the Sponsors Forum were two creations that helped us get the job done. The Sponsors Forum not only allowed us to co-opt the resources of our commercial partners to inclusive ends, the conversation also generated a competitive dynamic among the companies to improve their own performance in diversity and inclusion.

The Diversity Board helped nudge the sceptics over the line. The fact that the most senior people inside (and outside) the organisation were supporting diversity and inclusion and were assessing the work being undertaken by an inclusive yardstick, was an important motivator for all concerned, including for the Diversity and Inclusion team who could believe that the top people were supporting them. One modification I would make to the Management Committee Champions and Diversity Board Members would be to *interview* for the positions. This then starts from a position of success rather than request. It also makes the position more desirable and the person who is appointed to take it just as seriously as their day job.

Inclusive design

Physical infrastructure and property is one of the biggest organisational cost line items. Adapting it to meet accessibility compliance requirements is therefore often highly expensive. Hence the importance of inclusive design, the importance of forethought about how we can make environments work for all people. Rather than additional cost in transitioning the Olympic environment to the Paralympic environment, as was required in Athens, for example, we applied the Paralympic environment to both Games.

Next time you acquire new property, or do a redesign, or invent a new process, think in advance about how that environment will work for all your people and customers – and not just those you currently have. Upwards of 20 per cent of people have a disability, many of us have children, and all of us get old. Make those environments work now and save in the long run.

Personalised customer service

By coaching 200,000 people to 'talk to the person' we not only provided enhanced customer service, we created a culture of devolved decision-making that led to multiple other benefits. By employing the KISS mantra, and setting clear frameworks and parameters, unleash people to be themselves, and personalise the customer connection as a result. A flexible, tailored customer-focused approach was better able to respond to diverse customer needs. People could resolve issues quickly rather than rely on lengthy escalation. This attitude of empowering people and trusting them even extended to our final Ceremony dress rehearsal. Rather than try to ban cameras and phones in a social media age, we simply appealed to their good nature to #savethesurprise, and everyone did.

The ultimate game-changer is attitude

The overall strategy was simple and effective. The process of understand, lead and deliver and the interventions of workforce, procurement and service delivery combined to offer an effective framing of the issues. This allowed simple communication and a good chance of creating a new norm. The 22 projects provided tangible evidence of inclusion being created and a tolerance of risk allowed people the freedom to innovate and take part, claiming their own piece of the organisation.

London 2012 demonstrated that social change is possible in an extremely resource-constrained commercial environment where attention grabbing for a 'side issue' was not easy. But Inclusion 3.0 game-changers do not require a sledgehammer. A quiet intervention is fine, as long as it is profound and strategic. Many executives are content to accept, rather than change the system, because that creates least resistance and gives them most chance of being accepted. That's mere technical change and doesn't change the rules of the game. To change paradigms is hard and dangerous. You can get shot down. London 2012 gave us a defined period of time in which to stay alive and demonstrate results, and for that alone, I am thankful.

Takeaways – the tools: game-changers

1 We used existing tools that were already present in a more effective way. Examples include information that was then benchmarked or the guaranteed interview scheme that was given resuscitation. The game-changer was the new method.

2 Necessity is the mother of invention. We created new tools (out of necessity that positively impacted our outcomes) including Talent pools and the Leadership Pledge. The game-changer was their introduction.

3 The tools we used and created are not specific to the Olympics and Paralympics but applicable and transferable to most organisations.

Notes

1 http://www.disabilitysupportnetwork.org.uk/support-for-jobseekers/ what-disability-symbol-two-ticks-employer.

2 Full text in Appendix, p 314.

3 https://www.competefor.com/business/login.jsp.

4 http://www.diversityworksforlondon.com/.

The lessons: failures

25

We tend to learn more when we fail than when we succeed. When we fail we also make ourselves vulnerable, which helps other people relate to us by slicing through the professional veneer we coat ourselves in for supposed protection. There are so many good reasons to fail yet fear of failure holds us back all the time. In this context, the importance of courage was not to encourage recklessness, but to help people, as Shakespeare identified, 'be not afeard'.

Looking back on mistakes made, it is now abundantly clear that many Diversity 101 approaches fail, even by their own standards. Many 2.0 tools failed too. However, while Inclusion 3.0 methods were largely successful, there are still two areas, 'information load' and 'pie enlargement', where the jury is still out. If we analyse the three main areas of intervention, the failures tended to be least in the area of workforce and procurement, and most in the area of service delivery. This makes sense. Service delivery was a new area, it was huge and complex and we were experimenting.

Workforce failures

Early training

When I took on the Diversity and Inclusion role there was a training programme already set up that I honoured. That was a mistake. On 23 May 2008 the all-staff email invitation came out from HR and despite the fact that the training company was very good, and the effort and care was genuine, I still felt uncomfortable that we were patronising our people. I saw the reaction in the training room. I felt it, I heard it, and I sensed it. I remember cringing and physically placing myself near the door. That physical response told me everything I needed to know.

It took us some time to make up for this mistake. I had to re-run all my one-to-one meetings, especially with the people who were more likely to have prejudices about 'diversity' or 'inclusion' and whose prejudices had to some extent been reinforced by the training. They were unfortunately some of the people we would most rely on to deliver. They tended to be disproportionately represented in frontline operational roles where the Games would be consumed by the clients.

We managed to isolate the training as being outside the general approach we were adopting, but it had been an unnecessary time and cost distraction, thankfully early enough in the journey to recover from. I took some directors to the theatre to watch the musical *Avenue Q*, which includes songs such as *Everyone's a little bit racist*. It was effective in reminding them that we were doing things differently and the training had been a mistake. The later Diversity and Inclusion coaching programme was 3.0. For example, the Games Maker training was groundbreaking and challenged and surprised people.

Procurement failures

Following up non-compliant suppliers

We had asked suppliers several requirements such as completion of the Diversity Works online assessment and guaranteed interviews for disabled people. Following these up was a time sink and our negotiating power decreased as the Games approached and we ran out of time.

We should have pushed our partners harder to do the follow-up for us. That was the agreed model. In one sense we were just the front-end marketing machine for the existing Diversity Works programme (run by the mayor) and the Guaranteed Interview Scheme (run by government). With more time we should have gone over the heads of any civil servant not pulling their weight to ministerial level where they would have taken a more holistic view and made things happen. This is something another organisation not under the time pressures we faced could have done.

Lack of declaration

We had good statistics for our workforce, partly because we were building on established norms that individuals tell us their ethnicity and so on when completing a job application. This norm did not exist in procurement and we were only partially successful in creating it. With a poor response rate, our results were at risk of being statistically insignificant and us not being able to tell the supplier-diversity story. We were not asking the correct questions to the correct people. Often the people answering the Diversity and Inclusion section would not know the answers or not be in a position to ask the business owners.

We made completing the Diversity and Inclusion questions compulsory half-way through the journey but this in itself would not create the new norm. We should have either done this from the start or invested in more education about the value of supplier diversity. Some suppliers got it. Many small businesses understood that telling us more about them was good, such as Brickwall Films who produced some of our best short videos. Others continued to think we may discriminate against them or did not answer the questions out of ignorance or lack of familiarity.

Service delivery failures

Ticketing

While the ticketing programme remains one of the best successes of the Games from an inclusion perspective (see Chapter 16) there was one aspect we could have improved upon. One regret was not limiting the number of event sessions an individual could apply for even more so, and earlier in the process. We limited the number of sessions people could apply for in the initial round to 20. By the end, we were limiting the number of tickets, let alone sessions, to four only. We could have started limiting the number of tickets people could apply for much earlier in the process and then possibly (although not guaranteed) allowed a greater number of people to have obtained a smaller number of tickets each. To some extent this is hypothetical, and hindsight is a wonderful thing. We live and learn.

Audio description/enhancement

This is commentary of the sport/action, predominantly designed for visually impaired people so they know what is going on. Although there were unprecedented successes, such as the Opening Ceremony where people could often understand what was occurring for the first time ever, there were also failures. Due to lack of comprehension, attention and extreme complexity of delivery over multiple venues, we over-promised and under-delivered. We also made the mistake of changing the information during the Games, which added to the confusion and anger of those affected. Goal ball, for example, was a problem to begin with but was rectified. The irony here is that the technical officials, regulating a sport for visually impaired athletes, were against commentary for visually impaired people as they felt it was distracting. Only when we had sealed the commentators in a sound-proof box could we proceed.

Pride House

One Monday morning, Jean Tomlin, HR Director, and I were presenting to the team from the Sochi 2014 Winter Olympic and Paralympic Games. It was early, granted, but there was a Russian man in the back right-hand corner who was asleep. He had leaned forward to the extent that his forehead was resting on the table in front of him and he occasionally made sounds. I suspect to this day that he was drunk, or at least hung over; our presentation style is not that bad. When I mentioned the possibility of London hosting a Pride House for LGBT customers he suddenly sat up and exclaimed what a great idea it was. Really? Jean and I looked at each other for reassurance, before he continued: 'Yes, it's a great idea, because then we would know where they all are.'

As far as I am aware, Sochi did not proceed with a Pride House. Actually, London did, and credit goes to Chad Molleken, Lou Engelfield, Emy Ritt and colleagues at the Gay Games who made this happen, but it was a fraction of the original plan. This is a shame as London could have hosted a spectacular Pride House and really made a statement about LGBT inclusion in the world's biggest event. But it was not to be. The reasons? The same reasons as besets London Pride every year – politics, poor management and a collective *Guardian*-reader syndrome mentality that supposes the equality battle is already won in London and therefore why bother?

Communications

The award-winning LOCOG communications team was tactically brilliant, but inclusion remained nebulous for some of them. It was usually when things went wrong that the penny dropped – the Logo launch film, the Adidas launch and ticketing over-demand, for example.

The communications challenge was enormous, and the risks very high, therefore the response was defensive, but I would argue too defensive. This was the most high-profile and risky project in the UK's recent history and it was played out in real time in a newly digital age under the glare of the infamous British press. It is no surprise that the Communications team were wary of anything, literally anything, that could be perceived as a risk to the project. Unfortunately, this led to an extremely conservative attitude that saw Diversity and Inclusion as a potential risk, alongside sustainability or any other programme that could lay us open to criticism or accusations of failure against our perceived targets or goals.

Like many others, I understood Diversity and Inclusion to be the exact opposite – a risk-mitigating mechanism. Frustratingly, other organisations were crying out for the kind of programme we were implementing. When the results started to arrive other companies were even more interested in talking about it. For a company that was in a lower profile, less risky position, the good news Diversity and Inclusion stories were valuable property. At the World Economic Forum in Davos in January 2012, several companies were parading their Diversity and Inclusion success stories that were in many ways a fraction of the London 2012 accomplishments. It was very much glorification of the uninvolved. I taught a Harvard Business School Class in April 2013 and virtually all of the well-read students were learning of the London 2012 inclusion strategy and outcomes for the first time.

Communication (such as the Business Charter, for example) is how you grow the market for inclusion and generate a positive catalyst for change. Instead, the *Daily Mail* set the agenda with articles such as, 'Will Britain take Gold for the most PC Olympics ever?'[1] and these were never really challenged. My view was and remains that 'doing nothing' is a risk. A controlled telling of the story would mitigate that risk. This book is in part a response to the great story we had to tell that was simply never told. In the future, inclusion should be embedded in communications in the same way it was embedded in HR and every other department.

Knowledge management

The Olympic Games Knowledge Management programme (OGKM) was the International Olympic Committee's initiative to capture Games learning and transfer it to the next Games. It was an admirable and necessary aim. It is quite amazing how each new Games literally starts from scratch in many areas. In some ways this is understandable, even desirable – a new country will have new, perhaps unique, circumstances. A new age, in a time of rapid technological change, will require new tools.

This was the first time an Olympic and Paralympic Games had ever undertaken inclusion as a specific work stream and, as evidenced in this book (Chapter 2), we persuaded the International Olympic Committee and

International Paralympic Committee to come on board. For the first time, Diversity and Inclusion is an officially recognised function of an organising committee and was included in the Knowledge Management process; for example, the LOCOG Overlay Access File was transferable to other Games.

However, although we ticked the boxes, inclusion will only live if it is understood, led on and systemised. I am not yet convinced of this. As we have discussed, sports bodies lack the commercial imperative to act. Furthermore, without drive from the top, it will depend on the leadership capacity of the individual organising committees to what extent they pick up the baton. Crucially, the International Olympic Committee and International Paralympic Committee should make Diversity and Inclusion a key area for all future bids to address in their submissions.

There are many signs to be hopeful. The International Paralympic Committee has embraced inclusion and are now preparing their first-ever strategy. Rio 2016 has indicated it would like to continue the work, if only in response to social pressures seen throughout the country in 2013. Let us watch this space.

There will be more failures and that's good

Overall, the failures were more outside the tent, for example not pushing sports bodies or the sponsors more, or because of vested interests. I had an illuminating meeting with the French Consul in London. He was a wheelchair user and was impressed with our stance on a range of accessibility issues that he said were years away in France. He wanted the meeting to gain tangible examples of things that worked that he could use to increase his confidence to challenge colleagues back at the Embassy.

It is worth reminding us all that this was played out in real time. That gave credibility to the experiment, reminds us that leadership takes courage, and requires an appetite for calculated risk. This was a high-stakes game, with the whole world watching. It would be impossible to write this book before the end of the Games, not simply because of time, but because of lack of perspective. With that perspective, two big questions remain for Inclusion 3.0 practitioners.

Monitoring

Information is necessary in order to make fact-based decisions. However collecting information can be burdensome. The approach we undertook, due to lack of time and money, was to tweak existing data collection systems rather than set up new processes. This had the effect of embedding inclusion through the line in a system people paid attention to, rather than creating a separate system they could ignore. Monitoring was a success at LOCOG, and we continually pushed the boundaries and challenged our stakeholders to do the same. The Diversity and Inclusion team were successful in emphasising that diversity was the tool to measure inclusion. LOCOG knew that inclusion was the ultimate goal.

An additional real challenge remaining, however, is the paradox of data collection and 'categories' versus infinite diversity. People hate being put into boxes, understandably so. But information needs to be segregated somehow for the purposes of analysis. In some ways LOCOG grew too fast to have fixed levels and departments. We were indicative of the way organisational design is headed with flexible multi-layered teams that can 'swarm' a problem. It makes monitoring more challenging.

And where do you stop? Traditionally, race, gender and even sexual orientation were categories people could identify with. But with infinite diversity how do we capture complex multiple identities such as accent, looks and size? In the future, we will have to approach it the other way round. Rather than adding additional characteristics to the measurement scale, it will be about recognising the infinite nature of those characteristics in the first place. We need to work out how to allow individuals to express their own unique DNA better than any monitoring form presently can. Big-data experts need to help us understand how we then measure it.

There will always be an issue with categorising people into boxes. Even if you are measuring infinite diversity, you still have to group those people into boxes large enough to get significant results. How else can policy be made and improved? Everyone is unique and different, but statistics are based on patterns within and between groupings and this will continue to be debated for years to come. And big data could work against inclusion, as this is an area where people will make cognitive shortcuts and assumptions based on Facebook and Twitter before they have 'objectively' assessed candidates' skills.

Zero-sum game vs enlarging the pie

Inclusion 3.0 offers a series of game-changing tools that can enlarge the pie. Inclusive design, for example, genuinely benefits everyone and is not at the expense of anyone else. This is important in demonstrating to the sceptics that it is not always a zero-sum game.

The zero-sum game implies that there are winners and losers, whereas 'enlarging the pie' implies that everyone is a winner. I think the dichotomy is really between short-term and long-term, or local and global scales. Enlarging the pie may not be immediately felt as such if people's immediate experience is change that represents at best some amount of inconvenience and at worst having to give something up *right now*. I'm not questioning whether something isn't really a zero-sum game, I'm wondering how you convince somebody that her immediate experience of 'this sucks' is worth it in the long run. The best way to enlarge the pie for everyone is through actionable inspiration. Not everyone agrees with, or can attain, economic growth. But actionable inspiration speaks to everyone.

However zero-sums remain, especially in times of economic crisis. Can we always guarantee an enlargement of the pie and that no one will ever lose out? 'Seat kill' or all-women shortlists suggest that some people will indeed lose out. In these situations, potential non-disabled ticket holders or male politicians will have to forego their self-interest in the interests of wider society. Maybe it is that while zero-sum games do exist, they are not as frequently occurring, or as costly when they do, as people think. We need more research and more discourse in this space. It would be a tragedy if infrequently occurring zero-sum games were disproportionately highlighted at the expense of pie enlargement case studies – and real inclusion was jettisoned as a result.

Failures are not an excuse to avoid the work

In any work on proposing a new way of achieving inclusion, it is essential to acknowledge limitations. I think information in an information age and dealing with the zero-sum situations that remain are two such limitations of Inclusion 3.0. They do not, however, reduce the validity of the rest of the work whose success has been demonstrated throughout this book. In any ambitious programme, failure to some degree was inevitable. There will be failures not mentioned above that I was not even aware of, but overall I remain pleasantly surprised that the successes were far more in number and depth. When we do fail, however, it makes us human and opens us to learning. We can always improve. And the work goes on.

Takeaways – failures

1 The five-year experiment proved the inadequacy of Diversity 101 and 2.0 approaches, as evidenced in the initial training. It also showed that while 3.0 strategies in some cases worked brilliantly, there are still two conundrums we need to better understand concerning the zero-sum game and the burden of reporting.

2 Some of the failures were inevitable, which we can take heart from and should not be a deterrent from future experimentation; for example, demand modelling for ticketing. Some were more avoidable, for example communications.

3 Inside the tent, more under our control, there were fewer failures than occurred outside the tent. It is important to judge one another on what is under our control first, while acknowledging but not dwelling on failures outside our control.

Note

1 Stephen Wright, *Daily Mail*, Saturday, 10 September 2011, p 3 'Will Britain take gold for the most PC Olympics ever?' – re our volunteering booklet.

Stephen Wright and Daniel Bates, *Daily Mail*, Monday 2 April 2012, p 11 'Diversity targets are driving up bill for the Olympics' – re Toronto speech.

The applications: no more excuses

26

A s I finished the draft of this book, two bombs exploded down the road at the Boston marathon, killing three innocent people and injuring 264. The two suspects lived two blocks away from me in Cambridge, Massachusetts. The manhunt that resulted in their death and capture went past my front door. The terrorism that followed London's bid victory in 2005 had come full circle.

Terrorism is one of the terrifying and depressing aspects of society that seems beyond our control. At the other end of the scale, our individual actions are within our control, yet they are rarely of significant magnitude to impact the system (unlike, ironically, those of the Boston bombers, the Tsarnaev brothers). That leaves the organisation as the principal agent for change.

Paul Deighton, LOCOG Chief Executive, told me repeatedly to judge him on what was within his control. A bomb on the Boston marathon is not under his control. The diversity of his organisation is. I would not wish to link the two explicitly, at the risk of trivialising the issues. But for anyone who still wonders why we should care about Diversity and Inclusion, I encourage you to look around you at the increasingly diverse world emerging all around us. And then you have to make a choice, to connect or to disconnect.

Sometimes we need to disconnect. I need to go cycling through remote Scottish highlands, or just be on my own in a house without sound. But that is only to sustain myself for the next encounter with people. People, after all, can be exhausting. But anyone who wants to make the world a better place must do so in collaboration with others. Leadership is a group process. It is rarely a solitary activity. If everyone created systemic change in his or her organisation, then the collective output would really change the world. Surely there is a link between organisational togetherness and societal togetherness? Organisations, after all, are little salami slices of society.

I am not suggesting that achieving real inclusion is easy. Practitioners of Diversity and Inclusion have a tough job. If we are determined to leave the world a little better than when we found it, we are necessarily embarked on a process of change. And, as we have discussed, many organisations and individuals don't like change. Change is harder, adaptive work, rather than routinely technical. Change is more effort and, if not done carefully, can make you more enemies than friends. But as Winnie the Pooh once said, 'You can't stay in your corner of the Forest waiting for others to come to you. You have to go to them sometimes'.

A key part of the successful implementation of Inclusion 3.0 at London 2012 relied on re-framing the conversation. Rather than lobby people as to why they should engage in diversity, we found it more effective to ask professionals why they wouldn't. If it is free or minimal cost, if it is systemic and doesn't require time or costly additional initiatives, and if it actually makes the overall results better, why wouldn't you?

Why wouldn't you? Here are seven arguments you could make to disconnect, to avoid responsibility for achieving real inclusion, and seven reasons why you might want to connect, and persevere instead.

1. Because the Olympics and Paralympics were unique

In one sense the Games were a victim of their own success. Considering the potential for problems, or even tragedy, it is a double delight they went so well. But because they went so well people all over the world, in less high-profile organisations, or in more mainstream economic sectors, can define London 2012 as the 'other', in a similar fashion to that we discussed in Chapter 6.

However, this is a false dichotomy. Defining London 2012 as the 'other' removes the responsibility for individual agency. It fails to analyse what is transferable. In other words, it's an easy excuse, a cop-out. The theory contained in this book is directly transferable to almost any organisation I know and/or have worked with. Which organisation would not want to understand the world around it more? Which professionals would not want to improve their leadership style, and precisely which manager would not wish his or her team to deliver more?

Furthermore, many of the tools we developed are also transferable. Directly transferable processes include guaranteed interviews for target groups, talent pools to fast-track skilled people, group interviews to reduce subconscious bias and implicit associations, online procurement to reduce costs, inclusive design to creative environments that work for everybody and a series of 'nudges'[1] that anyone at any level can exercise at any time.

Perhaps you are reading this now and have simply enjoyed the luxury to date of not facing the circumstances we faced, and so have not been compelled to enter such uncomfortable territory? I understand there are vested interests and political pressures to ignore what is contained in this book, but they do not by themselves reduce the validity of the argument. If London 2012 can do it, with all the challenges it faced, then so too can your organisation. Moreover, many of the concepts and methods developed would work even better in organisations that have the benefit of hindsight and, most likely, more time and resources as well.

2. Because you don't have the resources

A reason offered by diversity practitioners themselves, let alone anyone else in the organisation, for aborting change is lack of resources, especially in a difficult economic climate. To organise and lead a comprehensive organisation change process across thousands of people is no easy task. How much resource is required? What is the ratio? Organisations worldwide are currently reducing HR staff ratios. If diversity teams are a subset of HR (usually on a ratio of at most 1:10) then we can see that at first look the challenge is even greater.

But what is the diversity team? Or for that matter the HR team? I had a team of three paid staff and eight free secondees matrix managed with seven external stakeholders. The 'resources' have to be expanded creatively. That's why our Diversity Board, chaired by our Chief Executive, was crucial, as was our sponsors' forum where we built allies across suppliers and clients. Our staff networks allowed staff to push beyond their personal best and lead change as part of their day job and our stakeholder relationships are crucial to moving us all along in tandem.

At the Harvard Women's Leadership Board in April 2013 I asked the audience who had direct responsibility for Diversity and Inclusion within their own organisation. About a quarter of the hands shot up. I responded by saying that all hands should have been up, for it is everyone's responsibility. Change is delivered through individual accountability, but change starts with collective leadership.

If you were to graph market capitalisation of Fortune 500 companies and plot their progression towards real inclusion, I doubt there would be a correlation between their resource endowment and their progress. In fact, as many diversity indices worldwide demonstrate, often bountiful resources result in complacency, rather than real inclusion. Sixteen out of the 30 corporations that make up the current Dow Jones Industrial Average started during a recession, ranging from Walt Disney (began during the recession in 1923–24) to Hewlett-Packard (began in 1938 during the Great Depression) to Microsoft (began during the 1975 recession).[2] These three organisations are also three of the most inclusive in the United States.

Diversity and Inclusion may not always be free but the resources required are not large enough to permit inaction; the benefits of real inclusion outweigh the costs. Even if you did throw resources at 'the problem' there is no guarantee they would be used effectively. Indeed experience to date suggests they have been used ineffectively. If we have a lack of resources then we can think creatively about how we can expand our resource base, through building allies, looking at partnering, and effectively performance managing what we already have.

3. Because you don't have the time

The third reason you may not pursue real inclusion is lack of time. An organisation will have a set business plan or strategic vision and competing interests will be in competition for airtime and prominence in the plan. We were conscious on any day of the week (including weekends) how many days there were to go before we had to stage the biggest show on earth.

But can't deadlines actually help? Can't they force decisions to be made and conversations to be had, rather than allow proposals to drift into the next quarter or the next planning meeting? Parts of East London had remained a wasteland since the end of World War Two. Successive governments, of right and left, and councils with various people strategies had come and gone and nothing much had changed. The winning of the bid forced conversations, forced joint working and decisions have been made, in my view for the better.

We can decide whether we interpret deadlines as fear-inducing or issue-resolving. By adopting systemic approaches to inclusion, it takes far less time than individual multiple initiatives. Real inclusion minimises time costs. It just requires more thinking time, but this is done in the bath while listening to your favourite music, not as an opportunity-cost during the day.

4. Because you lack buy-in

Lack of management buy-in could be a reason to stick with technical work. The Chief Executive doesn't get it. The management team doesn't care. It's true that if your organisation's top team is actively hostile to Diversity and Inclusion you are going to have a tough time. The British military before 2000 actively sought out and dismissed lesbian and gay personnel. Some FTSE 100 companies still don't sufficiently acknowledge the need for female talent in the boardroom. But what is their true understanding of the change we propose?

Leadership is required, and it's a call to action, not a corner office. Anyone can exercise it at any time. Of course the Chief Executive and the management team have more authority, and that can make leadership easier. But anyone can exercise leadership and a Real Inclusion practitioner has to exercise a tremendous amount of leadership in the first place, in order to convince the group to move forward with a change agenda it believes will add value to the business.

We can determine how effectively we challenge senior colleagues and those with authority. We need to be courageous, we need to be creative. Diversity and Inclusion can be low cost (or even free) and massively value adding if done right. The challenge for practitioners is to make senior colleagues get that it's a 'no-brainer'.

There is one other factor that is free, in infinite supply and completely within our own control. And that's attitude. Diversity and Inclusion's biggest dependency is attitude. And with the right attitude, Diversity and Inclusion really can make a difference.

If we believe something is really important, then we can prioritise it. Our 'Leadership Pledge' was voluntarily signed by 96 per cent of London 2012 hiring managers, committing them to hiring more inclusively than they otherwise might. Our General Counsel champions disability inclusion and our Sports Director champions age diversity. None of them have to do this. It's about engaging people with the question of how they can add value to the organisation at large. What can they do to improve the situation to benefit us all?

5. Because it is not a business imperative

Of all the multiple demands on professionals striving to run a business, isn't inclusion simply another time sink on the 'to-do' list? If you believe in diversity 'initiatives', then it is. But if you believe in systemic inclusion, just make it a part of every bullet point. You will have to think deeper, there may be a zero-sum battle for space going on inside your brain if you are under stress, but I have tried to offer evidence throughout this book of why real inclusion makes business sense. For your customers, who are in most cases already ahead of you. For your employees, who you want to attract, retain and leverage. For growth, from unlocking barriers to unlocking new markets. For better decision-making and calling out our blind spots. And for ethics. If nothing else, aren't ethics always an imperative?

We could also use the opportunity to reflect on what is a business imperative anyway. I would argue that all the elements of the business case for real inclusion are business imperatives – customers, employees, growth, decision-making and ethics. I would, therefore, argue that real inclusion is a business imperative, for the sake of the above.

6. Because it is too nebulous and the results are unquantifiable

For busy minds unwilling to engage in real inclusion, it will remain nebulous. All I can offer is to make the complex reality as simple as I know how. Everything we tried to do employed the KISS mantra. From the framing 'Why wouldn't you?' to the process 'understand, lead, deliver', to the interventions 'workforce, procurement, delivery'.

I have offered ideas throughout the book, from monitoring to RAG scores, from statistics to engagement scores. We can determine the diversity of the workforce in numbers, we can quantitatively measure the supplier diversity of the procurement system and we can measure aspects of service delivery. In the final analysis, however, some of the most impressive, value-adding aspects of the project and its legacy were qualitative, from the ceremonies to the customer service offered by the Games Makers to the changed career trajectories of thousands of people.

I have tried to make the definition clear, the approach clear and the results measurable. I would point out that there are several business 'initiatives' undertaken daily that are less quantifiable than inclusion. They somehow go ahead anyway.

7. Because there is no urgency

One winter evening I was wasting time on Facebook and came across the page of an old flame. Now well into his forties he had changed his profile picture to a shot of him as a very handsome man in his early twenties. He only came out in his thirties and is still single. The page reached out to me and reminded me of the fierce urgency of now. We don't want to have to look back over photos past and dream what might have been. Happiness comes from the present, by fully engaging all of our being in the environment in which we find ourselves. Anything that is a barrier to that happening is a regret.[3]

Dave Morris dedicated his life to inclusion. He used to remind me frequently that the value of diversity was as infinite as the cost of its destruction. It was something I shared with the mourners as I read his eulogy at Mile End Park where only the month before we had recruited hundreds of local people into the organisation and changed their lives. When he died in April 2010, only two months after meeting Desmond Tutu, it was a tragedy. But it was all the more tragic because he never got to see the results of his work, the most diverse and inclusive Games ever.

When my dad died suddenly in February 2012, I had no comprehension that he would miss the opening ceremony we had all been working so hard to deliver. In the same way a school child looks to the parent or teacher for validation, I suppose I was hoping to achieve that from my dad. But it never came. The solace that comes from tragedy, and can only be appreciated some time later, is that in moments of grief, we have the opportunity to think deeper and reason clearer. We truly gain a sense of perspective.

In one sense, the organisation that fails to adapt will die. This is a natural process, as in nature. We need diversity, to amplify and select. So in one sense Inclusion 3.0 champions can relax, safe in the knowledge that they are on the right side of history. The moral imperative, however, comes from the people left behind, trapped in organisations or systems unwilling or unable to change. It could take until 2075 for women to reach parity with men on corporate boards, even in the 'Western world'.[4] I would suggest that our current reality demands a more immediate response than Diversity 101 or 2.0 can ever offer. If an organisation is to have any hope of catching up with the world around it, real inclusion is a pressing imperative.

So for a multitude of reasons, and for the sake of honouring those who are no longer with us, there remains the fierce urgency of now.

I took the train and ferry to Long Island, New York, to see my friend Brooke, an inspiration for what is possible. Brooke was hit by a car on 4 September 1990 on the way home from school, her first day of junior high. Formerly a dancer, she is now a quadriplegic person, paralysed from the neck down, who uses her tongue and a 'touchpad' on the roof of her mouth in order to control her movements in a wheelchair. She casually told me about the ending of the technology production for this system. I was shocked to hear of technological *regression* in a time of unprecedented advancement. Without this technology she has found movement, as well as use of a computer, significantly harder. This is one of those issues that cannot be dropped. Every minute she is without that technology, which used to exist, is a minute that makes my life worse.

We've talked about the system, now let's talk about you

Above lie seven valid reasons to disconnect. To not undertake real inclusion. People are busy, and as free agents I respect that. I would, however, humbly suggest that all of these seven objections could be overcome with the right attitude. That is not to suggest that the factors are unimportant, of course they are. But we are too often seduced by the luxury of resources and time and over-dependent on top-down management, without truly questioning our own capacity for leading change in the organisational process.

So I do not for one minute deny that the Olympics was in some ways unique, or that resources, time and management are all important. I do not deny that there are other urgencies, climate change, mergers and acquisitions, personal bereavements or other imperatives, not least paying the mortgage or putting your kids through school. I appreciate that real inclusion could always be further refined, researched and tested till it is crystal clear. But at what point do we decide to lead? When do we start creating Paradise today? Jerusalem is not yet built.

There are increasingly few excuses for not engaging in inclusion. No more excuses could imply that we are coming from a compliance perspective and hunting down the wrongdoers. There may be a moral case for that in some instances, but increasingly we have laws. No more excuses is intended more as a mirror. A mirror to hold up to those organisations who realise they must change but either lack the courage, the creativity or the talent to do so.

You can choose to lead inclusively

In Part One I said there were three interwoven themes: inclusion as a method of leadership (Inclusive Leadership), how inclusion made the world's biggest and most complex event even better (London 2012), and how inclusion can also add significant value to your organisation.

Inclusive leadership is increasingly a prerequisite because the world is increasingly diverse and without managing that world, it will manage you. Even if your current organisation is still relatively homogeneous, your customer base is not. Even if you still think your customer base is similar, they are being influenced ever more by diverse forces at a global scale over which you have no control.

Diversity is not a universal panacea, it is problematic. While the straight-jacket of corporate culture can be suffocating, none of us wants to work at the zoo either and so we need leaders who can make sense of the mess. Throughout the pages that precede this I have tried to show how inclusive leadership played out – an appetite for risk and a willingness to put out fires, a recognition of subconscious bias and a desire to solicit the discretionary effort from all of our people.

At the final Diversity Board, Paul Deighton said, 'LOCOG has proved that Diversity and Inclusion not only is the right thing to do but makes commercial sense in the private sector.' Inclusion at London 2012 made sense because it was good business. It was a net benefit, not a cost. 'Everyone's 2012' made 'London 2012' a better Games, indeed the best Games ever. Very few people would disagree with that.

What did people care about? How did we fit real inclusion into their agenda, make it part of their agenda, make it part of their mission? The business case focuses largely on commercial arguments and the commercial demands always revolve around numbers. In the final analysis, however, it is perhaps the emotional case, rather than the business case, that draws out people's discretionary effort and brings real inclusion alive. Ironically, therefore, there is a business case for an emotional response. Beyond the numbers, it is the stories that recruit people to the cause of real inclusion.

The reason Desmond Tutu is the ultimate figure of real inclusion is because of his story. He reached out to members of a former apartheid government and included them in the new South Africa. Through his Truth and Reconciliation Committee they heard the stories, they forgave, they included and they moved on. In Myanmar in June 2013, I had the privilege to meet Aung San Suu Kyi. Again, her story is one of real inclusion. In Nay Pyi Taw on 7 June 2013 she recounted Burma's history and discussed its future. The first thing she said was 'it starts with inclusiveness'. Besides economic and social development, Myanmar needed to include the military 'as part of us' in order to create a future, in spite of its past.[5]

At the Opening Ceremony, Seb Coe said these are a Games for Everyone. At the Closing Ceremony he could say these were a Games by Everyone. We know now what we are capable of. As Seb said, 'when our time came, we did it right'. Men and women are more skilled for having worked on London 2012. Having that diverse workforce was not just an end in itself, however. It is about the output being more than the sum of those parts, and about the fact that those men and women will now take their whole selves to their next challenge. That's legacy.

You are responsible for your attitude and for the work you choose to do

Too often, the public discourse around diversity is negative, from immigration restrictions to the terrorists who murdered the soldier Lee Rigby in London in 2013. If there is one thing London 2012 did for the benefit of all of us, it was to reflect the positivity of diversity and show the world what real inclusion looks like. An American, a New Yorker no less, said the following online. I don't know this person. I don't know their gender, ethnicity, sexual orientation. I don't know their age, belief or whether they are disabled or not. I don't know whether they are rich or poor, liberal or conservative, right or left. But I know from online blogs, media, friends, colleagues and travelling that they speak for millions of people around the world. In November 2012 'chelseachamberlainc' said 'as a New Yorker, I don't think anyone could possibly top the awe-inspiring and poetic beauty in… London 2012… no matter how many fireworks or drummers you've got, Britain shared with the world a meaningful story displaying their national pride of the country they've become. What's better than that?'

But inclusion is not an end game. In the same way we have moved on from 'diversity for diversity's sake', the world is constantly evolving, and so must our responses to its challenges. There is always the possibility of retrenchment, like salmon falling downstream. In many ways, legacy is still up for grabs. That is one of the main reasons I have written this book. If you have come this far, you will appreciate what can be achieved, but you will also appreciate how we can take nothing for granted. We need to partner with each other, if only to build collective courage, to brainstorm collective creativity and to exchange infinite diverse talent that can take us places we could never reach alone. Only by doing so will real inclusion live, and our achievements not regress.

We have talked a lot about systems in this book. The ultimate system is that of life. We are born, we live, and we die. Change can happen through natural selection; diversify, amplify, select. Change happens through cohort replacement, such as will happen in Italy's dysfunctional corporate sector as the octogenarians move on. Relying on these systems in a passive sense is an option. But activating human agency to improve the situation for now is the challenge, the fierce urgency of now. If we set out to change the world with mere ideals we may fail. If we start in our own organisations, we can win for ourselves and for society at large.

The English poet WH Auden said 'you owe it to all of us to get on with what you are good at'. Self-actualisation is the greatest gift you can give someone. More accurately, it is the greatest goal you can encourage them to attain themselves. To attain it through inspiring courage, by supporting leadership, and by holding people accountable for delivery. To empower people, especially those who have not been empowered before, is not only a moral imperative and a minority interest – it is in the interests of the majority too. If we enlarge the pie, we can all sit at the table.

Takeaways – no more excuses

1 The theory contained in this book is applicable to your organisation: We can all better understand, we can all improve our leadership style and we can always deliver more.

2 Many of the tools are applicable to your organisation. Choose the ones most relevant to your circumstances, from a guaranteed interview scheme in recruitment, to a more transparent procurement process and peer review of customer service deliverables.

3 The real business case emphasises the removal of barriers, rather than the time and cost sink of new initiatives. In the final analysis, the main barrier to achieving real inclusion may well be you.

Notes

1 Thaler and Sustein, *Nudge: Improving decisions about health, wealth and happiness* (Yale University Press, 2008).

2 Recession may be a good time to start a business [online] http://bizfinance .about.com./od/startyourownbusiness/a/startup-in-recession.htm

3 See also, letter to my great-uncle Richard, Appendix, p 323.

4 Hagel, John, Seeley Broan, John and Davidson, Lang, Measuring the Forces of Long term Change: the 2009 shift index Deloitte Development 2009. Also see Catalyst press release 29 March 2006 '2005 Catalysts census of women board directors of the Fortune 500 shows 10 year trend of slow progress and persistent challenges'.

5 World Economic Forum, Aung San Suu Kyi private session, Nay Pyi Taw, Myanmar/Burma 7 June 2013.

APPENDICES

LOCOG Leadership Pledge

'Our vision is to use the power of the Games to inspire lasting change.

- The Olympic values are excellence, friendship and respect.
- The Paralympic values are courage, determination, inspiration and equality.

'I am committed to deliver a memorable Games, with a lasting legacy that truly encompasses the world in a city; where each individual in LOCOG takes personal responsibility for an inclusive approach that is fully integrated into every business decision.

'I will ensure that my team includes as much diverse talent as possible, meeting or exceeding LOCOG's aspirations.

- I will hire talented disabled people.
- I will hire talented local people from a range of cultural backgrounds.
- I will run my team inclusively, respecting all, including women, LGBT people, younger and older people.

'I will ensure my staff attend the diversity and inclusion induction sessions and I will push beyond my personal best to deliver a legacy of inclusion.'

In December 2010, the Leadership Pledge was extended to include all staff at LOCOG and was incorporated into the induction process on new starters' first day, when staff were given the opportunity to sign the pledge.

Full workforce diversity and inclusion results

Paid staff results, September 2012

D & I strand	LOCOG target zone	Actual role acceptance
BAME	18–29%	40%
Disability/LTHC/Deaf	3–6%	9%
LGBT	5–7%	5%
Female	46–54%	46%
Under 30	20–30%	36%
Over 50	10%+	15%

The retention rate for the LOCOG paid workforce during the Games was extremely high with fewer than 100 permanent and temporary staff leaving their roles. This figure is too low to have any significant impact on the existing workforce figures, therefore LOCOG can be confident that the diversity of the paid workforce was maintained throughout the Olympic Games and Paralympic Games. This supports our belief that increased diversity within an organisation does not lead to higher attrition rates.

Volunteer (Games Maker) results, August 2012

D & I strand	LOCOG target zone	Application 'pool'	Actual role acceptance
BAME	18–29%	17%	18.15%
Disability/LTHC/Deaf	3–6%	3.4%	4.14%
LGBT	5–7%	3.2%	3.75%
Female	46–54%	57%	56%
Under 30	20–30%	52%	37%
Over 50	10–15%	20.3%	32%

At its peak during the Olympic Games, LOCOG's Games-time volunteer workforce numbered approximately 70,000 people. In the table, the breakdown both at application stage and role acceptance stage is broken down as a percentage of the overall volunteer application/accepted pool. LOCOG achieved and surpassed its target recruitment levels in each category with the exception of LGBT, where under-reporting may have disproportionately affected the results. In the case of gender and age, we surpassed the upper limit of the target zone. In particular, the percentage of the volunteer workforce over the age of 50 was more than double the target level. The overall retention rate of the volunteer workforce, meaning those who finished Games-time responsibilities and their full term of engagement, was approximately 96 per cent.

Contractor Workforce results, September 2012

D & I strand	LOCOG target zone	Actual role acceptance
BAME	18–29%	50%
Disability/LTHC/Deaf	3–6%	9%
LGBT	5–7%	3%
Female	46–54%	41%
Under 30	20–30%	63%
Over 50	10%+	8%

The LGBT, female and over-50 target levels were all just below the lower levels of the LOCOG target zones. As with the volunteer workforce, we can assume a higher level of under-reporting in the LGBT group.

Host Boroughs workforce participation, August 2012

Six Host Boroughs	Target zone	Actual %
Six Host Boroughs total	15–20%	23.3%

Finally, LOCOG hoped to benefit the residents of the six East London Host Boroughs and, as such, established a target recruitment zone of 15–20 per cent of the total workforce to come from these communities. The actual rate of 23.3 per cent exceeded the target level.

Workforce functional area benchmarking tool

Overall Rank
YOUR SAY 7 – Overall

Position	Functional area
1	Facilities
2	Human Resources
3	Culture, Ceremonies & Education
4	Communications & Public Affairs
5	Finance
6	Legal
7	Strategy & Programme Management
8	Brand & Marketing
9	Transport
10	Sport
11	Security
12	Games Services
13 =	Client Services
13 =	Commercial (neg + other)
13 =	Technology
16	Procurement
17	Venues & Infrastructure

Disability
YOUR SAY 7 – Disability

Position	Functional area
1 =	Facilities
1 =	Legal
3	Human Resources
4	Brand & Marketing
5	Culture, Ceremonies & Education
6	Technology
7 =	Communications & Public Affairs
7 =	Strategy & Programme Management
9 =	Client Services
9 =	Commercial (neg + other)
9 =	Procurement
9 =	Finance
9 =	Transport
9 =	Security
9 =	Sport
9 =	Venues & Infrastructure
9 =	Games Services

Departments were ranked on the diversity of their recruitment.

Procurement RAG tool

LOCOG used the RAG (Red, Amber, Green) communication and assessment tool, which enabled the Diversity and Inclusion team to interact and cooperate with different Functional Areas on the challenges and key successes they had in implementing diversity and inclusion as a part of their specific tenders. RAG was used for both qualitative and quantitative assessment.

Following an evaluation sheet based on the RAG tool below, the Diversity and Inclusion team judged each bidder performance in this area before the result was sent to the Procurement team.

Evaluation response	Definition	Implication	Actions
GREEN	Supplier proposal is acceptable	Willing to sign off contract award to this supplier	None
AMBER	Issues within the supplier's proposal, but these can be resolved	Willing to sign off contract award to this supplier, subject to specific conditions being met	Detail the conditions that must be met by the supplier (eg clarification, provision of further evidence, required changes prior to contract start date)
RED	Significant and insurmountable issues within the supplier's proposal	Not willing to sign off contract award to this supplier	Provide rationale for the 'Red' evaluation response, referencing specific details of the supplier's proposal that have raised concerns

Our aim was not to discount bidders that lacked an understanding regarding diversity and inclusion (Red or Amber) but to help them move forward to Green, which meant good practice regarding diversity and inclusion in keeping with the Games' vision to inspire lasting change.

22 projects one pager

The purpose of the 22 projects was to help make the often-intangible 'inclusion' idea as tangible as possible in order to facilitate inclusive delivery. These 22 projects were identified as the core service delivery projects that could help London 2012 distinctively deliver on the diversity and inclusion promise.

We created an analytical communication tool to headline successes, identify challenges, and leave behind a lasting legacy of diversity and inclusion work:

- Successes: communicate with stakeholders the key achievements in the diversity and inclusion promise.
- Challenges: flag key diversity and inclusion issues/risks/areas of concern to appropriate manager. Identify areas of challenge, and draw attention to diversity and inclusion-specific needs in each project.
- Legacy: create records of key milestones, challenges and risks to help future OCOGs and other organisations understand how to achieve what London did in delivering the 2012 Olympic Games and Paralympic Games.

Every month in the lead up to the Olympic and Paralympic Games, the Diversity and Inclusion team, in partnership with a representative from each Functional Area, provided assessments of their project. These assessments incorporated the following criteria:

- Overall score using the RAG (Red, Amber, Green) communication and assessment tool.
- Areas reported in three sections: successes, challenges/lessons learned, legacy.

These responses were captured and reported to the Chief Executive Officer, Directors and Diversity Board.

The mascots, Mandeville and Wenlock

FIGURE A.0

More information at http://en.wikipedia.org/wiki/Wenlock_and_Mandeville
See the film at http://www.youtube.com/watch?v=KatN365jaBg

Pin badges

Sexual orientation: Pride pin badge, launched June 2010

FIGURE A.1

Disability: Inclusion pin badge, launched March 2011

FIGURE A.2

Age pin badge, launched June 2011

FIGURE A.3

Gender and gender identity pin badge, launched September 2011

FIGURE A.4

Faith pin badge, launched November 2011

FIGURE A.5

A letter to my great-uncle Richard

The Guardian, 27 July 2013.

I never met you, and no one ever talked about you, except Mum from time to time, late at night, when we were alone together, and we had drunk a few glasses too many. She never talked about you with Dad or my sisters. Yet I have always been aware of you, and this weekend I will think of you again. You lived in the wrong place, Berlin, at the wrong time – the 1930s – with the wrong sexual orientation, although they didn't call it 'gay' in those days. You were way ahead of your time in believing that this shouldn't be a barrier to enjoying a full and happy life.

Like me, you became a lawyer and used your skills to work for gay equality. You were remarkably brave to get involved with Magnus Hirschfeld's Institute for Sexual Research and to campaign for the decriminalisation of gay sex in Germany, although you didn't see it that way at the time.

But it meant that the Nazis could find out about you when they shut the institute in May 1933 and seized the names and addresses of supporters. You were unlucky to have a brother-in-law – Mum's adored father – who was a loyal Nazi party member, and who had become rich by means no one talked about either. He was involved with supplying the Wehrmacht and had to be above suspicion. You had become an embarrassment, maybe even a liability, to the family.

Mum heard that you 'disappeared' at some stage in 1934 or 35. You were arrested, but she was only a girl at the time and nobody told her why. What is clear, though, is that when they came for you, nobody in the family tried to help you.

When there was no more news about you from whichever camp you were in, nobody made any further inquiries. You were considered a non-person. Did you survive? Unlikely, given the way gays were worked to death in the camps and certainly none of your family ever heard from you again.

Your brother-in-law, my grandfather, loved England and regretted the war with the country. He would have been pleased that his only daughter married an Englishman, and that her children would grow up English. He did not long survive its ending, so I never met him either.

But when I learned about you in my early 20s, as I was trying to come to terms with my own homosexuality in a world that was still hostile, you inspired me. Dad always blamed Mum's side of the family for my 'condition'. When I went on my first momentous Gay Pride march back in the early 70s, and others in later years, I was doing it for you too. When I visited a concentration camp in the 90s, I also shed some tears for you.

You, and grandfather, would have been amazed that earlier this month the British parliament passed a law to allow gay people to marry, going further and faster for gay equality than Germany, where today you would feel much more at home. He would not have been too happy that his only grandson turned out to be gay and much more like you than him.

Nor would he have been too pleased that I have a lovely partner, whom I will soon be able to call my husband, who is non-Aryan, and who feels as fully at home in my family as I do in his. But I'm sure you would be delighted and so this weekend, when we raise our glasses in celebration, we'll drink a few for you.

Your great-nephew,
Peter

REFERENCES

Bohnet, Iris (2010) Gender equality: a nudge in the right direction [online] http://www.ft.com/intl/cms/s/0/59d7d2f6-d6a7-11df-98a9-00144feabdc0. html#axzz2Twnzq0YI, *Financial Times*, 13 October

Covey, Stephen (1989) *The Seven Habits of Highly Effective People*, Simon & Schuster

Crook, Mona Lena (2008) Quota laws for women in politics: implications for feminist practice, *Social Politics*, **15**(3), pp 345–68, http://crook.wustl.edu/pdf/social_politics_2008.pdf

Dasgupta, Nilanjana (2013) 'Thriving Despite Negative Stereotypes: How In-group Experts and Peers Act As Social Vaccines to Inoculate Women's Self concept and Achievement', WAPPP Seminar, Cambridge, MA, 18 April

Hansen, F (2003) Diversity's business case doesn't add up, *Workforce*, April, pp 28–32

Heifitz, Ron and Linsky, Marty (2002) *Leadership on the Line*, Harvard Business Press

Kennedy, John F (1956) *Profiles in Courage*, Harper and Brothers

Liswood, Laura (2010) *The Loudest Duck*, Wiley

Louganis, G (2006) *Breaking the Surface*, Sourcebooks

Magnay, Jacquelin (2012) http://www.telegraph.co.uk/sport/olympics/9627757/London-2012-Olympic-Games-comes-in-at-377m-under-budget-government-announces.html, *Telegraph*, 23 October

Page, Scott (2007) *The Difference*, Princeton University Press

Pages, Carmen and Priras, Claudia (2010) *The Gender Dividend: Capitalizing on womens' work*, Inter American Development Bank

Pellegrino, Greg, D'Amato, Sally and Weisberg, Ann (2011) *The Gender Dividend: Making the case for investing in women*, Deloitte

Phillips, Katherine (2013) 'Can Female Leaders Mitigate Negative Effects of Diversity?: The Case of National Leaders', Women and Public Policy Program Seminar, Cambridge, MA, 14 February

Porter, Michael and Kramer, Mark (2011) Creating Shared Value, *Harvard Business Review*, January: http://hbr.org/2011/01/the-big-idea-creating-shared-value

Said, Edward (2003) *Orientalism*, Penguin

Sandberg, Sheryl (2013) *Lean In*, A A Knopf

Sardar, Ziauddin (2008) *The Language of Equality*, Equality and Human Rights Commission

Thaler, Richard H and Sunstein, Cass R (2008) *Nudge: Improving decisions about health, wealth, and happiness*, Yale University Press

Trompenaars, Fons and Hampden Turner, Charles (2012) *Riding the Waves of Innovation*, Mc-Graw Hill

Younge, Gary (2000) The badness of words, *The Guardian*, 14 February

INDEX

(*italics* indicate a figure or table in the text)

DEDICATION

In memory of Cedric John Frost, died 28 February 2012, aged 65 years.

David Morris, died 18 April 2010, aged 51 years.
'The value of diversity is as infinite as the cost of its destruction.'
Dr R Roosevelt Thomas Jr, died 17 May 2013, aged 68 years
For all men and women who work on these issues, often against the odds and without sufficient recognition.

CPSIA information can be obtained at www.ICGtesting.com
Printed in the USA
BVOW01s0912150114

341756BV00008B/1/P